Praise for *Exploring Vacation and Etiquette Themes in Social Studies*

"Resor manages to address three of the most important yet often overlooked dimensions of social studies education at the secondary level: use of primary sources in the classroom, an emphasis on social rather than political history, and the need to inject an element of entertainment into instruction. This work stands as a first encouraging step toward reforming social studies education in the twenty-first century." —**Chris Snow**, 2010 University of Chicago Outstanding Educator Award; National History Club Association Sponsor of the Year; history teacher, Henry Clay High School (Lexington, KY)

"Resor's book is an innovative and unique approach to teaching thematic units. Excellent resources are provided for European and American history from medieval times to contemporary. The information is easily adaptable to any time period." —**Sharon E. Graves**, Kentucky Teacher Hall of Fame, Eastern Kentucky University Distinguished History Alumni, 2014 Gilder Lehrman Kentucky History Teacher

"This book, with its many examples and resources, provides middle and secondary history and social studies teachers an excellent avenue for engaging students in the study of history. The topics are authentic and meaningful in the *here and now* for middle- and secondary-age learners. Additionally, with the current goal for students to demonstrate twenty-first-century skills, this text offers teachers numerous primary source documents for lessons that help students analyze, think critically, communicate, and become more aware of and informed about their world." —**Rodney White**, professor emeritus, Social Studies Education, Eastern Kentucky University

Exploring Vacation
and Etiquette Themes in Social Studies

Exploring Vacation and Etiquette Themes in Social Studies

Primary Source Inquiry for Middle and High School

Cynthia Williams Resor

ROWMAN & LITTLEFIELD
Lanham • Boulder • New York • London

Cover image credits: Photo. Highland Beach, Maryland, 1930–1931. Courtesy of Scurlock Studio Records, ca. 1905–1994, Archives Center, National Museum of American History, Smithsonian Institution; U.S. Travel Bureau Poster. Works Progress Administration Federal Art Project, 1936–1938. Work Projects Administration Poster Collection. Courtesy of the Library of Congress; Painting. Krimmel, John Lewis. "The Country Wedding," 1820. Courtesy of Wikimedia Commons.

Published by Rowman & Littlefield
A wholly owned subsidiary of The Rowman & Littlefield Publishing Group, Inc.
4501 Forbes Boulevard, Suite 200, Lanham, Maryland 20706
www.rowman.com

Unit A, Whitacre Mews, 26-34 Stannary Street, London SE11 4AB

Copyright © 2017 by Cynthia Williams Resor

All rights reserved. No part of this book may be reproduced in any form or by any electronic or mechanical means, including information storage and retrieval systems, without written permission from the publisher, except by a reviewer who may quote passages in a review.

British Library Cataloguing in Publication Information Available

Library of Congress Cataloging-in-Publication Data Available

ISBN: 978-1-4758-3197-9 (cloth : alk. paper)
ISBN: 978-1-4758-3198-6 (pbk. : alk. paper)
ISBN: 978-1-4758-3199-3 (electronic)

∞™ The paper used in this publication meets the minimum requirements of American National Standard for Information Sciences—Permanence of Paper for Printed Library Materials, ANSI/NISO Z39.48-1992.

Printed in the United States of America

To my parents, Douglas and Virgie Williams.
Thank you for the family vacations and your efforts to teach me good manners.

Contents

	Author's Note	ix
	Introduction	xi
Chapter 1	Social History and Thematic Instruction	1
	Why Social History?	2
	Key Concepts Related to the Study of Social History	5
	Thematic Instruction	10
	Conclusion	11
	Notes	11
Chapter 2	Vacations	13
	Defining the Concept of Travel for Leisure	14
	Was Medieval Pilgrimage a Vacation?	15
	Vacationing in American History	19
	In the Classroom: Introducing the Theme	29
	The Primary Sources: Medieval Pilgrimage and Collective Memory	30
	The Primary Sources	35
	The Primary Sources: The "Rules" of Vacationing in America	39
	Extending the Theme	48
	Notes	50
	Additional Resources	53
Chapter 3	Manners and Etiquette	55
	The Vocabulary of Proper Behavior	57
	Relationships to Sociology, Psychology, Anthropology	58
	The History of Advice Manuals	58

	The Eighteenth Century Dilemma—Does Outward Behavior Reflect Inner Beliefs?	60
	Etiquette in the United States	63
	In the Classroom: Introducing the Theme	70
	The Primary Sources: Manners and the Enlightenment	70
	The Primary Sources: Courtship and Dating	75
	Extending the Theme	87
	Notes	87
	Additional Resources	91
Chapter 4	Exploring More Themes	93
	Choosing a Theme	93
	How to Research a Theme	94
	Keep the End in Mind: The Essential Question	94
	Doing the Research—Secondary Sources	94
	Doing the Research—Locating Primary Sources	96
	Reading and Interpreting the Primary Sources	99
	Creating Themed Units and Lessons	101
	Conclusion	102
	Notes	102
	Works Cited	103
	Index	109
	About the Author	115

Author's Note

Visit the companion website **teachingwiththemes.com** for the following:

- More primary sources, texts, and images related to the themes of vacation and manners
- Student reading guides included in this book that can be downloaded and edited
- Answer keys for the student reading guides; password protected: **vgw82*4BLEU**
- Additional resources and teaching ideas related to vacations and manners
- Information about future publications by this author
- A feedback form; please share your experiences and suggestions using the themes, primary sources, and recommendations in this book

Introduction

Social studies teachers are often disappointed by students' lack of interest. Early in my teaching career, a student expressed both his disinterest in what I was teaching and surprise that I thought studying history was both important and exciting by saying to me, "Wow, you really do like this stuff, don't you?" I was forced to acknowledge that my beloved discipline of history was not something students looked forward to learning, and I began a career-long quest to try to make my students love history.

I reflected on my own experiences as a student and began to search for new approaches to social studies content. As a middle and high school teacher, I found many resources that provided general teaching strategies, but most lacked the detailed, content-specific information I needed to develop strategies into quality social studies units. This book seeks to address both of these issues—the dilemma of how to make social studies relevant to students and the need for resources that provide in-depth but focused content information for use in the middle and high school classroom.

The following chapters provide historical overviews of two social history themes—vacations and manners—that are relevant to life in the twenty-first century and the past. Primary sources, teaching suggestions, and resources are provided for each theme, and the book's companion website, **teachingwiththemes.com**, provides additional information. I believe that by focusing on the study of the everyday lives of humans and connecting those topics to the bigger themes in other academic disciplines and modern life, history can become more relevant to our students.

Why Social History?

I love history, but that love developed outside the classroom. My history classes were okay, but we studied the usual, and often dull, political narratives. I didn't really understand—or care—what a bunch of men did to govern societies distant in place and time. The historical people and events in those history classes were like numbers in a math book—mostly flat, colorless, and dull.

Historical novels made history come alive for me. In middle school, I worked as a student volunteer in the school library and discovered George Orwell's *Animal Farm*, the historical romances of Victoria Holt, and the fantasy epics of medieval historian J. R. R. Tolkien, just to name a few. The historical figures in novels were both men *and* women who had thoughts, dreams, and adventures. Their lives represented time that I could measure, in days or years. The characters in novels discussed things I thought were interesting—clothing, manners, customs, houses, personal relationships.

In high school, my outstanding social studies teacher Shane Abbott captured the complexity of the past, and my attention, by introducing primary sources describing daily life. To this day, I remember the excitement of reading a source about the events in the Roman Colosseum, imagining I was actually there and wondering why these stories were never included in textbooks. But social history primary sources were rarely used in my other high school and college history courses.

My journey from a historical-novel-reading teenager to a proponent of social history themes in the classroom occurred at the same time social history was emerging within the discipline of history. While I was reading novels in middle school (1970s), the "new social history" was beginning to be recognized among professional historians and within university departments of history. Most of my undergraduate (1980s) history professors had written their dissertations before social history was popular; they taught what was expected at the time, rarely veering from a focus on the political events of the past. My love of novels lured me into graduate literature classes, my years as a high school teacher kept me searching for lessons to interest my students, and an opportunity to return to graduate school to earn my PhD in history (1990s) expanded my content knowledge. These experiences helped me to develop the thematic approach to middle and high school social studies described in this book.

Why Teach Thematically?

When I reflect on my experiences teaching middle and high school, I see that two of my most successful units were thematic, even though I didn't realize it at the time. My first attempt at thematic instruction was a unit developed for a high school elective humanities course. Many of the college-bound students in my high school were unable to fit a "fun" and "not required" elective into their packed, pre-college schedule. The students who chose to take my course were a unique mix of students who included the academically uninspired, struggling learners, college-bound and not-college-bound students, lovers of social studies, and students who had taken one of my other courses (not always successfully) and decided that my class was as good a place to be as any other.

Since the curriculum and standards for this course were not state or district prescribed, I identified various topics that I had always wanted to teach but could never fit into a traditionally offered social studies course. I asked students to suggest unit topics. Video cameras were still a very novel form of technology in the 1990s, and the group wanted to "make a movie." I created a unit called Creativity, inspired by a themed issue from *Utne Reader*.[1] We read about creativity and applied what we learned in various creative projects. The students researched the concepts upon which drama and soap operas were based and created their very own video-recorded drama.

I didn't know that books had been written on thematic learning; I didn't know there was a name for what I was doing. My overall goals were broad and vague—but I did know that I wanted students to read and analyze texts and do engaging activities that would trick students into learning, and I wanted to explore interesting topics with my students and challenge myself to learn new information and try new teaching strategies. Looking back, I see that I created a course organized around themes. Sadly, my humanities course only existed one year due to staffing and scheduling issues.

Another memorable attempt at interdisciplinary, thematic instruction using primary sources was the combination of history and literature within my junior level US History class. I purchased classroom sets of three historical novels—*Uncle Tom's Cabin* (1852), *The Jungle* (1906), and *Hiroshima* (1946). The novels provided the themes for my history units on America before the Civil War, the Progressive Era, and World War II. To make a long story short, reading all of *Uncle Tom's Cabin* was a disaster—the book was too long and the language was too archaic. Only the gory parts of *The Jungle* were a hit with students. But with the final novel, *Hiroshima*, I stumbled upon the perfect combination: short enough for students to read, language that students understood, and plenty of action and horrific detail—three important lessons learned, long before "reading in the content area" strategies were widely known.

I used that winning combination when I later taught sixth grade in a self-contained classroom. As both the social studies and the literature teacher, I was able to combine history and literature/English language arts in units on Ancient Greece and the Middle Ages. We read *The Bronze Bow* (1997) by Elizabeth George Speare as we studied ancient culture. We read *Redwall* (1986), a medieval fantasy novel by Brian Jacques, as we learned about the Middle Ages. During the medieval unit, my daily read-aloud for the students was *The Hobbit* by medievalist J. R. R. Tolkien. Students were able to really imagine the historical contexts using the novels and analyze the difference between myth and historical reality, and a few students who had not been novel-readers before became passionate readers of medieval fantasy.

Aligning to the Standards

The savvy teacher might ask, "How is this approach to be justified in a standards-driven curriculum?" Instruction using primary sources recommended in this book aligns with two current sets of national standards and with place-based pedagogy.

Literacy Instruction

Reading, writing, speaking, and listening, and literacy skills specific to the social studies, were considered important long before the publication and adoption of the *Common Core State Standards for English Language Arts and Literacy in*

History/Social Studies, Science, and Technical Subjects.[2] While controversy currently rages about the origin and adoption of these national standards, most recognize that the literacy skills outlined are important for students to learn.

The primary source sets provided in this book can be used to teach the literacy skills described in the *Common Core*. Many resources are already available that are tailored to teaching and learning these literacy skills. Therefore, choosing specific teaching strategies that best meet the needs of your students and your local and state curriculum requirements is left up to your professional judgment.

Social Studies Standards

National social studies standards have long been problematic because opinions vary across the fifty states about the role of history and social studies education in the development of society. As with the *Common Core Standards*, social studies standards often become a battleground in the culture wars between liberals and conservatives. As I write this, my own state of Kentucky is in a multiyear transition in which "new" state social studies standards have been written and proposed in the hopes of pleasing both sides, but, in reality, they will probably please very few. Therefore, I have used the most current publication of the National Council of Social Studies, *College, Career, and Civic Life (C3) Framework for Social Studies State Standards: Guidance for Enhancing the Rigor of K–12 Civics, Economics, Geography, and History*,[3] as a reference.

This document was written to closely align to the *Common Core Standards for Literacy* and at its core is the "Inquiry Arc"—a four-dimension process that promotes both critical analysis and content-specific learning. The entire publication is available for free online, so there is no need to review its contents in great detail. But the four dimensions (in bold below) are important to note because they are used as an organizational tool for the thematic chapters that follow.

Developing questions and planning inquiries is the first dimension in *College, Career, and Civic Life (C3) Framework*; student inquiry is focused upon compelling and supporting questions. A compelling question is a renaming of Jay McTighe and Grant Wiggins's essential question. According to McTighe and Wiggins, essential questions are overarching questions with three important characteristics—they reflect the key inquiries within a discipline, can be applied over multiple units or disciplines, and serve as a conceptual framework for learning both concepts and discrete facts.[4] These three characteristics are also the foundations that underlie thematic instruction. The following themed chapters are built around essential questions.

The second dimension, **applying disciplinary tools and concepts**, is related to both literacy skills and the specific skills used by historians. But inquiry does not occur in a vacuum; historians must have a deep and wide knowledge within their field of study. Each chapter includes a broad summary of a theme in European and American history. Each theme has relevance outside of the context of Western civilization, and the exclusion of other world civilizations is attributed only to my lack of expertise and the necessity to offer an affordable book that weighs less than ten pounds.

Third, so that students can become adept at **evaluating sources and using evidence**, each chapter includes primary source sets that provide evidence for answering the chapter's essential questions. The majority of the primary sources included in this book are texts, but the interpretation of non-text primary sources such as photographs, fine art images, cartoons, video and sound recordings, and objects of daily life is also very important in the classroom. Texts are the focus for several reasons.

One is that the *Common Core Standards for Literacy* concentrates upon reading and writing texts. Also, the reproduction of images in print increases the cost of a book due to space required for printed images and charges for copyright permissions. Furthermore, publication limitations require that color images be reproduced in black and white, making many images difficult to analyze. Therefore, additional visual resources for the themes of vacation and manners are provided on this book's companion website. This allows for fast "clicking" instead of slow typing of complicated URLs, easy updates of changing web addresses, and an opportunity to update resources with references to newly digitized sources. "Fair use" copyright rules allow teachers to project large, color images from the Internet on their classroom computers for student analysis.

Finally, the *C3 Framework* Inquiry Arc engages students in **communicatng conclusions and taking informed action**. Communication of conclusions can take many forms, both written and oral, inside and outside the classroom. But taking informed action on events that happened in the past can be a challenge. The "action" component of social history can involve studying the history of themes in the local community or state; analyzing the theme in one's personal or family life; investigating the theme in the modern world locally, nationally, or internationally; or using what is learned to take action within the classroom, school, or community.

In this book, taking action is framed as place-based education. Both themed chapters conclude with suggestions for extending the theme to the present in classroom, school, and community settings.

Place-Based Education

Place-based education is an interdisciplinary approach to education that "immerses students in local heritage, cultures, landscapes, opportunities and experiences," with a special focus on service projects for the local school and/or community.[5] Many social studies curricula ignore the history of issues within their own communities in an effort to "cover" a national or international political narrative. In contrast, the themes of manners and vacations discussed in this book have relevance to students as individuals and are also significant to students in their own community and culture, both in the past and the present. Suggestions are provided to help students make these local connections.

How to Use This Book

This book may be used in several different ways. In a utopian world, where teachers are able to make all of their own curriculum decisions, this book could serve as a guide and resource for redesigning a social studies curriculum around themes relevant to the present and future lives of students. But most of us have not found this teachers' Land of Cockaigne.[6]

It is more likely you will find inspiration to incorporate at least one thematic unit in your courses or social history themes and activities in your existing units. You may also discover connections to other disciplines, especially English/language arts, and be inspired to collaborate with other teachers to develop themes together. Even if you are unable to overhaul your curriculum to reflect the themes of vacations or manners, you are sure to find interesting anecdotes and at least one primary source in the collections provided that can make your students look at their everyday life with new eyes.

The themed chapters on vacations and manners provide two sets of essential questions that can be used to focus instruction and as the basis for discussion, writing assignments, or culminating projects. A historical overview of each theme provides in-depth context for the teacher. Two primary source sets for each theme are designed to assist students in answering relevant essential questions. The primary sources are short excerpts, but teachers and students are encouraged to consult the endnotes for references to the full texts, many of which are available online. I have edited some of the more difficult-to-read primary sources to make them more accessible to middle and high school students, but I kept the meaning and language as close to the original as possible.

The reading guides included provide students with the support they need to ask meaningful questions and cite relevant evidence to support their answers. The answer keys and downloadable versions of the reading guides are provided on the book's companion website.

The last chapter provides recommendations for locating quality books, articles, and primary sources related to social history themes. Guidance for developing social history units and lessons focused on essential questions and the interests of your students is also included.

Many excellent books and articles describe well-researched and effective teaching strategies, and this book does not attempt to reinvent the work of those authors. Some suggestions for appropriate teaching strategies are included, but this book depends upon your professional expertise as a teacher to choose the teaching strategies that best suit the needs of your students.

I can't promise that following the advice in this book will make all of your students' standardized test scores dramatically increase, solve every classroom management challenge, prompt your administrator to give you a pay raise, or inspire increased school funding. I would be selling snake oil if I made those guarantees. Ultimately, I hope this book will provide inspiration to learn more about your own favorite social history themes and ignite a new love for the discipline that you teach. Your knowledge and enthusiasm can help convince students that social studies courses are worthwhile.

Notes

1. "Are You Creative?" Themed issued of *Utne Reader*, March/April 1992.
2. Common Core Standards Initiative, "English Language Arts Standards," accessed April 28, 2016. http://www.corestandards.org/ELA-Literacy/.

3. National Council of Social Studies, *College, Career, and Civic Life (C3) Framework for Social Studies State Standards: Guidance for Enhancing the Rigor of K-12 Civics, Economics, Geography, and History*, 2013, accessed April 28, 2016, http://www.socialstudies.org/c3.

4. Jay McTighe and Grant Wiggins, *Essential Questions: Opening Doors to Student Understanding* (Alexandria, VA: Association for Supervision & Curriculum Development, 2013). For an overview see "Essential Questions: Opening Doors to Student Understanding," http://www.ascd.org/Publications/Books/Overview/Essential-Questions.aspx.

5. Center for Place-Based Learning and Community Engagement, "What Is Place-Based Education?" accessed April 28, 2016, http://promiseofplace.org/what_is_pbe.

6. The Land of Cockaigne was a mythical utopian world for working people.

CHAPTER ONE

Social History and Thematic Instruction

The quarrels of popes and kings, with wars and pestilences in every page; the men all so good for nothing, and hardly any women at all, it is very tiresome; and yet I often think it odd that history should be so dull, for a great deal of it must be invention. The speeches that are put into the heroes' mouths, their thoughts and designs; the chief of all of this must be invention, and invention is what delights me in other books.

—Stated by Miss Catherine Morland in *Northanger Abbey* (1818), by Jane Austen[1]

Many students sitting in middle and high school history classrooms would probably agree with the seventeen-year-old Catherine Morland, even though over two hundred years and Miss Morland's fictional existence in a novel by Jane Austen divide them. Modern teenagers might also agree with Miss Morland on what they enjoy, if one translates Miss Morland's preferred reading of novels, poetry, plays, and travel accounts into their modern equivalents—fiction in the form of novels, video games, music lyrics, and the stories of human lives in television and movies. Both historical and modern poetry and prose categorized as "fiction" are often set in the past, and as Miss Morland pointed out, it is the "thoughts and designs" of the human characters that really make the reading interesting.

This book is about teaching the "thoughts and designs" of humans in history. The "quarrels of popes and kings," political history, and functions of government that bored Miss Morland are the focus of a large majority of social studies instruction in middle and high schools. These are considered important subjects and are the primary focus of most textbooks, instructional materials, and a majority of standardized test questions. But this book offers an alternative approach.

The following chapters introduce two social history themes, along with primary sources and suggestions on how to incorporate and teach those themes in a middle or high school classroom. The purpose of this thematic approach to teaching social studies is threefold.

First, the examination of themes from social history encourages critical analysis of not just the past, but also the present lives and culture of students. Students already have knowledge of the themes discussed in this book—vacation, travel, and struggling with correct manners. Through formal study of these experiences in the past, students can better understand their own culture and how social class, sex, gender, and technological change impact their everyday lives.

Second, thematic instruction, as promoted in this book, incorporates several effective and currently prominent pedagogies—literacy instruction as outlined in the *Common Core Standards for Literacy*, the most recent standards framework published by the National Council of the Social Studies, and place-based learning.

Finally, this approach to teaching seeks to remedy the problem that Catherine Morland and modern students have with history. By starting with topics or issues that are applicable to the everyday lives of humans, and connecting to the bigger themes from life or the other social studies disciplines, history can become more relevant.

Why Social History?

Social history not only provides a historical background for everyday experience, it also gives students an analytical perspective to examine their own lives.[2] Students begin with concepts and experiences that they already know and apply them to a study of the past. Think of the study of social history as acquiring a new pair of glasses. If we never wear these social history glasses, we can only see our lives, culture, and society through the lenses created by our own culture.

In other words, we see what we are taught to see by our experiences with our family and friends, schools, mass media, and regional and national cultures—a concept defined as enculturation. Sometimes the lessons learned through enculturation are very obvious and straightforward; other times we absorb lessons on how to act and react without even realizing it. To complicate matters, our own personal experiences are impacted by how the mass media (television, Internet, social media, and printed publications) frame and interpret them for us.

Furthermore, our original lenses, or ways of seeing, through which we view the world, are specific and unique not just to our culture, but to our historical era. We may view human experiences very differently from cultures in the past, or we may have surprising similarities to past cultures. In order to critically analyze and assess our own actions, beliefs, and the culture around us, we must be able to step back and view our world in an objective way. Donning a pair of "social history glasses" and examining social themes in both the past and present can help students to develop a framework of critical analysis. We can teach our students to see beyond their original lenses and to look at, describe, and analyze their cultural assumptions instead of just taking for granted the world as interpreted by their culture.

Social history crosses all disciplines of study, not just the social studies. Social historians draw upon the sources and methods of all types of history (political, economic, intellectual), social sciences (geography, sociology, psychology, anthropology), and the humanities (literature, theatre, art). The themes of social history are also connected to the disciplines of science, technology, mathematics, economics, communication, and medicine. For example, the study of manners originated in the disciplines of sociology, psychology, and anthropology. Eighteenth-century concepts of behavior were influenced by the new discoveries of anatomists about the nervous system. The history of vacations is also a story of the changing technology of transportation and the shift to an industrial economy, and is even related to the history of medicine as many early resorts promised "water cures" at mineral or hot springs.

Despite the emergence of social history as a prominent area of academic study at the university level in the 1960s and its continued growth in the following decades, the study of social history has been slow to enter middle and high school classrooms. Several reasons exist for this slow entry into the classroom.

Social history topics are difficult to squeeze into narrowly defined teaching units that are often required by state or national standards. The causes and effects of social history do not always lend themselves to the well-defined eras that are traditionally taught because social history often focuses on patterns that develop over decades or even centuries.

Furthermore, social history themes may lack the clear narrative and specific "memorizable" events to which teachers and testers are accustomed. Educators may find that quick-to-grade objective assessments and standardized multiple choice questions do not flow easily from units that concentrate on social history.

Finally, teachers—through no fault of their own—may not have had the preparation and training in their university social studies and history classes to teach thematically or recognize the value of social history in the classroom. As an academic discipline, social history is still relatively new. New methods of study at the university level are often slow to enter the K–12 classroom, especially in a discipline as dedicated to the past as history.

The following paragraphs describe the framework of the thematic, social history chapters in this book. First, social history itself is defined and its development as a subdiscipline in history is examined. Next, two closely related and overlapping concepts—cultural history and popular culture—are discussed. Finally, six key concepts related to the themes and activities in the following chapters are explained:

- the shift of language over time
- social stratification
- agency
- sex and gender
- generational change
- the implications of studying history before and after the invention of the printing press

Social History Defined

Social history can be defined in two ways. First, social history is often defined as the study of the lives of groups of ordinary people, the people who are *not* of the elite, the wealthy, and politically powerful. This type of social history is commonly referred to as "history from the bottom up."[3] Social history is also defined by contrasting it to "traditional" history—the study of political events, formal institutions, or great people, usually great men. Because social historians do not focus on political power, which throughout most of history has been held by men, and in Western history, white men, they are more likely to study the lives of women, people of color, and the working and lower classes.

Second, social history can focus on what shapes a society as a whole and large-scale social processes. One might think of this as the "big changes" approach that focuses upon the turning points in historical eras, such as the social changes associated with the Industrial Revolution. Social historians of this type may ask how and why changes in human behavior occur. Social historians differ widely in their interpretations of these changes, differences based on using varied methods of analysis and diverse primary sources. Social historians generally agree that social conditions and changes interact with other historical processes such as political technological developments.

The study of social history is a recent development in the discipline of history. In the late 1800s and early 1900s, historians began to incorporate sections or chapters in larger works dealing with popular characteristics and everyday life and began noting that social forces were a factor in political change. The phrase "new social history" began to be used in 1960s and 1970s to refer to the type of social history that became prominent in those decades and that adapted the quantitative research methods and theories of the social sciences—sociology, anthropology, and economics—to history.

Previous to this movement, historians generally used qualitative research methods. In simplified language, the "old school" historians read primary sources from the time period and made informed conclusions based on the documents. But because descriptions of and writing by the majority of ordinary people throughout history are rare or do not exist, the new social historians began to use quantifiable social statistics from land and tax records, church registries, wills, probate proceedings, census data, or voting records that referenced ordinary people. This new type of history often depended upon the statistical analyses provided by the new technology of the era—computers.

More recently, social historians have begun to use the products of popular culture as primary sources: photographs, television shows, comic books, or everyday objects such as toys or tombstones or household furnishings. Social historians still use traditional text and printed sources, interpreting them in new ways. For example, personal diaries, previously considered as limited in their use as historical primary sources because they represent only one individual, have been used individually and collectively by social historians to gain insights into an era. Laurel Thatcher Ulrich's Pulitzer Prize–winning *A Midwife's Tale* (1991) focused upon the twenty-seven-year diary of a late-eighteenth- to early-nineteenth-century Maine midwife who had been ignored by previous historians.

Cultural History and Popular Culture

Cultural history and popular culture are key concepts related to the study of social history. Cultural history is a term that can have several different meanings. First, cultural history may be used as a synonym for intellectual history—the study of the thoughts and ideas of the educated elite of society. This type of history examines the historical contexts of the works of great philosophers, theologians, or political theorists—Plato, St. Augustine, Rousseau, John Locke, and Karl Marx, for example. The works of the intellectual elite may interact with popular culture, but one must be careful not to assume that what is current in academic culture at any point in time automatically reflects the views and daily culture of average individuals.

Second, cultural history can refer to a method of doing history that analyzes the subjective meaning of primary source texts, a method adopted from postmodern literary theorists. Sometimes one will see this second type of cultural history called "history with a literary turn." A short explanation in everyday language can be hard to find and some historians have been very critical of its application in the discipline of history. In very simplified terms, the "literary turn" means different texts, which are distributed and read in different ways and can mean different things at different times to different people; there is no single, objective way to interpret a text. When first introduced in the 1960s and 1970s, these primary source analysis methods derived from the study of literature and language were controversial but now are commonly used by historians.

Finally, cultural history can refer to the study of how groups of people in the past understood their daily experiences. The culture of groups of people is often analyzed with reference to a cultural continuum (figure 1.1) with a minority of

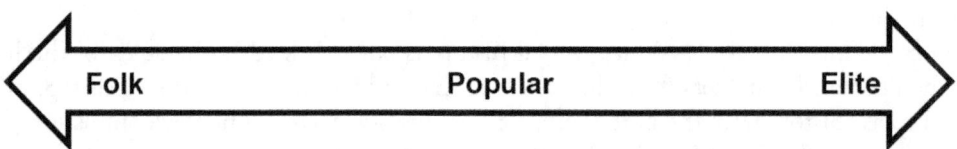

Figure 1.1. The boundaries between folk, popular, and elite culture are fluid and often overlap.

elite, wealthy, or powerful people at one end and a minority termed folk culture at the other. The wide middle expanse in the center of the continuum is characterized as popular culture. Elite culture is associated with great wealth, an expensive education, arts patronage, and if one wishes, extensive leisure time to travel widely and the money to sponsor charities or pursue costly pastimes anywhere in the world.

On the other hand, folk culture is local, isolated, and governed by one-on-one personal relationships. Parents, grandparents, learned people of the community transmit the culture to youth, not formal schools or universities. Folk cultures are oral cultures (not literate), small scale and rural, which provide isolation from outside influences. The unique characteristics of a folk culture and elite culture can affect or be affected by popular culture in some circumstances, but both are distinct from the wide middle section of the continuum—the popular culture.[4]

Popular culture is the culture of the majority or the masses of people in a society—it is what a large part of a population believes or does, and the objects that symbolize, are shared, or are needed to participate in the popular belief or activity. In the modern world, popular culture is spread by mass media paid for by commercial or political interests, through such items as magazines, best-selling books, social media, Internet, television shows, or movies.[5] Since the popular culture of the mass media is pervasive in the twenty-first century, products of the mass media are examined in several chapters of this book. Sometimes, this middle zone of "popular culture" is automatically associated with "the middle class," a connection that may or may not be correct, depending upon the time period studied. Issues related to the study of "the middle class" are important and discussed below and in the chapters in this book.

Popular culture is not a modern phenomenon; it existed in the premodern world before the invention of the printing press and mass communication. Archeologists have discovered molds for the mass-production of small clay religious figures in ancient Egypt and Tibet that would have been available and affordable to a wide section of the population.[6] Medieval epics were performed orally for a wide range of audiences, not just the nobility. But the challenge for historians of the premodern era is attempting to distinguish between popular and elite culture.

For example, many medieval sermons and treatises on Christian theology, written by clergy within the Roman Catholic Church, have survived. These were produced by an elite, intellectual culture, written in Latin, a language foreign to most of the population of Europe. One can't assume that the average illiterate peasant knew the official theology contained in these written documents. But a large part of this elite culture was transmitted, in oral and artistic forms, to the peasantry in order to convert them to Christianity. The social historians' job is to try to determine the process of this transmission and how these messages were received by people who have left no written records.

Three commonly held assumptions about popular culture should be discussed with students.

First, one must not assume that the elite culture of a historical era represents the views or tastes of the majority of the people of the age. For example, what is considered the "best" literature or art of a historical era and subsequently included in literature or art textbooks may not have been popular at the time that it was produced and could have had little effect on most people in that era.

The art of Vincent van Gogh was not highly praised or widely purchased in his lifetime. The majority of van Gogh's nineteenth-century contemporaries would not have recognized his art or his name. But subsequent generations view it as great, groundbreaking art. An original van Gogh painting today is in the realm of elite culture; only the wealthiest individuals or museums can purchase his original paintings. But van Gogh is also a part of the popular, mass-produced culture of today, on posters, calendars, magnets, and coffee cups.

Products and ideas of elite culture can be immediately influential in elite circles and quickly reproduced in ways that are accessible to a popular audience. For example, the works of Sigmund Freud were published for an elite audience, in journals and books for academic specialists in the late nineteenth and early twentieth century. By the 1920s, Freud's works were being translated from German and popularized in mass media publications, magazines and books for nonspecialist readers in America, impacting the popular culture of the twentieth century. The plays of William Shakespeare were both a product of a learned elite culture and immediately popular and widely attended by people of all walks of life in Shakespeare's era and in subsequent generations.

Second, one must also be careful not to assume that culture is always transmitted "downward" from the elite to the lower classes. Elite culture can be influenced from "below." For example, the practice of men and women "dating" originated in the lower, working classes of American cities in late-nineteenth-century cities and was adopted by young people of the elite classes that wanted to be free of the constraints of the formal courtship.[7]

Finally, the lines between elite, popular, and folk culture are not rigid barriers. A person might move between elite and popular culture. The intellectuals of Renaissance Europe, such as Dante and Petrarch, were a part of an elite culture, well educated, and fluent in Latin. They were bilingual, also fluent in vernacular Italian, and able to participate in the popular culture of Italian cities.[8] But a person's "native" culture is likely to have an impact on how that person perceives the "nonnative" culture. A historian of popular culture might ask, what did Dante and Petrarch think about the popular culture of town festivals in which all people of the community participated? Or in today's terms, how might a person raised outside the elite society that patronizes the arts feel about donating millions of dollars to build a museum or theatre for the ballet or opera?

The complexity of popular culture both today and in the past is what makes its study so exciting. When students are encouraged to analyze the products of popular culture of the past, and ask questions about their production, distribution, and reception by different groups of people, they acquire skills that can be applied to their own popular culture. The objects may have changed from small, clay religious tokens and oral performances to printed materials, such as broadsides, penny press novels, newspapers, and magazines, or to the visual and audio products of television, motion pictures, and the Internet, but the questions we can ask about the cultures that produced them and their impact upon people are often the same.

Key Concepts Related to the Study of Social History

"That's just semantics"—Defining Key Terms and Concepts

The phrases "that's just semantics" or "it's just semantics" are often used, usually as critical comments that translate into "you are making a distinction that really doesn't matter." But words *do* matter when studying history. Simplified, semantics is a broad discipline that studies the meaning of words and phrases. Words may seem similar, and may even be used interchangeably in some contexts, but have distinct meanings. For example, sex and gender are related words with distinct meanings that are often used interchangeably. Social history and popular culture can have different meanings in different contexts. In educated study and discussion, clarity is important.

Furthermore, the meaning of words changes over time. New words that come into common usage can represent new patterns of behavior, new types of power or institutions, or new or changing social relationships. Old words are abandoned that no longer apply to modern life. Learning the history of a word and the context in which the word originated can provide useful insight. The history of the meaning and use of particular words is similar to the study of social change—it occurs slowly and is hard to perceive if viewed over a short period of time or attached to one year or point in history.

Another factor to consider is that commonly used words may have a different or distinct meaning in academic study, referred to as discipline-specific lexicon. For example, *social class* in daily usage is usually a combination of two distinct economic and sociological terms—social class and social status. And to compound the problem, different scholars may use the same terms differently or interchangeably; if a term that is the focus of academic study is not carefully defined and used consistently, then confusion may result.

The *Oxford English Dictionary* is an important tool in the study of the history of key words. The history of this twenty-volume work is a lesson in itself. The volumes began to be published in 1884, after twenty-seven years of work. This dictionary is a historical dictionary that demonstrates the origins and development of the meaning of words over time using short quotations from various time periods. Libraries may have a complete collection, and it is also available online.

Teachers can introduce students to the *Oxford English Dictionary* by choosing a "new" word in the English language such as "hard drive" or an old word that has come to have a new definition such as "computer" or "intercourse." Ask students to compare the meanings of the word over time, its origins, when the word began to be used in the English language, and whether the word is still commonly used, considered archaic, or has taken on a new meaning.

Which People Are We Talking About?—Social Stratification

Social stratification, social ranking based on characteristics such as wealth, occupation, or prestige, is an essential concept in the study of social history. Different words and expressions throughout history have been used to describe the grouping of people in hierarchical social categories—estates, rank, order, social class, and socioeconomic class. And depending upon the era or point of reference, different categories have been recognized—bourgeoisie and the proletariat; upper, middle, and lower classes; white and blue collar; and elite and working class are just a few examples. Students should be familiarized with the key concepts related to social stratification.

The study of social stratification began in the disciplines of economics and sociology with the work of Karl Marx (1818–1883) and Max Weber (1864–1920) and two key terms emerged from their work—*social class* and *social status*. Marx's key contribution to the study of social stratification was identifying the economic basis of class systems and the linking of social classes and political process. While one may disagree with his political theories, these key concepts became the basis for future study of social stratification.

Weber furthered understanding of social stratification by noting that many social class distinctions were not purely based on income or occupation. In other words, Weber made a distinction between *class*, which is based on economic position or income, and *status*, which is based on very subjective and often very hard-to-define factors. Status groups think of themselves as a social community with a common lifestyle and develop common customs related to everyday functions such as eating, dressing, or speaking. These customs are used to rank people within the status group, as well as used to exclude people from the group.[9]

Class and status are related. Status is usually determined by class (how much money one has or earns), but individuals or groups of people can shift to a different status by learning new customs or manners. Advice manuals and etiquette books depict the manners of the middle and upper status groups, the people who had the most money or held the most political power or both. When the economy changes, as it did in the 1700s and 1800s as industrialization increased, new classes of people whose income was based on new types of jobs caused changes in the status structure. These changes were reflected in the rules of behavior prescribed in advice manuals. In other words, books and articles published advice for how a person born in the working class should act in a professional, middle-class setting. At the same time, these publications served as guides on how to exclude people who did not have the "correct" manners.

What exactly does middle class mean? The term "middling sort" was first used in seventeenth-century England, and the meaning can vary depending upon who is asked and what time period is referenced. Prior to the 1700s, middle class described a small group of people between the nobility and the peasants and usually referred to the merchants that lived in towns. So applying the modern concept of middle class to groups of people prior to the eighteenth century is an anachronism. Furthermore, the professions included in the middle class changed as economy and social structure shifted from agricultural to industrial (1700s and 1800s) to postindustrial era (1900s to present).

Modern concepts of middle class also vary. American class structure models vary depending upon whether they are based on purely economic distinctions or seek to include differences in status or prestige. To further confuse the matter, a modern individual might consider his or her status to be middle class, while actual earnings would put that person in the working class—an example of the simultaneous subjective and objective nature of social groups.

For example, a 2012 Pew Research Poll measured *status* when it asked "If you were asked to use one of these commonly used names for the social classes, which would you say you belong in: the upper class, upper-middle class, middle class, lower-middle class or lower class?"[10] The answers of respondents were subjectively based on how each individual chose to define her or his status. On the other hand, the "income calculator" provided by the same organization on a different site determined *class* very objectively by asking for one's actual income and the number of people in the household.[11]

The Choices of the Individual—Agency

How do humans react to historical events or trends? What is the effect of political actions, the economy, technological change, or culture on humans? In other words, are people blank slates who believe and accept the messages of popular culture or do people analyze and reject some or all of these messages? These questions are related to the concept of agency.

Agency is the ability of a person to make her or his own choices and decisions. A social historian must consider whether ordinary people, including the poor, exploited, and oppressed, have agency. Political histories of "great men" usually assume that these powerful political leaders made choices in their own lives, as well as choices for entire nations of people. But can regular people make choices in their lives, or are they passive beings that must follow the patterns created by laws, the economy, or culture?

In the study of American slavery, some historians assumed that slaves were docile and accepting of their fate, without the freedom, will, or energy to rebel or make decisions. Other historians argued that slaves did have a degree of agency in their lives, arriving at these conclusions by reading sources differently or by consulting additional primary sources not written by the free, white observers of slavery, such as the biographies of ex-slaves or the quantitative analysis of plantation records.

Furthermore, the social historian might analyze the types and extent of the choices that were available to a group of people in a given historical era. Using the previous example, the American slaves might not have been able to choose freedom, but they may have had choices open to them, such as how they might practice their religion in order to preserve their dignity.[12]

The Very Different Histories of Men and Women—Sex and Gender

In the quote at the beginning of this chapter, the fictional Catherine Morland notes that there are "hardly any women at all" in history books. She is right! Through time, the population was usually made up of an equal number of females and males, yet men are portrayed as the main characters in history. Women are invisible or, if visible, assumed to have little agency. The study of social history enables women to take their equal place since social history shifts the focus away from political events that have been dominated by men.

If students complain that the themes examined in this book are "girl stuff," you can note how women and men participated equally in every theme in this book. Male and female roles and assumptions about these concepts may have been very different, and the examination of those differing roles can be the topic of critical analysis and provoking discussions. The questioning of three assumptions about sex and gender underlie the activities in this book: gender polarization, androcentrism or male-centeredness, and biological and religious essentialism.[13]

Gender polarization is the assumption that men and women are psychologically opposite and fundamentally different, aside from the obvious biological differences in their bodies. In order to understand gender polarization, one must differentiate between the concepts of sex and gender.[14] *Sex* is defined as the biological differences between males and females—their chromosomes and internal and external sex organs. *Gender* refers to the characteristics that a culture defines as masculine or feminine.

Different cultures ascribe different "rules" for genders, so masculine and feminine qualities across time and culture can change. Gender polarization operates in two ways. First, it creates a mutually exclusive set of characteristics for males and females—masculine traits are expected to be displayed by biological males; feminine traits are expected to be displayed by biological females. Second, any person or behavior that crosses these lines is characterized as problematic—unnatural or immoral in the eyes of religious authority, or biologically abnormal or pathological from a scientific perspective.

In a gender-polarized society, men and women are expected to display the emotions and behaviors of their assigned gender, an expectation that is nearly impossible to meet and inconsistent in an American society that claims to value freedom. Both men and women are made to feel insecure and vulnerable, constantly working to prove that they are "real" men or women. Men who cross boundaries, often referred to as "sissies," are punished more often than women, or the "tomboys," who cross gender boundaries.[15]

Androcentrism is the assumption that men are inherently the dominant or superior sex. This male-centered perspective assumes that male experience is the neutral standard or norm and the female experience is a deviation from this norm. In Western culture, in both pre-Christian Greek and Roman societies, and Christianized Europe, men did hold most of the economic, legal, and political power. In the history of the Jewish, Christian, and Muslim faiths, the deity is male and the proscriptions for women are largely based on the model of the weak nature of the first woman, Eve, who was tempted and sinned in the Garden of Eden. The assumption that men are dominant and superior is often confirmed by the argument that it has "always been that way" throughout both Western and non-Western cultures, and is therefore assumed to be correct and true, or "natural."[16]

Biological and religious essentialism describes the efforts to support or prove that these first two assumptions, male and female differences and male dominance, are natural. Even after the advent of scientific research and reasoning, conclusions were made that assumed male dominance. For example, Herbert Spencer's (1820–1903) "progressive" theory of evolution concluded that the existence of a class- and sex-based division of labor in society was biologically natural. He argued the theory that came to be known as Social Darwinism: that biology molded social classes and the male and female sexes to fit the roles that they were expected to hold in the culture of the late nineteenth century. It was Spencer who coined the phrase "survival of the fittest" to fit the belief that reform movements and government should not make efforts to relieve the suffering of humans.

Even today, scientifically valid research and theories can be interpreted in ways that justify male dominance or exaggerate male and female differences. For example, evolutionary theories have explained that the differentiation in labor by sex in preindustrial societies was created by the biological demands of birth and childcare. Women did not hunt or fight because they were often limited by pregnancy or the care of children. Even though this theory does not apply to our own, and very different, postindustrial society, it is often evoked to describe and justify the predominant role of men.[17]

While examining the themes and primary sources that follow, ask students to notice how the pronouns *he* and *she* are used in historical sources and ask why *he* is used to describe all people; why schooling throughout history was stressed for men but often optional, substandard, or even discouraged for women; why a majority of authors of primary sources were men; why women were expected to act one way, men in another manner; how the different clothing of men and women encouraged or limited their role in society.

The purpose here is not to criticize men or to value a past society as "good" or "bad," but to learn to wear a new pair of cultural glasses that can be used outside the classroom to evaluate modern society. It is easy for students to assume that because the roles of males and females have changed so much when compared to the past, that all is equal in modern society, but gender polarization, androcentrism, and biological and religious essentialism are still present. Challenge students to examine assumptions in their own culture about the roles of men and women.

The Slow Pace of Change in Social History—Generational Change

Studying social history in the classroom can be difficult because changes in behavior over time usually occur slowly; are often difficult to identify in a very specific, concrete manner; and rarely fall on specific dates or neatly on a timeline. Students may struggle to conceive of changes in social history since they may be accustomed to learning specific dates and discrete lists of causes and effects.

In a single lifetime, seemingly unconnected and unimportant events that are considered trivial to an individual are a part of a larger pattern of cultural, technological, economic, or political changes. In many cases, the history of a cultural or social idea may stretch back in time for centuries and across different cultures. For example, the symbols used in ancient Egyptian architecture and mortuary monuments appear throughout Western history into the twentieth century. However, framing the shifts in social history themes in terms of a "generation" can be useful by helping students place change in terms of the life cycle of humans.

Social changes can be framed using the concept of *familial generations*. A familial generation is from the birth of a parent to the birth of a child and was around twenty years for most of history, but it has been climbing since the eighteenth century to about thirty years in industrialized nations today. So, for example, the grandparents of a student today are removed by two familial generations, or approximately sixty years and products of the culture of the 1950s or 1960s (at the time of publication). The Civil War is removed by about six generations. Using an example of a family tree, easy to obtain in the era of online genealogy research, can assist in illustrating both the distance in time of past eras and the continuity of social history themes.

In sociology, a *social generation* or a *cohort* is a group of people who were born in the same date range and share the same experiences. In historical eras when technological, economic, or intellectual changes have occurred quickly, a generation of young people may have very different life experiences, thus making their daily lives and attitudes different from their parents' or grandparents' generation. The younger generation may have greater opportunities to move to a higher socioeconomic status or may have opportunities to move to a different region of the country or world and thus adopt different ways of living. On the other hand, in preindustrial societies, the pace of change was generally much slower, so the lives of children, their parents, grandparents, and great-grandparents may have been very similar.

"Generation gap" is the term commonly used to describe the differing attitudes between children and their parents or grandparents. Students are likely to recognize at least one of the modern designated or named generations such as the baby boomers (1946–1964), generation X (early 1960s to early 1980s), and millennials (early 1980s–early 2000s). Middle and high school students at the time of the publication of this book fall into the newest named cohort—generation Z (1990–mid-2010s).

Ask students to list issues on which they disagree with their parents or grandparents, and a long list will be compiled very quickly. Encourage students to discuss *why* these disagreements occur, and they will very likely connect these points of disagreement to societal changes driven by technological, economic, or political change. For example "my parents want to restrict social media use" connects to "they didn't have cell phones or social media when they were young." To place the discussion in a historical context, brainstorm and discuss issues that caused disagreements between their parents or grandparents and their previous generation. For example, many American families before the 1950s did not own a car. How might the use of a family car cause conflicts between teenagers and parents in the 1950s?

After discussing how students' attitudes differ from those of previous generations of their family, ask the students to note issues in which they agree with the views and values of their family. This discussion opens an opportunity for the teacher to introduce and discuss the concept of *enculturation*, the process of learning (consciously and subconsciously) the expectations of one's culture. People learn values and behaviors from parents and family members, schooling, peers, and the mass media. Often, these values or ways of seeing the world are so embedded in the culture that it is difficult for a native of that culture to distinguish and recognize them.

The terms *cultural meta-message* and *subtext* describe the subconscious ways in which an individual subconsciously learns to "wear the glasses" of her or his native culture—the ways a society defines what is of importance and of value, which differences between people should be emphasized or overlooked. For example, historically, American culture has emphasized differences in race, ethnicity, sex, and gender more than it has emphasized differences in social classes. Social stratification exists in the United States, but it is not discussed and emphasized to the degree it was in medieval Europe.

Meta-messages can also be illustrated using the example of how children are taught to tell time and be conscious of the time by wearing a watch (or using the time function on a cellphone). Clocks are prominent in classrooms and workplaces; everything is carefully scheduled to begin and end at an exact time. Children don't just learn to tell time through formal lessons, they absorb the meta-message that their culture values time, timeliness, and doing things on a schedule.[18]

Social History Before and After the Printing Press

History is commonly organized by eras with specific or approximate start and end dates, and these eras often become the units in a history curriculum. History in the classroom can become fragments of time that appear to have no connection to what happened before or after. The Ancient World, The Middle Ages, Renaissance and Reformation, The Age of Reason, and the Enlightenment are commonly used for Western history. Earlier American history is divided into eras covering several decades—Colonial, Revolutionary, Early Republic, Civil War, and Gilded Age—until the twentieth century, and then it seems to fall conveniently into decades. This periodization of history is an anachronism, imposed on the past by scholars in order to study history.

Determining precise dates on which to begin and end an era is often the subject of contention among historians, and proposing new dates or eras or recharacterizing key elements with an era has been the thesis of many articles and historical monographs. For example, the "Early Modern Period" begins in the 1300s, 1400s, or 1500s and ends in the 1500s, 1600s, or 1700s, depending upon which historian is consulted and what factors are used to define the era. To further confuse the issue, the time over which social and cultural change occurs is much longer and slower than political change.

Social history crosses the lines of traditionally recognized eras. While references to commonly known eras are used in this book, two reference points are especially important. First is the distinction between preindustrial society and the society that came after the Industrial Revolution. The production of simple necessities of life such as food, clothing, and shelter consumed most of the time of the majority of people before industrialization. The shift occurred between 1750 and 1850—earlier in England, later in parts of Europe and America.

The technological innovations of the era launched a period of economic growth in which the standard of living of a large part of the population improved. Mass-produced goods became available and changed the daily lives of the majority of regular people. Life during and after industrialization was not suddenly easy and carefree, but the nature of labor and leisure changed with the availability of affordable, mass-produced food, clothing, shelter, and items for the home, and the industrialized methods of transportation.

The second marker is the shift that started in the 1400s caused by the invention of moveable type printing and the development of cheap paper. These technologies began to make popular culture a larger, mass-produced phenomena, rather than regional or national. In the 1500s and 1600s, printed materials of all types began to be available to a wider audience, and literacy rates increased steadily.[19] Throughout the eighteenth and nineteenth centuries, printing technology improved, and later, the invention of radio, television, and computer communication created a popular culture that was accessible to a wide majority of the population.

This fifteenth-century shift is important to students and teachers who seek to read and analyze primary sources. Primary sources before the printing press were handwritten and copied and only available to the small elite minority of the population who were literate. Therefore, the study of written sources raises important issues that must be addressed when examining the lives of everyday people.

Printed primary sources in the transitional period between the fifteenth and seventeenth centuries may have reached a wider swath of people than ever before, but one can't assume that printed texts represented all social stratifications. Even in the nineteenth, twentieth, and twenty-first centuries, everybody did not read everything, and the historian must assess who read what and for what purpose.

Thematic Instruction

Thematic instruction is difficult to define precisely using published education literature because it is so often associated with or a component of several other instructional approaches and strategies, most commonly interdisciplinary or integrated instruction. For example, in a review of literature on the subject published in 1994, Kathy Lake identified seven elements common to integrated curriculum models: a combination of subjects; an emphasis on projects; the use of a wide variety of source material, not just textbooks; highlighting relationships among concepts; *thematic units*; flexible schedules; and flexible student grouping.[20]

A definition of interdisciplinary/integrated instruction published in 1998 is as follows: "related terms used somewhat interchangeably to indicate the bringing together of separate disciplines around common themes, issues, or problems."[21] But variations of thematic instruction have probably existed for as long as teaching and schools have existed. One could argue that it originated with the progressive education philosophy in the late nineteenth century.

Models of this type of instruction were especially popular during the 1990s.[22] These texts covered all aspects of designing and assessing interdisciplinary/integrated classroom units and whole-school curriculum, how to select appropriate themes and activities, and how to overcome common challenges. But as a whole, these texts are relatively content neutral. As several authors noted, gaining the in-depth content knowledge needed to design and teach interdisciplinary/integrated instruction is one of the most common barriers to implementation, yet this topic is beyond the scope of pedagogy-centered books. This is the gap that this book is intended to fill for middle and secondary social studies teachers: detailed content and relevant primary sources with guidance on how to develop one's own thematic social studies units.

The combination of elements usually included in interdisciplinary/integrated instruction has not gone out of style in more recent, twenty-first-century education publications. Well-known education scholars have highlighted essential elements of the interdisciplinary/integrated instruction approach in recent publications:

- Carol Ann Tomlinson, differentiated instruction expert, repeatedly emphasizes the need to allow student choice in the classroom.
- Robert Marzano and Debra Pickering, authors of several texts that describe research-based strategies, stress the importance of connecting to students' lives, allowing for student choice, and making real-world applications.
- Brigid Barron and Linda Darling-Hammond summarized recent research and described several successful project-based and problem-based learning approaches, all versions of interdisciplinary/integrated instruction.[23]

The interdisciplinary/integrated instructional approach has received a twenty-first-century makeover in recent years, now often described as project-based learning. Project-based learning includes the essential elements previously included in the integrated approach, updated to include many of the newest education expectations, such as differentiation, and twenty-first-century skills, such as collaboration, communication, and critical thinking.[24]

Since many different terms have been used for thematic instruction over decades and the label has included a wide range of educational strategies, it important to define it precisely for this book. **Thematic teaching** *is the selection and highlighting of a theme through a unit, or a course, or a series of courses within the social studies, or crossing disciplinary lines in other courses. The theme should be recurrent through human history and present in modern life. It can be a topic, such as vacations or manners, or the theme can take the form of an overarching question, called essential questions or compelling questions in the current publications.*

Ideally, the theme should be something about which students already possess some knowledge in their daily lives or in their community so that connections made to the theme are immediately relevant. While interdisciplinary/integrated instruction is usually associated with the progressive philosophy of education, thematic instruction can be associated with any educational philosophy, depending upon the theme that is chosen and the instructional strategies that are used in the classroom. Any teacher, at any point on the spectrum of educational philosophies, can incorporate thematic teaching. And even though thematic teaching is most often associated with elementary classrooms and middle schools that use the team-based approach, it is possible within an individual course, or across courses, in a high school setting.

The advantages of thematic teaching, as described in the literature, are numerous.

- Students learn better when experiencing knowledge in a larger context in order to see relationships and connections
- Larger themes and concepts more closely resemble how we experience life outside of the school and classroom
- Themes can be chosen that are student-centered and incorporate the needs, interests, and perspectives of the students
- Carefully selecting knowledge related to a theme can help teachers narrow down the overwhelming amount of information that is available in any discipline[25] (consider the thousands of years of written history—so much history, so little time to teach it!)

When thematic instruction is used in the study of history, it has the following additional benefits:

- Students make connections between seemingly distant and irrelevant events, people, and cultures in the past to their daily modern lives.
- Students analyze their own modern culture and community through new eyes, in this case, through the "social history glasses."
- Thematic instruction might inspire students to become more interested in history and social studies.
- The disciplinary tools of history and social sciences that are stressed in current teaching standards—questioning, analysis, critical reading, and writing—can be incorporated in a more meaningful way.
- Teachers may discover new professional inspiration while exploring themes relevant to both the classes they teach and their personal interests.

Conclusion

When one considers human history thematically, over centuries or millennia, instead of chopped up into discrete political time periods and instructional units, a new way of looking at ourselves, or society, and the history of humans develops. Both change and consistency in daily life become more evident, and this realization encourages a reexamination of modern assumptions and daily routines in a new light.

Social history is about examining the lives of average people, often using evidence from unlikely places. Social historians look for patterns in all sorts of primary sources, ask questions about the patterns they see, and seek answers about when the patterns originated, their causes, and how they changed or stayed the same over time. Teaching students the methods of the historian, as well as how to look through the lenses of critical analysis, will encourage them to think critically about their own lives and culture and the "primary sources" of the modern world that influence their thoughts, beliefs, and actions.

Notes

1. Jane Austen, *Northanger Abbey* (1818), in *The Works of Jane Austen* (London: Allan Wingate, 1962), chapter 14, 824.
2. Peter N. Stearns, "Social History Present and Future," *Journal of Social History* 37, no. 1 (Autumn 2003): 14, http://www.jstor.org/stable/3790307.
3. Gary J. Kornblith and Carol Lasser, "More Than Great White Men: A Century of Scholarship on American Social History," *OAH Magazine of History* 21, no. 2 (April 2007): 8.
4. Fred. E. H. Schroeder, "The Discovery of Popular Culture Before Printing," introduction in *5000 Years of Popular Culture, Popular Culture Before Printing*, ed. Fred. E. H. Schroeder (Bowling Green, OH: Bowling Green University Popular Press, 1980), 3–15.

5. Michael Schudson, "The New Validation of Popular Culture: Sense and Sentimentality in Academia," *Critical Studies in Mass Communication* 4 (1987): 51–68; and John Tosh, *The Pursuit of History: Aims, Methods and New Directions in the Study of History*, 6th ed. (London and New York: Routledge, Taylor & Francis Group, 2015), 206.

6. Schroeder, "The Discovery of Popular Culture Before Printing," 4.

7. Beth L. Bailey, *From Front Porch to Back Seat: Courtship in Twentieth-Century America* (Baltimore, MD: Johns Hopkins University Press, 1989), 13–18.

8. Peter Burke, *Popular Culture in Early Modern Europe* (New York: New York University Press, 1978), 28.

9. Dennis Gilbert, *The American Class Structure in an Age of Growing Inequality*, 9th ed. (Thousand Oaks, CA: Sage, 2015), 1–18.

10. Rich Morin and Seth Motel, "A Third of Americans Now Say They Are in the Lower Classes," Pew Research Center, September 10, 2012, accessed May 4, 2016, http://www.pewsocialtrends.org/2012/09/10/a-third-of-americans-now-say-they-are-in-the-lower-classes/.

11. Richard Fry and Rakesh Kochhar, "Are You in the American Middle Class? Find Out with Our Income Calculator," Pew Research Center, September 10, 2012, accessed May 4, 2016, http://www.pewresearch.org/fact-tank/2016/05/11/are-you-in-the-american-middle-class/.

12. Kornblith and Lasser, "More Than Great White Men"; and Eugene D. Genovese, *Roll, Jordan, Roll: The World the Slaves Made* (New York: Vintage Books, 1976).

13. Sandra Lipsitz Bem, *The Lenses of Gender, Transforming the Debate on Sexual Inequality* (New Haven, CT: Yale University Press, 1993), chapter 1.

14. The distinction between the words sex and gender is a fairly recent development. The use of the word gender to describe social or cultural distinctions and differences, instead of biological ones, originated in the United States in 1945. *Oxford English Dictionary Online*, s.v. "courtesy, n." "gender, n.," June 2016, http://www.oed.com/view/Entry/77468?rskey=ZwrspE&result=1.

15. Bem, *Lenses of Gender*, chapter 4.

16. Ibid., chapter 3.

17. Ibid., chapter 2.

18. Ibid., 140.

19. Schroeder, "The Discovery of Popular Culture Before Printing," 3–15.

20. Kathy Lake, "Integrated Curriculum." School Improvement Research Series VIII (Portland OR: Northwest Regional Educational Laboratory, 1994), accessed April 28, 2016, http://educationnorthwest.org/webfm_send/528.

21. Arthur K. Ellis and Carol J. Stuen, *The Interdisciplinary Curriculum* (Larchmont, NY: Eye on Education: 1998), 174.

22. Susan Kovalik and Karen Olsen, *ITI: The Model, Integrated Thematic Instruction* (Federal Way, WA: Susan Kovalik & Associates, 1993); Robin Fogarty, *The Mindful School: How to Integrate the Curricula* (Palatine, IL: Skylight Publishing, Inc., 1991); Robin Fogarty and Brian Pete, *How to Integrate the Curricula*, 3rd ed. (Thousand Oaks, CA: Corwin Press, 2009); Patricia L. Roberts and Richard D. Kellough, *A Guide for Developing Interdisciplinary Thematic Units* (Upper Saddle River, NJ: Pearson, 1996, 2000, 2004, 2006); Arthur K. Ellis and Carol J. Stuen, *The Interdisciplinary Curriculum*; Samuel S. Wineburg and Pamela L. Grossman, *Interdisciplinary Curriculum: Challenges to Implementation* (New York, NY: Teachers College Press, 2000).

23. Brigid Barron and Linda Darling-Hammond, "How Can We Teach for Meaningful Learning?" in *Powerful Learning: What We Know about Teaching for Understanding*, ed. L. Darling-Hammond (San Francisco: Jossey-Bass, 2008), 11–70.

24. Buck Institute for Education, "Why Project Based Learning (PBL)?" accessed April 28, 2016, http://www.bie.org.

25. Ellis and Stuen, *The Interdisciplinary Curriculum*, 69–70.

CHAPTER TWO

Vacations

How are our individual perceptions of vacation destinations impacted by others?

- What is the effect of popular culture and mass media on our individual thoughts and ideas of vacation? How do fiction, travel guides, advertising, movies, television, and the Internet impact our conceptions of vacation?
- Do we, as individuals, really have agency, or are our ideas and decisions a product of our culture and collective memory?

How did cultural expectations and economic realities impact vacation in the past? Are those factors still present today?

- In the past, what groups of people had vacations? Why did people take a vacation or travel for leisure? Why did people choose different types of vacation?
- Did ethnicity, race, sex, religion, or social class impact the decisions of individuals to take vacations and vacation destinations?

Vacations . . . students and teachers dream of summer vacation. Getting away from the everyday routine has been a desire of people throughout time. But the places we go, the reasons we want to visit, what we do when we get there, and the amount of time for vacation varies greatly. The concept of travel away from home for pleasure in medieval Europe and nineteenth- and twentieth-century America is the focus of this chapter.

An examination of medieval pilgrimage, generally considered travel for purely religious reasons, can offer insight into the travel of preindustrial people who were also seeking diversion from the routines of daily life. Student analysis of primary sources can shed light upon medieval popular culture and the unique challenges of reading sources produced before the printing press. Until the industrial era, most leisure travel was possible only for the wealthiest elite. But the massive economic and technological changes caused by the Industrial Revolution made a vacation possible for more and more people beginning in the nineteenth century. Popular media and advertisers, then and now, make it appear that everyone can and should take a vacation, but one's gender, social and economic status, race, and ethnicity shape both conceptions of and access to vacation.

Studying vacation as a theme through time can illustrate the concept of a *cultural circuit*[1]—a continuous interrelationship between myth and reality that involves every discipline within the social studies. Vacation is related to tourist destinations on the map (geography) that evolve over time. At the same time, individual experiences and widely circulated accounts of travel from both the past (history) and present (current events) influence what subsequent visitors think about that destination.

Figure 2.1. This photograph and its original caption, "An American Family Launches a Pilgrimage through Lincoln Land," captures the relationship between the family-centered focus of the post–World War II era, the promotion of heritage tourism featuring American history, culture, and patriotism, and the concept of tourism as a pilgrimage.
Source: Ralph Gray, "Vacation Tour Through Lincoln Land," National Geographic 101, no. 2 (February 1952): 149. Reproduced by permission from William Ralph Gray / National Geographic Creative.

A collective memory is drawn upon when thinking about vacation and destinations; popular conceptions often include stereotypical views of the people at travel destinations and of other travelers to those destinations based on their sex, gender, social class, race, and ethnicity (sociology). Another layer of complexity is added to this cultural circuit when travel and vacation is commercialized—packaged, advertised, and sold for profit (economics). Collective memories of vacation are manipulated in advertising and government promotion (political science) of tourism in order to sell more vacations to more people. Historians and other social scientists seek to unravel these connections, often aware that it may never be possible to accomplish the task, but still eager to attempt the challenge.

Defining the Concept of Travel for Leisure

The ancient Greeks and Romans used the word ἰστορία, often translated to mean "history," to describe the urge to travel in order to locate places and objects of historical interest; a type of educational tourism. For example, around 83 AD Plutarch used the word ἰστορία when he described an encounter between two travelers at Delphi "for the purpose of investigation and sight-seeing."[2] Pausanias (c. AD 110–c. 180), a Greek geographer who lived in the time of the Roman emperors Hadrian, Antoninus Pius, and Marcus Aurelius, wrote *Description of Greece*.[3] This educational guidebook described the monuments of the golden age of Greece, as much as three- or four hundred years before his own time. His interest in travel was similar to that of a modern American who tours sites important in American history before the Revolution. Pausanias didn't just repeat the information provided by the local tour guides, he often criticized their inaccuracies and provided additional information for the reader, much like a modern travel guide writer today.

Terms used for leisure travel before the mid-1800s were traveler, tour, resort, or a summer stay, and the word *vacation* only referred to a break that a student or teacher took from school. But in the mid-nineteenth century, the meaning of "vacation" shifted; the term began to be used to describe a time set aside for the purpose of recreation. Newspaper and magazine articles used *vacation* when describing the advantages of restoring oneself physically and mentally from the demands of work in a new, fast-paced, urban environment of an industrialized society.[4] For example, an article in a July 1855 *New York Daily Times* claimed that due to "incessant brain-work, unaccompanied by proper exercise of the muscles and by sufficient open-air amusement" the health of American businessmen was declining and vacations were recommended.[5]

Tourism is a concept closely related to vacation but with slightly different connotations. Vacation is the time away from daily life; tourism is something people do while on vacation. Tourists travel to destinations for entertainment or to visit cultural, historical, religious, or natural sites. According to historian Richard Gassan, tourism can also be defined much more precisely as "a kind of travel that creates an illusion of novelty while remaining within a narrow range of societally defined boundaries."[6]

The three "societally defined boundaries"—a destination that people want to visit, transportation systems and facilities that allow tourists to get to the destination, and a cultural infrastructure [7]—are useful in an analysis of tourism in the past. These three elements continually interact in a cultural circuit, each promoting the growth or decline of the other. For example, the cultural infrastructure is the information about the destination that provides tourists with a reason to visit and an expectation of what one can expect to see and do.

After the visit, the tourist shares the experience with friends back home. Additional information about a destination also circulates within a culture, transmitted through the published or personal accounts of other tourists, works of art, guidebooks, promotional and advertising material, and through all forms of the popular media of the era, including newspapers, magazines, television, movies, and more recently websites and social media.

If a destination becomes popular, transportation is improved and more hotels, restaurants, and attractions are opened; when a destination becomes less popular, the destinations and tourist infrastructure decline and close. The cultural circuit between tourist destinations, how government and private enterprise supports tourism infrastructures, and how a culture values and defines vacation and tourism waxes, wanes, shifts, and changes over time, sometimes repeating the same ideas for centuries. This is one of the most interesting aspects of the study of vacation over time.

Was Medieval Pilgrimage a Vacation?

A pilgrimage is "the physical journey from one's normal place of residence to a religious shrine" in order to honor or request a special favor from a recognized holy being.[8] Pilgrimage is not unique to just one era or one religion. Many ancient and modern religions recognize pilgrimage. Pilgrimage is an important element in historical and modern Buddhism, Christianity, Hinduism, Islam, and Judaism.

Some might argue that Christian Protestant faiths exclude pilgrimage because of the rejection of the veneration of saints and relics, but many Protestants visit the Holy Land in order to see the places where Jesus and other biblical people lived and died. The Church of Jesus Christ of Latter-Day Saints maintains important sites in the development of the Mormon faith, encourages visits, and educates visitors in the history and faith.

A medieval pilgrim visited the religious shrines to honor or request favors from a saint, often represented at the shrine by a holy relic. A saint was a family member or apostle of Jesus, a martyr, a missionary, church leader, or an especially holy person who had died and was believed to act as an intermediary between humans and God. Pilgrims believed that the shrine of a saint was a point in the physical world that had a connection with the holy, spiritual world. The venerated saint might have lived, appeared, died, or been buried at the site or been associated with a miracle at the site. Churches usually held the relics of one or more saints—items that belonged to the saint or a piece of the body of the saint. It was the miraculous power believed to flow through the relics of saints that drew pilgrims.

Life was terrifying in the Middle Ages; medieval people had few defenses against illness, violence, or starvation, and a saint's protection and miraculous powers were sought by many people of all social classes. Medieval pilgrimages could be very short trips to numerous local shrines or journeys of many months to distant shrines, with many stops at the shrines of saints along the way. Over three thousand individual saints have been documented from the late Roman and medieval periods of history.[9]

The three most famous Christian sites in the Middle Ages, and still very popular today, are Jerusalem and the Holy Land (the region between the Jordan River and the Mediterranean Sea in which events of the Bible took place); Rome, the seat of the Roman Catholic Church; and the shrine of St. James, often referred to by its Spanish name, Santiago de Compostela, in northwestern Spain. When the crusading movement began in the late eleventh century, crusaders were also considered pilgrims with special permission from the Church to carry arms in order to conquer or defend the Holy Land.

If one is to consider pilgrimage as a form of vacation, or travel for recreation, then there must be evidence that pilgrims were motived by more than just faith. Pilgrimage is primarily a religious act, therefore, pilgrims' accounts tend to feature religious motives, not motives that might be associated with leisure or recreation. Many medieval pilgrims were monks, clerics, priests, nuns, or other employees of the Church. Therefore, the primary motive evident in their accounts of pilgrimage is religious devotion, reflecting their faith and obligation to the Church. But human actions are usually inspired by a mix of motivations.

Descriptions of nonreligious motives, such as a desire to escape the daily routine, see new things, and meet new people, can be found in works by churchmen who are critical of pilgrims who do not show the proper devotion. Jacques de Vitry (c. 1160/70–1240), a canon and bishop of the Catholic Church, wrote that "some light-minded and inquisitive persons went on pilgrimage to the holy places, not so much out of devotion as out of curiosity and love of novelty, that they might travel to unknown lands, and with great toil . . . might prove the stories which they had heard about the East."[10] A writer in the fifteenth century criticized the populace who wanted to go on pilgrimage out of a "curiosity to see new places and experience new things, impatience of the servant with his master, of children with their parents, or wives with their husbands."[11]

Information about travel by medieval merchants, envoys of the Church, secular rulers, and nobles who visited the Holy Land has survived, providing evidence that business, religious pilgrimage, and pleasure were often combined on one journey. The pilgrims in Chaucer's *Canterbury Tales* met new people and entertained themselves with stories on the journey to the Shrine of Saint Thomas Becket. Crusaders, armed knights who took the pilgrim's vow to fight for Christianity in the Holy Land, were also inspired by the adventure, riches, and exotic sites in the East.[12]

Not all pilgrims went voluntarily. Both lay and ecclesiastical authorities encouraged pilgrimage as a penance for sins or crimes. Thieves disguised themselves as pilgrims and preyed upon travelers along the road.[13] Because the lower classes of people were illiterate in the medieval era, their experiences were not recorded in their own words. But pilgrimages to local shrines were possible and encouraged by the Church, and we can assume that this silent majority of working people also had many different motivations.

A single primary source rarely provides a complete and explicit explanation of human motivation. Humans tend to record only part of their experience, the part that is most likely to be acceptable to their potential readers. Historians can also examine the motives of modern religious pilgrims and cautiously apply that analysis to historical pilgrimage. For example, sociologists have found that the modern pilgrims struggle to find the words to describe all of their motives for going on pilgrimage. Even when religious motives are primary, modern pilgrims will also note, often as asides to their main narrative, that they went for other reasons such as to see beautiful scenery, to visit famous locations, or to socialize with other people who have similar interests.[14]

Pilgrimage is a form of travel in which the three elements of tourism are present—shrines as destinations, a physical infrastructure to visit those sites, and a culture that promoted travel in the form of pilgrimage.[15] First, late Roman and early medieval Christians valued saints and the relics of saints.[16] Miracle stories were circulated, and the locations of these miracles developed into pilgrimage shrines. The oldest surviving written account of pilgrimage is from the year 333 by an unknown author from Bordeaux, France.[17]

Then, as more and more pilgrims sought to visit pilgrimage shrines, monasteries, churches, and private individuals on the route began to provide places to stay, food, souvenirs, and other services for religious, economic, and political motives. More stories about miracles and information on how to visit a shrine were circulated by sponsors of shrines and by pilgrims who had visited shrines, causing more people to want to visit. Many elements within medieval culture, both popular and elite, identified the shrines to visit, provided and improved the tourist infrastructure, and promoted pilgrimage.

Premodern methods of the promotion of medieval pilgrimage have parallels in modern tourism. In the Middle Ages, the monastic order or church that administered a shrine carefully recorded the miracles that occurred at the shrine or as a result of the saint's intervention in order to further "advertise" its shrine. These miracles were circulated in the form of stories of the deeds of the saint, a genre of writing called hagiography by modern scholars. Bishops, priests, monks, and clerics were motivated by faith, but one must also consider that well-known saints were fundraisers for the church. Shrines, saints, and their relics were depended upon to inspire cash donations by visitors to the shrine.

Pilgrims made donations for the redemption of their souls, the souls of their ancestors, and for the saint's favor in this life. This money was vital to both the Church and the wider community in which the shrine was located. This revenue was used for the maintenance and renovation of the shrine, the monastery or church, for the support of those who worked for the church, and improvements of roads, bridges, and other "tourist" infrastructure. Therefore, promotion of pilgrimage, the miracles of saints, and their shrines was in the religious *and* economic interest of both the Church and the wider community.

Just as a modern tourist spends money in the community surrounding a tourist site, the pilgrim ate meals, paid for places to stay, and bought souvenirs. The most common souvenir sold was the pilgrim's badge. These small tokens, usually metal and stamped with the symbol of the saint, could be worn on the clothing of the pilgrim to show where he or she had visited.

One of the best known and earliest was the palm of Jericho that pilgrims brought back from Jerusalem. The cockle shells worn by pilgrims to the shrine of St. James were first collected from the beach near Santiago. By the twelfth century, they were replaced by small lead badges in the shape of a shell. The sale of these souvenirs was regulated and taxed by the archbishop of Santiago.

Figure 2.2. St. James as a pilgrim, by Hieronymus Bosch. St. James wears the distinctive clothing of a medieval pilgrim—a long tunic called a sclavein, a wooden staff, and scrip to carry his belongings at his waist. The broad-brimmed hat turned up in the front, commonly depicted on pilgrims by the mid-thirteenth century, has a cockle shell badge, the symbol of his shrine. Bare feet were considered a type of penance, a self-punishment for one's sins. He is also carrying a knife and a book, not typical for a pilgrim. The book symbolizes James's status as an apostle; the knife symbolizes his role as Saint James, the Moor slayer, or may refer to the dangers on the pilgrim route. In the background, on the right, a pilgrim is being attacked. This painting is on the outside, left shutter of the three-panel triptych entitled *The Last Judgement*, painted in the late fifteenth or early sixteenth century.
Source: Hieronymus Bosch, The Last Judgement, *circa 1450–1516 via Wikimedia Commons. Original painting located at Academy of Fine Arts in Vienna, Austria.*

Lead badges, usually a small disc depicting the patron saint, were produced in large quantities for sale to pilgrims at many shrines. Pilgrims' badges were prized possessions, often believed to have miraculous healing powers and used by pilgrims as exceptions for certain taxes and tolls. Once back home, the badge, sewn to hats or clothing, symbolized one's devotion and further promoted the shrine and saint to others.[18]

Individual pilgrims returned from their travels and told their stories orally or in writing, inspiring others to go on pilgrimage and making pilgrimage more and more popular over time. Historian Jonathan Sumption noted that between the twelfth century and the fifteenth century, the numbers of pilgrims and accounts by pilgrims grew steadily. The infrastructure that served pilgrims grew, and travel to pilgrim sites became cheaper and easier because of improvements in transportation in the centuries of the high and late Middle Ages (c. 1000–1500).

For example, Venetian ship owners began to provide all-inclusive package tours, and the Venetian government, by the early thirteenth century, began to regulate the traffic in pilgrims. The package tour fare included food, lodging, all required tolls and taxes, guided tours of Jerusalem, and even special expeditions to the Jordan River.[19] In the mid-fourteenth century, the appearance of *Mandeville's Travels* made travel accounts even more popular. Purporting to be an account of the travels of Sir John Mandeville to Palestine, Turkey, Persia, India, and Egypt, the book was really a compilation of various previous itineraries with wild, fictional stories attributed to a man who probably never existed.

Over three hundred manuscripts survive, and the account was translated and circulated throughout Europe. Its popularity grew when countless editions were printed and distributed across Europe. The popularity of *Mandeville's Travels* inspired the publication of thousands of travel narratives and pilgrims' accounts over the next centuries. These narratives reflected a growing fascination with travel and pilgrimage and created new interest in the places described.[20]

Thus, information about pilgrimage became a part of the *collective memory*, also referred to as *social* or *public memory*. These terms describe the process in which individuals blend their own personal memories of places or events with the information provided by friends, family, and information from the wider culture, such as lessons learned in school or church, and perceptions absorbed from the media of the era. In other words, what an individual knows is mediated, or influenced, by the assumptions and beliefs of one's wider culture. Social memory that becomes distorted or disconnected from reality becomes a *social myth*—popular beliefs that are inaccurate, yet influence how we comprehend what we see, or how we interpret the actions of others.[21]

Modern "urban legends" can be helpful in illustrating this concept to students.[22] Often, these stories and assumptions about other places, or about the past, help to validate beliefs about our own culture. For example, the following observation from a fourteenth-century pilgrim's account helped to confirm the collective memories of previous experiences of Christian pilgrims and crusaders—that foreign cities and Muslims were not what they appeared to be. The author, a Franciscan friar, was warning others that while Eastern cities and Muslims might be interesting to the traveler, they were both deceitful.

> [Alexandria] although it shines in beauty to the person approaching, yet it has narrow, crooked, dark streets, full of dust and other filth and is in no place paved; in which there is a great abundance of everything except wine which is most dear there, because the perfect Saracens never drink wine, neither at home [or] publicly, but in private and hiddenly (sic.) they drink and that to a nauseating state.[23]

The concept of collective memory was first introduced by French sociologist Maurice Halbwachs (1877–1945) and based on his groundbreaking study using travel accounts written by Westerners about their trips to the Holy Land. He discovered that many of the facts that pilgrims included about the sites were incorrect and originated from accounts in previous historical periods. For example, François-René de Chateaubriand (1768–1848), a French writer and politician, published his account of his journey to the Holy Land in the early nineteenth century. In this account, he traced the footsteps of the First Crusaders, using a mostly fictional epic poem by an Italian poet, Torquato Tasso, called *Jerusalem Delivered* and published in 1581. An eighteenth-century account, based on historical fiction written in the sixteenth century, about a historical event in the late eleventh century, inspired by biblical accounts recorded in the first century, about events that took place during the life of Jesus believed to have happened around 33 AD—five layers of historical descriptions that combined myth, reality, and religious faith, all believed to be true in the nineteenth century. Halbwachs concluded that collective memory of the Holy Land proved to be more powerful than individual recollections.[24]

Even today, modern perceptions of the Middle East and the Holy Land are influenced by centuries of travel narratives, impressions from religious education, accounts of modern pilgrims, and the many forms of mass media. Collective memories and myths related to vacation and travel have an impact on how we see and interpret the people, places, and culture at modern tourist destinations; these cultural lenses can distort our view. When social historians view the past, they must be aware of their own lenses imposed by modern culture, as well as recognize collective memories that may distort the recollections of historical pilgrimage, vacations, and travel.

Vacationing in American History

Most Americans living before the mid-1800s could only dream of time away from work. In preindustrial America, transportation by foot, horse, or boat was slow, time-consuming and prohibitively expensive for the majority of Americans who made a living on farms or in small workshops where work was required on a daily basis. Leisure time was spent close to home. In 1786, the journey between Boston and New York, a journey of about two hundred miles, took from four to six days, depending on the weather and road conditions.[25] Today, on modern highways, this trip takes about four hours and only about one hour by plane. Working-class Americans did travel for family matters, for business, or to migrate, but usually not to relax.

Only the wealthy could afford to travel for pleasure before the mid-nineteenth century. The main destinations were resorts with mineral springs, "watering places," that provided both entertainment and water cures for a variety of ailments. White Sulphur Springs, Virginia, (now The Greenbriar in West Virginia) and Saratoga Springs, New York, were two of the best-known resorts. Many more regionally known resorts existed as well.

Bathing or soaking in the mineral spring water or taking the water internally were believed to have curative qualities and were part of a popular medical trend in the early nineteenth century called hydropathy. While some people visited for their health, many more visited these resorts for entertainment.

Nineteenth-century resorts offered as many different diversions as all-inclusive resorts today. Guests could enjoy the beautiful scenery; consume good food and drinks; play a wide variety of games and sports; attend concerts, theatre performances, parties, and balls; and socialize. Guests might rent a cottage or a hotel room for a week, a month, or the entire summer. It was not unusual for Southern planter families from the deep South to travel by riverboats and stagecoaches to resorts in states further north for the entire summer in order to avoid seasonal outbreaks of malaria in the year's hottest weather.[26]

Touring natural and historical sites was also popular among the upper classes before the Civil War, despite often challenging traveling conditions on rough roads. Tourism was already popular among wealthy Europeans of the late 1700s and early 1800s—imagine Jane Austen's Elizabeth Bennet traveling with her aunt and uncle to admire estate gardens and visiting Darcy's estate, Pemberley, in *Pride and Prejudice* (1813). Well-to-do Americans made the "Grand Tour" to visit cultural and historical sites in Europe.

By the 1820s, wealthy tourists, American and European, were also visiting American sites. Historical and cultural tourist destinations such as Niagara Falls, the Connecticut and Hudson River Valleys, and even the difficult to access Mammoth Cave, Kentucky, were visited and promoted in art and travel narratives. American artists such as Thomas Cole, Frederic Church, Albert Bierstadt, and Thomas Moran depicted the natural beauty of the American landscapes. Washington Irving, Nathaniel Hawthorne, and other writers described their visits to famous sites and added references in their fictional works.

Charles Dickens and other European tourists published accounts of their travels in the United States. The reform movements of the early 1800s encouraged the construction of reformed prisons, modern asylums for the deaf, blind, and mentally ill, and the new style of garden or rural cemeteries, and these also became popular tourist destinations.[27] Guidebooks and other publications described the beauty and history of famous sites and provided itineraries for the "fashionable" tourist. Paintings of tourist destinations, prints of the paintings, and publications promoted travel; improvements in railroads and canals made tourism easier and more affordable. The opening of the Erie Canal in 1825 made travel from New York City to the Great Lakes faster and provided easier access to Niagara Falls, as well as to midwestern destinations.

While most travel for pleasure before the Civil War was limited to the wealthy, religious camp meetings were an exception and gave working-class Americans opportunity travel from home and stay for several days. As with medieval pilgrimage, religious motives could be combined with the desire to socialize and see new things. Observers and participants in camp meetings also noted a wide variety of activities at camp meetings—religious experiences, socializing

Figure 2.3. Title page of *Picturesque America*. This two-volume set of books, with over 900 images and detailed descriptions, encouraged tourism by describing and illustrating American natural and cultural scenery. Many of the images first appeared in *Appleton's Journal*, and the books were published as a subscription book from 1872 to 1874. Subscribers agreed to a two-year commitment in which they paid small installments on the total cost of $24 and received sections as they were printed, which could later be bound into a book. By 1880, at least 100,000 subscriptions had been sold, and over a million copies may have been sold by the early 1900s. See Sue Rainey, *Creating* Picturesque America, *Monument to the Natural and Cultural Landscape* (Nashville, TN: Vanderbilt University Press, 1994).

Harry Fenn, "Dome of the Capitol," Picturesque America, *vol. 2, (New York: D. Appleton and Company, 1984), title page. (Courtesy of Eastern Kentucky University Special Collections and Archives, Richmond, KY.)*

between families and young single people, rowdy behavior often fueled with whiskey, and the business of supplying goods to the campers.

Early nineteenth-century camp meetings, led by traveling preachers, were common on the frontier where few churches had been formally organized. The Presbyterian Cane Ridge Revival in Kentucky lasted about a week in August 1801, one of the largest camp revivals of the Second Great Awakening. In the following decades, the Methodists and other denominations promoted camp meetings throughout the United States. Camp meetings usually lasted four to eight days and drew hundreds and sometimes thousands of people from as much as fifty miles away. After the Civil War, a few of the early nineteenth-century camp meetings locations became permanent middle-class vacation destinations.[28]

Vacations after the Civil War

The growth of railroads, canals, and improvements in American roads allowed more Americans to travel more cheaply and in more comfort. By the middle of the nineteenth century, upper-middle-class Americans began to take "vacations" at the seashore, in the mountains, in rural destinations, or at popular resorts.

As the century progressed, prosperity spread and the possibility of a vacation reached further down the economic ladder. More men and women from the middle class took short pleasure trips, influenced by numerous newspaper articles about resorts and other tourist destinations and the advantages of time away from work. Tourism and entertainment also became increasingly commercialized. Entrepreneurs such as Thomas Cook, Fred Harvey, and P. T. Barnum realized the economic potential of a growing market of middle- and working-class people seeking diversion, so they advertised entertainment and tourism experiences.

Throughout the nineteenth and first half of the twentieth century, the middle class grew to include a larger number of people, and the term was used to describe a wide range of people in different social and economic circumstances. In the nineteenth century, doctors, lawyers, business entrepreneurs, and bankers were the most prosperous members of the middle class. These professionals had excellent incomes but were often at risk of financial disaster in an economic downturn, which was common in the late 1800s. Ministers, skilled craftsmen, small businessmen, newspaper editors, teachers, and well-established farmers earned a wide range of incomes, but were also considered middle class.

By 1915, the growth of large corporations, mass retailers, and the government bureaucracy created a new, large group of white-collar employees who were distinguished from the working class because of their generally better education and salaried jobs that did not require manual labor. This group included factory supervisors and technicians, clerks, salespeople, bookkeepers, middle managers, and civil servants.

Incomes of those in the middle class widely varied depending on sex, age, race, location, and occupation.[29] By the late nineteenth and early twentieth century, many middle-class employees earned enough to pay the expenses for a short vacation and some employers were beginning to make least one or two weeks of paid or unpaid vacation a standard practice.

Middle-class vacationers in the late nineteenth century could choose from several types of vacations in all price ranges. Vacationers could stay in resort hotels, rented cottages, or boardinghouse rooms at mineral springs, the seaside, in the mountains, the countryside, or small towns. Many destinations offered sports and other activities such as bowling or billiards, opportunities to socialize, dance, eat, and rest.

By 1915, Americans could also vacation in the newly opened Florida resorts. Florida's boom started when one of the founders of Standard Oil, Henry Morrison Flagler, built a chain of resorts on the east coast of Florida from St. Augustine to the Keys.[30] Some Americans believed that leisure time should be spent in self-improvement activities at religious camps like Ocean Grove on the New Jersey shore, founded by Methodists in 1869, or at Chautauqua assemblies named after the first such meeting held at Chautauqua Lake in 1874. At these self-improvement gatherings, vacationers were exposed to cultural experiences and educational speakers, teachers, musicians, preachers, and other specialists of the era, as well as recreational activities that did not include alcohol, gambling, or other immoral pastimes offered at traditional resorts.[31]

Vacationers could also tour several different natural, historical, or model industrial sites. Civil War battlefields and the World's Fairs became popular destinations. The emerging tourist industry of this period promoted tourism to American historical and natural sites as a patriotic duty. In 1906, western booster groups introduced the "See America First" campaign. Western railroad companies saw the economic potential and launched extensive advertising campaigns. Railroad expansion and the introduction of the automobile drew more and more tourists westward, and by the 1920s, the National Park Service, along with the private tourism industry, made America's national parks a main American tourist attraction.[32]

Camping was another vacation option that grew in popularity with the introduction of the automobile. Camping allowed urbanites to enjoy nature and engage in restorative and physical activities such as reading, boating, fishing, or hunting. Campers also avoided the cost and possibly dissolute activities provided at resorts. In the early years of the automobile (c. 1910–1920), camping was limited by the poor condition of American roads and to families who could afford both a car and time off work. By 1920, the popularity of "autocamping," promoted by articles in magazines and newspapers, drove the creation of designated campsites in towns hoping to capture tourist dollars.

As automobile ownership became possible for people lower on the socioeconomic scale, campsites offered more and more conveniences, such as small cabins with cooking facilities, toilets, and running water. They also began to charge fees to screen out "undesirable" migrant and itinerant campers. These private camps evolved from simple cabins to the motel-hotels serving motorists along the highway. By 1945, the "motor court" or motel industry was well-established enough to attract large-scale development across the nation.[33]

As the number of potential tourists grew, the business of tourism expanded in post–Civil War America. Newspapers and magazines described vacation destinations and the healthful benefits of getting away from the fast-paced work environment and profited from advertisements for vacation destinations. As demand grew, the number and variety of vacation destinations grew. Resorts expanded, hotels that catered to a wider range of budgets were built, and small towns along railroad lines promoted themselves as vacation destinations for weary urban dwellers.

More and more inexpensive vacation destinations were available, and although the accommodations, food, and entertainment were often of poor quality, the increased availability enabled more people to pursue the middle-class ideal—at least a short vacation.

Railroad companies were especially active in the commercialization of vacation. Resorts and amusement parks were developed by railroad companies along or at the end of lines and new lines were built to service existing resorts. The railroad enabled urban wives and children to spend the summer in the country or at a resort location, while the father commuted to his job during the week and joined the family for the weekends. Promotional advertising by railroad companies stressed the ease of train travel, sometimes often with great exaggeration.

The career of Fred Harvey (1835–1901) exemplifies the interaction between the growth of the advertising industry, train travel, development of services for tourists, and the increasing numbers of Americans seeking to take a vacation. Early in his career, Harvey traveled extensively by train and realized that many hotels and restaurants that served railroad travelers were dirty, unreliable, and unwelcoming to customers, especially women. His businesses sought to remedy that problem.

At the peak of his career, he ran over sixty-five clean and standardized restaurants and lunch counters, sixty dining cars, twelve large hotels, including the Bright Angel Lodge at the Grand Canyon, and numerous newsstands and bookstores in railroad stations located along the country's largest railroad, the Santa Fe between Chicago and Los Angeles. He also heavily promoted tourism in the American Southwest. His services raised the standards of tourist services throughout the nation and encouraged more and more Americans to go on vacation.[34]

In the last half of the 1800s and early 1900s, vacationing was a sign that one had achieved middle-class status, but it was a luxury that was not typically available to working-class Americans. Working-class Americans' leisure time was measured in hours or a day, not a week or two away from home and work. In 1870, this widely diverse group of urban and rural people included farm laborers and some farm owners, textile mill workers, boot and shoe makers, railroad workers, draymen and hack drivers, domestic workers, and laborers in mining, manufacturing, and construction. Domestic service alone employed half of all female workers and eight percent of the nation's labor force.[35]

Instead of a vacation, working-class people might spend a day, afternoon, or evening at sporting events, theater productions, vaudeville shows, county fairs, or pleasure gardens like New York's Central Park, which opened in 1857. They might visit traveling shows and other commercial amusements such as circuses, menageries, or painted dioramas. Some traveling exhibitions and "dime museums" established permanent locations in major cities, offering "scientific" wonders, "freak" shows, entertainers, wax displays, and horror exhibits for the urban working class.[36]

By 1915, "day-trippers" could visit more than 1,500 amusement parks across the United States, conveniently located by public transportation and most urban centers.[37] The best-known example is Coney Island, located at the southwestern tip of Long Island, New York. In the 1870s, this area was a fashionable middle-class seaside resort, but developers and railroad companies realized the potential to attract working-class people from the city.

Many of the new attractions were enclosed in separate amusement parks—Steeplechase Park, Luna Park, and Dreamland. Visitors could go on thrilling mechanical rides such as the Ferris wheel, rollercoaster, carousel, or scenic railroad

Figure 2.4. Magazine advertisement for the Santa Fe Railroad promoting tourism to the Grand Canyon, 1909. Magazine articles and advertising increased interest in vacation and tourism. The text of this advertisement promotes the "winterless" climate of the American southwest, the comforts of the Pullman sleeping cars, the affordability of the trip, the El Tovar hotel on the rim of the Grand Canyon managed by Fred Harvey, and the availability of side trips around and in the canyon.
Advertisement, McClure's 34, no. 2 [December 1909]: 7. (Author's collection.)

or water rides through frightening and exotic artificial landscapes, play games of chance, visit "dime" museums and freak shows, eat and drink cheaply, socialize, and return to the city for work the next day.

Amusement park operators offered new amusements and rides every year in order to draw repeat customers. By the Depression, only about four hundred parks were still open, and many of these closed during the 1930s due to the poor economy and the decline of the interurban railroads that served many of the parks.[38]

The amusements of the working classes were often condemned by intellectual elites and the middle class and became targets of late-nineteenth-century and early-twentieth-century reform movements. The vacations and recreation of "working girls," young single women employed in offices, factories, and stores, were seen as a social problem. These single women often lived in boardinghouses in towns and cities and went, unchaperoned, to cheap dance halls, theaters, and concerts with men on "dates." Reformers created recreation centers, clubs, vacation societies, and vacation houses for young women where chaperones were present.

The young women, many of whom were recent immigrants, could learn "proper" middle-class manners and housekeeping skills for their future marriages. Efforts were also made to provide healthful summer vacations in the country or seaside for poor, urban mothers and their children. Many working women and poor mothers resented these lessons because the "proper" activities were seen as very dull and restrictive, and because the reformers often ignored the harsh economic realities of their daily lives.[39] Efforts to reform the leisure activities of working-class and immigrant men usually focused on temperance. Reformers believed the consumption of alcohol led to poverty, abuse of family, violence, and sexual immorality at work, at home, and during free time spent at popular working-class entertainments.

Ethnic minorities of any social class faced exclusion. Even Atlantic City, which catered to day-trippers and vacationers from every social class, was not racially integrated. As early as the 1890s, African Americans were beginning to open vacation facilities for African American tourists at destinations such as Highland Beach, near Annapolis on the Chesapeake Bay.[40] The lakeside resort of Idlewild, Michigan, was a vacation destination from 1912 to 1964 and attracted African American tourists from Chicago, Detroit, Indianapolis, and Cleveland. "Colored only" amusement parks were established beside segregated "white" amusement parks and at the end of city trolley lines that traveled through black neighborhoods. In some cases, African American businessmen built and operated amusement parks, such as Preston Taylor's Greenwood Park in Nashville, Tennessee, which was open from 1905 to 1949.[41]

Jews also faced exclusion on vacation and built their own vacation resorts, many located in the Catskill Mountains of New York, in order to attract the large New York City Jewish population. This area was sometimes referred to as the Borscht Belt, or Jewish Alps. Fleischmann's was one of the earliest Jewish resorts, opening in the 1890s. Working-class Jews unable to afford the expensive resorts vacationed in budget boardinghouses in the Catskills. Many of these resorts remained popular vacation destinations for Jewish families until the 1960s. The 1987 film *Dirty Dancing*, set at a fictional resort called Kellerman's, portrayed the final years of the Jewish resorts' popularity.

By the 1920s, paid vacations were extended to a majority of salaried workers. More and more employers accepted the advice of management experts that vacations renewed the spirit, energy, and efficiency of white-collar workers, but factory owners debated whether or not their workers were entitled to a paid or unpaid vacation. Companies began to establish vacation policies in the 1930s for primarily two reasons. First, in the face of growing union membership, companies realized that the establishment of more worker-friendly personnel and management programs would help to avoid costly labor disputes. Second, many companies came to believe the rested workers would contribute to increased productivity and profits. Almost 40 percent of wage earners had paid vacation policies in 1937, and the majority, but not all, of wage earners had paid vacations by the beginning of World War II.[42]

Despite hard times during the Depression, vacationing did not decline. As more Americans earned paid vacations, tourism was promoted by federal government and local communities eager for tourism dollars. Community advertising done by chambers of commerce and local business associations usually began with the promotion of business opportunities in national publications, self-published pamphlets, and booklets and grew to include efforts to attract tourist dollars.[43]

Federal New Deal programs also promoted tourism. The Civilian Conservation Corps built recreational areas, hiking paths, and cabins at hundreds of state parks. In 1937, the *American Guides*, produced through the Federal Writers' Project, produced guides to 48 states, as well as cities, regions, and major automobile routes. In the same year, the federal government created the United States Travel Bureau. This agency assembled and disseminated tourist related information for travel agencies, transportation companies, and tour operators.

The Bureau promoted travel in campaigns such as "Travel America Year" in 1940 and "Travel Strengthens America. It Promotes the Nation's Health, Wealth, and Unity" in 1941. Visitor centers were opened in New York, Washington, and San Francisco to introduce Americans to vacationing. The Division of Negro Activities produced guides listing hotels and motels for African American travelers.[44]

American involvement in World War II curtailed travel for the purpose of leisure for many Americans. But after World War II, the baby boom and economic prosperity resulted in the "golden age of the American family vacation." Between 1945 and the Oil Embargo of 1973–1974, rising rates of car ownership and the construction of the new federal highway system made a family road trip to cultural, historical, and entertainment destinations a middle-class standard.

The middle-class culture that promoted family justified spending money on vacation and, in turn, taking a vacation confirmed the middle-class status of the family and the ideals of family promoted in mass media.[45] Paid vacation benefits become widely accepted by employers and expected by workers. By the end of 1944, 85 percent of union agreements contained vacation benefits for workers.

By 1949, 93 percent of collective bargaining agreements contained vacation provisions. The length of service required to earn vacation time decreased, and longer vacations were granted for longer periods of service. But, despite the fact that an unprecedented percentage of Americans moved into the middle class in the 1950s, 25 percent of Americans lived in poverty, and the poverty rate of black families was more than 50 percent.[46] Even for middle-class African American and Jewish families, the family vacation was a very different experience because they continued to be banned from many hotels and tourist destinations.

The American Family Vacation in the Twentieth Century

The family vacation of the 1950s must be examined as a product of a very unique era in the history of the family. Several factors converged to create the child- and family-centered America of the mid-twentieth century. A culture was created in which marriage was celebrated, and the family was considered the essential institution of society. The 1950s family, idealized in TV shows like *Leave It to Beaver* and considered the "traditional" family model, was really a new phenomenon when compared to families in almost any other era.

Young families were encouraged to strike out on their own, breaking from extended family ties that had been the norm throughout the Great Depression and World War II, and the new postwar economic prosperity enabled them to do so. A new set of family values that focused on finding complete satisfaction and amusement within the nuclear family was stressed in the popular media. For the first time, men as well as women were encouraged to seek their identity and self-worth in familial and parental roles. Television shows, movies, and popular magazines touted the ideal child-centered family in a suburban home.[47]

The vacation destinations of 1950s and 1960s family vacations were similar to those of previous eras, but the focus of vacation promotion shifted to featuring and catering to families with children. Disneyland, first opening in southern California in 1955, was the product of the family-centered culture of the era. This theme park was advertised as a clean, orderly, family-oriented, and suburban middle-class alternative to what was perceived to be urban, lower-class, and unwholesome in amusement parks like Coney Island.

Walt Disney rejected the carnival or fairground atmosphere of freak shows; hucksters shouting to sell attractions, food, and souvenirs; and adult-focused entertainment. He denied entrance to those in the working class by setting the admission price beyond their reach. Instead, he created a childlike world centered on cute cartoon animals associated with his popular children's movies. Disneyland's Frontierland promoted the Davy Crockett mania started by the five-part Disneyland TV miniseries that debuted in 1954. Other western theme parks cashed in on the cowboy craze of the postwar years. For example, Knott's Berry Farm in southern California added a western ghost town in the 1940s.[48]

Visiting American monuments and historical sites was promoted as educational, a way to teach children about American history, identity, and patriotism. After the challenges of the Depression and World War II, Americans were seeking to reaffirm their national pride. The tourist industry and mass media responded to and encouraged the trend by publishing guides, maps, and accounts of heritage travel.[49] Heritage travel promotes the restoration of historical sites for tourism. In an effort to make these restored sites attractive to visitors, the past is often sanitized and homogenized, and negative historical events are ignored.

Postwar American families went on vacation in the family car. The cars of the fifties and sixties were roomy, economical because gas was cheap, and the family had the flexibility to travel any distance, visit many different locations, and change plans as needed. The family car was just one of the many consumer items marketed to the family. Car manufacturers created entire advertising campaigns focused upon roomy station wagons and sedans for family travel. Slogans like Ford's "There's no vacation like a Ford vacation" and "America's schoolhouse on wheels" and Mercury's "Home away from home for the entire family" promoted both the car and the concept of vacation.

Free road maps distributed by oil companies at gas stations depicted families on vacation and promoted tourist sites, as well as their brand of gasoline and family-friendly gas station restrooms. National chain restaurants like McDonald's offered predictable service and inexpensive, kid-friendly meals. Howard Johnson and Holiday Inn motel chains catered to families with clean rooms, air conditioning, free ice for the family cooler, swimming pools, and special offers allowing children to stay for free.

Figure 2.5. Heritage tourism in the 1950s. Tour of the US Supreme Court Building (used 1791–1800) at the Independence National Historical Park in Philadelphia, Pennsylvania. Heritage tourism, travel to cultural, historical, or natural sites to experience and learn about American history, was a popular choice for American family vacations after World War II.
Photo by Paul J. Schumacher, 1955, Catalog Number: HPC-001024. (Courtesy of National Park Service History Collection.)

Spending money on vacation was what middle-class Americans did to prove their status within middle-class America; taking a vacation showed that the family could afford leisure time away from home. The mass media of postwar America informed readers that buying a large family car, visiting vacation destinations, or purchasing special vacation gear was what an American was supposed to do to build the economy, fight the Cold War, and achieve greater satisfaction.[50] Banks promoted loans and vacation savings plans, sending the message that family vacations were expected, even if in reality the family's earnings could not cover the costs.

African American families were still frequently excluded or segregated at gas stations, motels, restaurants, and vacation destinations until the 1960s. Two travel guides, modeled on similar Jewish travel guides, provided advice to African American travelers. The *Green Book*, published from 1936 to 1966, and *Travelguide*, published from 1946 to 1955, listed hotels, motels, tourist homes, and restaurants, arranged by city within each state.

By the early 1960s, under increased pressure from African Americans and complaints of the NAACP to national companies that owned discriminatory hotels, restaurants, and gas stations, some barriers were removed. But many locally owned facilities refused to accept black customers. The Civil Rights Act of 1964 did not ensure equality, but it made discrimination illegal and allowed those discriminated against to take legal action.

Are You a Tourist or a Traveler?

A common theme throughout primary sources related to vacation and travel for leisure is commentary about the wrong kind of people acting in unacceptable ways or enjoying improper activities while on vacation. Medieval clerics criticized

Figure 2.6. Newspaper advertisement promoting vacation spending, 1961. The text states "There is nothing more aggravating than 'car trouble' on a vacation trip. A bad-acting automobile can squander your precious time and completely spoil your fun. If you need a new car anyway, why not buy it NOW and enjoy all the fine touring months ahead?" Advertisements such as this promoted vacations and vacation spending, even if money had to be borrowed.

Advertisement, "Kentucky, Your Vacationland," The Courier-Journal, Travel Section, April 30, 1961, 6. (Author's collection.)

pilgrims whose motives were not purely religious. The wealthy classes at nineteenth-century resorts commented on the manners and attire at resorts, separating the fashionable people who "belonged" from those striving to enter the upper classes.

When the price of a resort made it accessible to more people, the fashionable elite chose more exclusive and expensive vacation destinations away from the newly arrived middle classes. Resort vacations and leisure time were criticized by Americans who believed that hard work was a moral good and required for material success and that idleness was an indulgence that led to immorality. Many reform-minded people preferred the educational opportunities provided at religious or education camps. Men and women criticized women who did not act appropriately or modestly while on vacation because they socialized with men unchaperoned, participated in sports, spent too much on fashionable clothing, or swam in revealing bathing costumes.[51]

Figure 2.7. Cover of *The Travelers' Green Book*, 1960. These travel guides, published 1936–1966, provided information about lodging, restaurants, and other facilities that served African Americans. The full text of several editions is available online from the New York Public Library.
(Courtesy of The New York Public Library. A full text collection is available at http://digital collections.nypl.org/collections/the-green-book#/?tab=about.)

Figure 2.8. Segregated travel, 1943. A rest stop for Greyhound bus passengers on the way from Louisville, Kentucky, to Nashville, Tennessee, with separate accommodations for colored passengers.
Photo by Esther Bubley, September 1943. Farm Security Administration: Office of War Information Photograph Collection. (Courtesy of the Library of Congress.)

Middle-class vacationers and the intellectual elite criticized the "Sodoms by the sea"—urban amusement parks popular with the working class and immigrants.[52] Middle-class observers thought the working classes should be engaged in inexpensive, educational, or religious activities with the goal of self-improvement. Working-class and immigrant city-dwellers were instructed to spend their rare days away from work in nature or the countryside, instead of wasting money on childlike or even sinful urban activities—amusement parks, theatres, dance halls, ballparks, or saloons.

In the 1950s, when family vacations became an economic possibility for the largest number of Americans to date, Jewish and African American families were still excluded. The American mass media and advertisers promoted vacation spending, using depictions of middle-class white families as the national norm, creating an impression that everybody could achieve this American dream, even though the illusion didn't conform to the reality of the lives of many Americans.

Throughout history, as well as today, tourists have been criticized if they don't appear to fully appreciate natural, historical, or cultural sites. Complaints are made that these "rude" or "vulgar" tourists only want to buy souvenirs, take photographs, and brag to acquaintances back home. A recent trend, labeled "new moral tourism," is promoted as morally superior to "mass tourism" and echoes many of the same criticisms heard in previous generations.

The "new moral tourist" respects the differences of the culture and people by learning the local language and customs, seeks physical challenges and educational experiences, buys authentic local food and souvenirs that support the local economy, and respects the local natural environment. On the other hand, the "mass tourist" is criticized because he or she ignores the local culture, prefers prepackaged resort or cruise experiences, and is only seeking selfish pleasures such as relaxing, sunbathing, shopping, or engaging in mass entertainments such as theme park rides or shows.[53]

In the mass media, the "traveler versus tourist" imagery and other powerful tools of persuasion are often used to sell vacations. Promotion of vacation and travel, often for commercial gain, has shaped our conceptions in the past and today. Throughout the Middle Ages, the Church promoted pilgrimage for its spiritual value to pilgrims, but also for the benefit of the Church itself. Over the centuries of the Middle Ages, fewer barriers to travel, stories of returning pilgrims, and widely circulated and, later, printed accounts continued to promote pilgrimage for religious and nonreligious purposes.

Pilgrimage became an integral part of the popular culture. Nineteenth-century publications educated the new middle class about vacation—who should take one, the benefits, the places to see and avoid, where to stay, and how to react to the vacation experience. Since then, routes of transportation have improved, destinations for tourists have multiplied, and more Americans are able to afford a vacation. Those promoting vacation travel have become very adept at shaping our preconceived notions of vacation habits, expectations, and destinations so that we will continue to purchase vacations.

Travel accounts, travel guides, promotion of tourism by local, state, and national government, and paid advertisements teach people what to see and do, and in turn, the returned vacationer communicates expectations that inform and shape the perceptions of the next visitor, continuing the cultural circuit of influence. We make individual choices about the vacations we take or don't take, why we need to take them, and what we do, but our agency is shaped by layers of modern and historical perceptions of vacation.

In the Classroom: Introducing the Theme

Ask each student to write an answer to the following questions:

Describe your perfect vacation. Where would you go? What would you do there? How long would you stay? Why did you choose this vacation destination?

Note that these questions are worded in a way that does not assume all students have been on vacation. Vacations are still not affordable, possible, or a part of the culture of many American families. After students have written their responses, categorize the types of vacations they have imagined using the following categories. Some students may have a combination of activities, so ask them to choose their primary focus for categorization purposes.

- Relaxation and entertainment vacations: beaches, resorts, spas, cruises, or theme parks
- Nature or sporting vacations: camping, hiking, skiing, fishing, or hunting
- Touring vacations: visits to historic, cultural, or scenic sites
- Educational, religious, or spiritual vacations: learn new skills, volunteering, missions, retreats, or visits to religious sites

Assign students to small groups of two or three and ask them to discuss the factors that may have influenced their choices of vacations. After discussion, direct the groups to report their conclusions, listing the various influences so that the entire class can view and analyze the answers. It is very likely that students will note the impact of the media and the influence of their culture through friends and family in some manner. If not, give students hints and prompts to help them consider these influences. Discuss with students the manner in which vacation experiences are often idealized in the media and how the "perfect" vacation may be as much a media myth as a lived reality.

Next, ask students to list real-life factors that might limit their ideal vacation. Lists are likely to include lack of money, a shortage of time away from work or school, or family obligations. Finally, ask students to brainstorm what factors would have been likely to limit vacations of people in the past in general, or specifically in the time period that is to be studied.

The Primary Sources: Medieval Pilgrimage and Collective Memory

The lesson that follows and the primary source texts focus not on pilgrimage itself, but the impact of collective memory, how myth and reality merge in works related to travel and vacation and the challenges faced by historians who attempt to unravel these connections between sources. Students will need to understand the concept of religious pilgrimage and the key facts about medieval pilgrimage prior to engaging in the primary source lesson below. Many lesson plans are available that explore pilgrimage and its armed counterpart, crusade, and numerous accounts of medieval pilgrimages and crusade are available in translation, so these topics are not dealt with in depth here.

The influence of collective memory should be considered in the analysis of any narrative about travel, but especially in the analysis of premodern primary sources. Today, guidebooks, televisions shows, and travel maps are viewed as factual; they describe what to see and how to get there. Modern writers are still influenced by various cultural, economic, and political factors when making travel recommendations, but fact-checking is an easy process in the modern world, and blatantly false information is quickly exposed.

But in the prescientific era, "truth" was often measured in different terms. For example, in the Middle Ages, information from Greek, Roman, and biblical texts was considered true because it had survived over time or was inspired by God. Tradition was often regarded as true and rarely questioned. Critical analysis of documents was largely a product of a later era, the Renaissance. Therefore, surviving pilgrims' accounts and other medieval sources may not be "true" in the modern sense.

Avoid asking students to characterize information in sources as true or false, reliable or unreliable, because those binary terms oversimply history and human experience. Myths, collective memory, religious belief, and human misconceptions all must be explored in order to understand the human experience, past and present.

In the Middle Ages, it was common for authors to describe contemporary events using descriptions from sources that may have been written decades or even centuries before, often quoting word for word. The original source was rarely attributed or questioned for its accuracy or authenticity. Therefore, it is difficult to know the author's own personal thoughts or observations, the quality of his or her sources, or if what was described even existed in the author's time period. Today, authors would be accused of plagiarism or sloppy scholarship if quoted material was not analyzed and cited; the rules of scholarship have changed.

The author may have used information from previous works because he or she was unable to personally visit a particular site, but felt that the information should be included for future readers and pilgrims. Or maybe the author felt that the words of previous experts could describe the experience better or more accurately than new words. For example, many descriptions of religious sites are taken straight from the Bible because, for a medieval Christian, the Bible was the ultimate and certainly true authority in any matter.

Needless to say, by the Middle Ages many biblical era descriptions of locations were no longer accurate. Some medieval documents were intentionally created and falsely attributed to known experts for political or economic gain. In some cases, modern scholars can identify quoted sources and discover false attributions, but just as often original sources haven't survived, authors remain unknown, and scholars disagree.

Medieval hagiography, the stories of saints or other holy persons, is also a primary source related to pilgrimage that requires special consideration. The stories of the lives of saints (*vita* in Latin) are sometimes called biographies, but that is a very misleading label. A modern reader of the genre of biography expects factual information about the life of the individual that has been collected from primary source material—interviews, letters, and newspapers, for example.

The medieval hagiographer's goal was to describe a saint's holiness and the miracles performed; in other words, the goal was to demonstrate how the saint glorified God. Modern readers may question the "truth" of these stories for various reasons. Public school teachers must be especially careful to neither promote nor denigrate religious faith. In the author's experience, the best approach is to explain that when examining religious primary sources, the objective is not to determine the truth of sources for today's reader, but to determine how the sources were interpreted by their intended audiences.

To apply modern scientific skepticism to this medieval practice would be anachronistic. Medieval Europeans believed in saints and their miracles. Some may have criticized the promotion, abuses, or crimes connected to the cults of saints, relics, and pilgrimage, but those who questioned the underlying religious belief were rare and, if vocal, quickly condemned.

The following set of excerpts exemplify collective memory—a network of interrelated facts and myths about the ninth-century medieval king Charlemagne that became part of the religious and secular popular culture of pilgrimage and crusade in the twelfth century. These six excerpts, one from a historical ninth-century contemporary biography of Charlemagne and the remainder from twelfth-century manuscripts, demonstrate how lines between history, fiction, and religious belief and practice blurred and help students grasp the complexity of historical research. In the activity below, students are asked to characterize information as historical, fictional, based on religious belief, or a combination of these factors.

In the Classroom
This lesson should be conducted as an inquiry activity in which students are provided with only the basic information about medieval pilgrimage before reading, discussing, asking questions, and forming conclusions about the following sources.

Choose a reading strategy that best meets the needs of your students. I prefer that students read by themselves first, then form small groups for discussion. This method ensures that all students attempt the reading but also provides an opportunity for struggling readers to increase their understanding of the text during the discussion. Provide the students with the primary sources and the reading guide (figure 2.9).

After students have read the sources, ask them to discuss and compare their answers in pairs or groups, completing the reading guide *without consulting outside sources of information for clues*. Caution students that all of the information requested by the reading guide may not be contained in the sources. Direct each group to generate theories and additional questions they may have about the sources and how they are related to each other. The Question Formulation Technique[54] is an excellent model that can be used to teach students how to generate critical questions about primary sources.

After small group discussion, ask each group to share the best theory about the relationship of the sources and one or two of the group's best questions about the sources, and record those for the whole class to view. As a group, edit the list to clarify and remove redundant theories and questions.

Add the following essential questions to the list and define, explain, and discuss the concept of collective memory. Ask students to consider and discuss the following essential questions as they conduct their research, and alert students these questions are to be answered in a culminating assignment for the lesson. You may choose to have students answer one or all of the questions in an argumentative or informative/explanatory essay or in presentations or media projects.

- *How did collective memory impact medieval pilgrimage? How does collective memory impact travel and vacations today?*
- *Do we, as individuals, really have agency (making our own decisions about what to see and how to interpret it when we travel), or are our interpretations a product of the collective memory of our culture?*

Direct students to do research in order to find answers to the questions from the class list. To save time, consider assigning questions to groups so that all of the questions are addressed. Also, consider creating information packets for student research with key information about pilgrimage and the sources provided in this chapter and a list of preselected websites, as the quality of information on the Internet about the Middle Ages can vary greatly. Beware, for example, of anachronistic "Rules of Chivalry" on the web that originate from the role-playing game Rifts.

As students work, you can circulate and, when appropriate, ask questions such as the following examples to provide "hints."

- Charlemagne lived around three hundred years before most of these sources were written. How might the passage of time impact memories and historical information about his reign?
- A majority of people in the Middle Ages could not read or write. How did people know history, tradition, and their religion?

- Consider how written information was saved in the Middle Ages. How could this impact historical writing?
- How does a historian assess religious documents that describe religious beliefs and practices? What can a historian learn from these types of documents?
- What can you learn if you chart the locations mentioned in the sources on a map of Europe or a map of pilgrimage routes to the Shrine of St. James?
- Consider how historical events or historical eras are portrayed in modern movies or television shows. How are real events changed to make a movie more interesting or entertaining? Could a modern person assume that fictional events or people portrayed in television or movies were real?

After students complete their research to answer the key questions, ask groups to share their findings, conclusions about the relationship of the sources, and the role of collective memory in travel through the ages. Be sure to correct misconceptions about the content throughout the discussion and provide additional information about the sources that students may not have discovered.

Primary Source Information
Source A, an excerpt from Einhard's *The Life of Charlemagne*, is considered historical and factual, but clearly intended to present a very positive portrait of Charlemagne. The author was a scholar and court official in the reign of Charlemagne (c. 740s–814) and his son, Louis the Pious (778–840). This biography was written shortly after the death of Charlemagne in the ninth century.

The primary sources from which sources B–F were excerpted are all from the twelfth century, produced around three hundred years after the death of Charlemagne in regions that are now a part of modern France. The twelfth century was an era in which the traditions of pilgrimage became bound up with the concept of armed pilgrimages, or crusade, against Muslims in both the Holy Land and Spain. Jerusalem fell to the first crusaders in 1099, the Second Crusade took place in 1147–1149, the Third Crusade in 1189–1192. Several Muslim kingdoms still existed in twelfth-century Spain. Many twelfth-century crusaders were French nobles; French kings participated in the Second and Third Crusade. Furthermore, the French Capetian kings associated their rule with the legendary traditions of the powerful Charlemagne in order to legitimize their rule.[55]

The Pilgrimage of Charlemagne (source D) and *William in the Monastery* (source F) are epics, the equivalent of an action movie today. *The Song of Roland*,[56] another epic from the late eleventh or early twelfth century, is relevant to the discussion, but not excerpted here because it is widely known and taught in literature courses. Action movies, much like medieval epics, often have predictable and repetitive plots (cop versus criminal, heroic American versus evil foreign enemy, or Christian knight versus Muslim warrior) and similar devices for advancing the action (hand-to-hand combat, explosions, big battle scenes).

In some action movies and epics, the overall theme is quite serious; in others, the hero is also a comic. Action movies are consistently popular, and a particularly successful hero, like Indiana Jones or Luke Skywalker, will star in series of movies. Popular medieval characters were featured in many different epics, and some of the most popular characters were Charlemagne and his knights.[57] Epics, like movies, were performances, not just words on a page. Epics were recounted orally, by professionals, and captured the attention of the audience just as a hit action movie today.

Epics and action movies reflect myths and realities of the time period in which they were made, but can be set in a historical past portrayed as a combination of fiction, myth, and historical fact. For example, American films from the Cold War era often featured antagonists from the Soviet Union; the antagonists in more recent action films are terrorists, often from the Middle East. Both reflect American concerns about the security of the nation in the time period the movies were produced.

The historical epic *Spartacus* (1960) was set in first-century Rome. But the overall theme echoed concerns that America would decline like ancient Rome under a burden of slavery and oppression, just as modern Americans were confronting the oppression of African Americans and the fear of communism. Some of the characters in the film were loosely based on historical people and events, others were not. This combination of fiction, myth, and fact merges and becomes largely real for the epic's listeners or film's viewers.

The Pilgrimage of Charlemagne, *William in the Monastery*, and *The Song of Roland* are historical fiction set in the late eighth and early ninth centuries, but reflect the twelfth-century secular and religious culture of pilgrimage and

PRIMARY SOURCE	A	B	C	D	E	F
Date of document						
Type of document - is the document 　　a factual historical account? 　　fiction? 　　based on religious belief? 　　combination? what parts are factual, fictional, or religious						
Author of document (if known)						
PEOPLE IN THE SOURCES *If the person appears in the source, describe the role of the person in the source.* *If a person is not mentioned in a source, leave the box blank.* *If you are not sure, mark with ?*						
Charlemagne, Charles, King Charles the Great (c. 740s – 814)						
Charlemagne's queen						
Roland						
Turpin						
Other soldiers, Paladins, or Peers of Charlemagne, Franks						
William of Orange, St. William, Count William						
Names for enemies of Charlemagne and his warriors						
Pope Callixtus (c. 1065 - 1124)						
Saint James						
Unnamed pilgrims						
What relics or pilgrimage shrines are referenced?						
SUMMING UP A. How are these sources related? What themes are evident in all of the sources? B. What questions do you have about these sources or the relationship of these sources?						
ESSENTIAL QUESTIONS A. How did collective memory impact medieval pilgrimage? How does collective memory impact travel and vacations today? B. Do we, as individuals, really have agency (making our own decisions about what to see and how to interpret it when we travel,) or are our interpretations a product of the collective memory of our culture?						

Figure 2.9. Reading Guide—Medieval Pilgrimage.

crusade. Some characters probably really existed between the ninth and twelfth centuries, others did not. Details from medieval epics came from popular culture, historical traditions, and religious stories of saints; then, in turn, these epics, what we could call "historical fiction," were often wholeheartedly adapted into subsequent medieval "historical" chronicles.

Modern historians are more careful to authenticate the source of information included in history books, but in modern popular culture, myths still can be incorporated into our conceptions of reality. For example, Harry Potter's Platform 9 3/4 at King's Cross Station in London is an imaginary entrance to the train that goes to the imaginary Hogwarts School of Witchcraft and Wizardry. Yet modern-day tourists can have their photo taken at a very real version of this imaginary location. Is it possible that at some time in the future, a photo of a tourist at Platform 9 3/4 may cause someone to believe that it was a historical place with significance beyond a popular set of novels?

The *Pilgrimage of Charlemagne* and *William in the Monastery* have been included because they are epics with comedy, very different from the somber *The Song of Roland*. The *Pilgrimage of Charlemagne* is a type of epic called a "gab." A gab begins with a boast or jest, followed by a challenge to perform the deed. The person challenged then succeeds at the challenge and pardons the challenger. The boasting of the gab was generally associated with drinking alcohol, a tradition that was documented to have taken place during the long evenings of Germanic warriors and was certainly carried on in the Middle Ages.[58]

The excerpt (source D) is from the opening scenes of this epic. Charlemagne decides to travel to the Holy Land because he is goaded by the queen's statement that Hugo the Strong of Constantinople is braver and richer than Charlemagne. But he tells his key knights, the Twelve Peers, who accompany him that he has been inspired by three dreams to make the pilgrimage to Jerusalem.[59]

In reality, Charlemagne never visited the Holy Land. Einhard, a contemporary of Charlemagne, did not mention a trip to the Holy Land. Einhard's medieval biography only noted that Charlemagne was interested in the Holy Places and relics. Around 998, almost 200 years after Charlemagne's death, the monk Benedict of Saint Andrew's in southern Italy claimed that Charlemagne had been to Jerusalem and Constantinople and had brought back relics of St. Andrew for the Italian monastery, probably to make a case for the importance and authenticity of the relic.

Charlemagne's pilgrimage to the Holy Land was reported by three chroniclers of the First Crusade, which began nearly three hundred years after his death.[60] One noted that "these most valiant knights and many others (whose names I do not know) traveled by the road which Charlemagne, the heroic king of the Franks, had formerly caused to be built to Constantinople."[61] In a twelfth-century "history," the church of St. Denis used Charlemagne's pilgrimage as evidence that their relics, a piece of the Holy Cross, a nail used on the cross, and the crown of thorns, were authentic.[62] The author of *The Chronicle of Pseudo-Turpin* (source 2) stated that Charlemagne was inspired by dreams to go to Spain and that he made a pilgrimage to the Holy Land.

William in the Monastery is one of twenty-four surviving twelfth- and thirteenth-century epics in the series of epics about the deeds of William of Orange and his family (not to be confused with the Dutch and English leaders of the sixteenth and seventeenth centuries). Scholars believe there were historical models for this epic hero but do not agree on which eighth-century William was the model; it is likely that the William of the epics was modeled on several different people and traditions, both real and mythical.

William of Toulouse was likely to have been a principal model, as known facts about his life are similar to some events in the epics. He became a duke in 790, served under Charlemagne's son Louis during Charlemagne's lifetime, and was known to have fought Saracens. He founded the abbey of Gellone in 804, retired there as a monk in 806, and died in 813.[63]

The characters in the epics related to William are often comical, but like the characters in *The Song of Roland*, they are still ideal medieval knights who love their king, God, battle, and glory. William loves to fight, treasures his horses and his sword, and has a quick temper that often puts him in dangerous and comical situations. Sometimes his love of lively adventures outweighs his duty to religion in these epics, making him more like a modern action hero.

Sources B, C, and E are excerpted from the *Book of St. James*, a five-part work centered upon pilgrimage to the shrine of St. James and believed to have been put together as one work between 1140 and 1172. Within the work, authorship is claimed by Pope Callixtus II (c. 1065–1124), and the manuscript is often referred to as the *Codex Calixtinus*, but modern scholars agree, for various reasons, that the book could not have actually been written by that pope.

The five books were probably written at different times in the twelfth century by different unknown authors, and sections of the work may predate the twelfth century. Scholars have varying opinions about the primary purpose of the *Book of St. James*. Endorsement of the cult of St. James and of pilgrimage to his shrine, the promotion of the Spanish Church and Compostela, efforts to advance the Cluniac monastic order that established monasteries and hosted pilgrims along the routes through France, or as encouragement for crusading efforts against Muslims in both Spain and the Holy Land are all provided as purposes by scholars and all may be involved.[64]

Two parts of the *Book of St. James* are not excerpted here. The first part, also referred to as the *Book of St. James*, is a collection of various liturgical pieces to be used on dates important to St. James—his martyrdom on July 25 and the miraculous relocation of his bones from the Holy Land to Spain on December 30. The third part is a collection of various texts that glorify St. James, including the story of how his relics arrived at Santiago de Compostela.

The remaining three parts of the *Book of St. James* are excerpted below (sources B, C, and E). The second part, *The Miracles of Saint James* (source 3), is a collection of twenty-two miracles of St. James. Most of the miracles are associated with pilgrims. Pope Callixtus II (1065–1124) is listed as the recorder of these miracles, but scholars believe that the collection was not compiled in its final form until 1140–1172.[65]

St. James was often referred to as the Moor-slayer, and this association contributed to his popularity in the crusade culture of the twelfth century. He is often portrayed as ready for battle, mounted on a white charger, armed with a sword, and carrying a white banner with a red cross. His first miracle was believed to have occurred in the ninth century when he appeared on a Spanish battlefield and led the Christians to defeat the Spanish Moors.[66]

In the fourth part, commonly known as *Pseudo-Turpin*, the narrator presents himself as Archbishop Turpin of Rheims, one of the Twelve Peers of Charlemagne who accompanied him to Spain in the late eighth century. There was a historical bishop of Rheims named Turpin (c. 748–c. 795–800), but this account could not have been written by the historical Turpin because it is not written in the Latin of eighth century. Furthermore, events and characters mentioned in this account are fictional, taken from epics, or historical figures who lived in the two hundred years after Charlemagne's death.[67] Bishop Turpin is also a main character in *The Song of Roland*.

Pilgrim's Guide to Santiago de Compostela (source E) is the final part of the *Book of St. James* and described the major routes across France and the Pyrenees Mountains to the shrine, recommended relics and shrines to visit on the way to Compostela, and gave advice about the regions through which the pilgrim would pass.

(I highly recommend the complete version of all of these sources to teachers and students. All are accessible and interesting to the modern reader when compared to many other medieval sources.) The full text of *The Pilgrim's Guide to Santiago de Compostela* and *The Pilgrimage of Charlemagne* are available on the Internet, although the translation of *The Pilgrimage of Charlemagne* was made over one hundred years ago and the language is difficult. All of these primary sources are available in newer, critical translations in affordable paperback editions.

The Primary Sources

Source A
The Life of Charlemagne (written c. 817–836) by Einhard (c. 775–840)[68]

At a time when this war against the Saxons was being waged constantly and with hardly an intermission at all, Charlemagne left garrisons at strategic points along the frontier and went off himself with the largest force he could muster into Spain. He marched over a pass across the Pyrenees, received the surrender of every single town and castle which he attacked and then came back with his army safe and sound, except for the fact that for a brief moment on the return journey, while he was in the Pyrenean mountain range itself, he was given a taste of **Basque** treachery. Dense forests, which stretch in all directions, make this a spot most suitable for setting ambushes. At a moment when Charlemagne's army was stretched out in a long column of march . . . these Basques, who had set their ambush on the very top of one of the mountains, came rushing down on the last part of the baggage train and the troops who were marching in support of the rearguard and so protecting the army which had gone on ahead. The Basques forced them down into the valley beneath, joined battle with them and killed them to the last man. They then snatched up the baggage, and protected they were by the cover of darkness, which was just beginning to fall, scattered in all directions without losing a moment. In this feat the Basques were helped by their light weapons and by the terrain. On the other hand, the heavy equipment and rough ground hampered the **Franks** in their resistance. In this battle died Eggihard, the King's steward; Anselm, the Count of the Palace; and Roland, Lord of the Breton Marches, along with a great number of others. What is more this assault could not be avenged there and then, for, once it was over, the enemy dispersed in such a way that no one knew where or among which people they could be found.

Key Terms

- **Basque**—an ethnic group of a region that spans the Pyrenees into what is now northern Spain and southwestern France. Scholars are not certain if they were pagan, Christian, or Muslim in the time of Charlemagne.
- **Franks**—soldiers of Charlemagne.

Source B
The Chronicle of Pseudo-Turpin—Part 4 of the *Book of St. James* (twelfth century)[69]

Chapter 1—About the Apostle's Apparition to Charlemagne

Suddenly Charlemagne saw a path of stars in the sky, beginning in the **Frisian Sea** . . . to **Galicia,** where the body of Saint James lay buried and undiscovered. Looking upon this stellar path several times every night, he began to meditate on its meaning. A knight of splendid appearance, more handsome than words can describe, appeared to Charlemagne one evening in a vision . . . [and said] "I am Saint James the Apostle, disciple of Christ . . . and my body lies forgotten in Galicia, a place still shamefully oppressed by the **Saracens.** I am deeply disturbed by the fact that you, who have conquered so many cities and nations, have not liberated my lands from the Saracens. So I have come to tell you that, just as the Lord has made you the most powerful of the kings of the earth, he has chosen you from among them to . . . liberate my lands from the hands of the Muslims. . . . After you, all peoples from sea to sea will walk there as pilgrims, begging forgiveness for their sins and proclaiming the greatness of the Lord, his virtues and the marvels that he has performed, from your own time until the end of the present age."

Chapter 20—About the Person and Strength of Charlemagne

There must be those who would like to hear about his Charlemagne's deeds in more detail, but telling them is for me [the author] a great and overwhelming task. . . . Nor can I explain how he conquered diverse lands and cities, subjugating them to the name of God or how he established many abbeys and churches around the world, placing the bodies and relics of many saints . . . and how, as emperor of Rome, he visited the **sepulcher of the Lord** and brought **the wood of the cross** back with him, which he later distributed to many churches. My hands and pencils would crumble before I could finish this story.

Key Terms

- **Frisian Sea**—southeastern section of the North Sea.
- **Galicia**—the northwest part of the Iberian Peninsula, in Spain.
- **Saracens**—medieval Christian term for Arabs or Muslims.
- **Sepulcher of the Lord**—the Church on the site believed to be where Jesus was crucified and the empty tomb of Jesus, where he was believed to have been buried and resurrected from the dead.
- **The wood of the cross**—relics; pieces of the cross on which Jesus was crucified.

Source C
The Miracles of Saint James—Part 2 of the *Book of St. James*; also referred to as the *Codex Calixtinus* or *The Book of Pope Callixtus II* (twelfth century)[70]

10. A miracle of Saint James Written Down by His Excellency Pope Callixtus II
In the year of Our Lord, one thousand one hundred and four, while a certain pilgrim was returning from Jerusalem and was sitting on the edge of the ship . . . he fell from the ship into the open sea. While he was appealing to Saint James, one of his companions threw down his shield from the ship to him in the sea, saying "May the most glorious Apostle James, whose help you invoke, assist you."

The drowning man grasped the shield and for three days and three nights, with St. James leading . . . swam through the sea's waves, following the wake of the ship, until he came unharmed to the desired port. He then told everyone how Blessed James had guided him from the moment when he had called to him by holding his head with his hand.

This was accomplished by the Lord and it is miraculous in our eyes.

12. A miracle of Saint James Written Down by His Excellency Pope Callixtus II
At the beginning of the year of Our Lord one thousand one hundred six, a certain soldier in **Apulia** became swollen in the throat. Since he could find no recovery of his health from any physician, he entrusted himself to Saint James and said that if he could find a shell, which pilgrims are accustomed to bring back with them on their return from [the shrine] of Saint James, and if he could touch his ailing throat with it, he would immediately be cured. When he had found one on a certain pilgrim

who happened to be his neighbor, he touched he throat with it and he was cured. Then he set out toward the threshold of Blessed James in Galicia.

This was accomplished by the Lord and it is miraculous in our eyes.

Key Terms

- **Apulia**—region in southern Italy.

Source D
The Pilgrimage of Charlemagne (twelfth century)[71]

One day, in the **Church of St. Denis,** Charles put on his crown and crossed himself. His sword with its pommel of pure gold was girt about him and in his company were dukes, lords, barons, and knights. He looked at his wife, the queen, who wore her crown with great splendor, and taking her by the hand, beneath an olive tree began to speak forcefully to her. "My lady, have you ever seen any man on earth with a sword or crown more becoming than mine? With my lance I shall conquer yet more cities." The queen lacked sense and made a foolish reply. "Emperor," she said, "you think too highly of yourself. I know someone even more dashing than you when he wears his crown in the company of his knights. When he puts it on his head, it suits him better than yours." When he heard these word, Charles was very angry. Because the **Franks** had heard what she said, he bowed his head low. "Come, Lady, where is this king? Tell me who he is . . . if the Franks agree, I shall accept their judgement. But if you have lied to me, you will pay dearly, for I shall cut off your head with my sword of steel."

"Emperor," said the queen, "do not be angry. This man has greater wealth than you, more gold and more money, but he is not so valiant or such a brave knight on the battlefield or so capable of putting an enemy to flight." When she realized that Charles was so enraged, the queen deeply regretted her words. . . . The queen said, "I have often heard of King Hugo the Strong, Emperor of Greece and Constantinople. He holds all Persia as far as Cappadocia and there is not finer knight from here to Antioch. Apart from yours, there has never been such a company of men as his."

After wearing his crown and making his offering at the main altar, the Emperor of France returned to the hall of his palace in Paris, taking with him Roland and Oliver, William of Orange, and brave Naimes, Ogier of Denmark, Gerin and Berenger, Archbishop Turpin, Ernaut, Aimer, Bernard of Brusban and the brave Bertrand, and a thousand knights from France.*

"Lords," said the Emperor, "Listen to me. If it pleases God, you will visit a far off kingdom to seek Jerusalem and the land of the Lord God. I wish to worship **the cross and the sepulcher.** Thrice have I dreamed this, so I must go. And I shall seek out this king of whom I have heard. . . . I shall not return until I have found him.

* In medieval accounts, Charlemagne is often accompanied by the Paladins, also referred to as the Twelve Peers.

Key Terms

- **Church of St. Denis**—a Benedictine abbey located north of Paris. The church was closely associated with the kings of France and many were buried there. In 1140, the church was rebuilt by Abbot Suger and is considered the first Gothic church.
- **Franks**—soldiers of Charlemagne.
- **The cross and the sepulcher**—the cross on which Jesus was crucified, and the empty tomb of Jesus, where he was believed to have been buried and resurrected from the dead.

Source E
The Pilgrim's Guide to Santiago de Compostela—Part 5 of the *Book of St. James* (twelfth century)[72]

St. William

If you go to **Santiago** on the Toulouse road, you should visit the body of the Blessed Confessor William. The most saintly William was a standard-bearer and an eminent companion of Charlemagne, a brave soldier skilled in war. Through his strength of character he brought to Christian rule the cities of Nimes, Orange and many others, and carried the **cross of God** into the Gellone valley, where he led the life of a hermit, and after a blessed death, Christ's confessor rests there honorably.[73]

Roland

Then at Blaye, on the coast, one should seek the help of St Romanus, in whose basilica rests the body of the blessed martyr Roland, who was of noble family, a count of Charlemagne the King, one of his twelve warriors, who girded with the zeal of faith, entered Spain to expel the perfidious pagans.

It is said that he was filled with such strength that in **Roncesvalles** he split a rock from top to bottom through the middle with a triple stroke of his lance, and when he blew his horn, the power of his breath split it down the middle. The split ivory horn is in the basilica of St Severinus in Bordeaux, and the church in Roncesvalles is built on the rock split by Roland.[74]

Charlemagne's Warriors

Then in the territories of Bordeaux, in the town called Belin, one must visit the bodies of the holy martyrs Oliver, Gondebaud King of Friesa, Ogier King of Denmark, Arastain king of Brittany, Garin Duke of Lorraine and many other warriors of Charlemagne, who after conquering pagan armies in Spain were slaughtered for the faith of Christ. Their companions brought back their precious bodies all the way to Belin and buried them there with great affection. They lie together in one tomb, from which wafts the sweetest fragrance which can make healthy the sick.[75]

The Basque Country has the highest mountain on the **Camino.** It's called the Pass of Cize and is a gateway to Spain. . . . The summit is called Charlemagne's Cross, because here Charlemagne, setting out with his armies for Spain, made a road with axes, picks and other digging tools. He first raised a cross and then knelt facing Galicia and poured out prayers to God and St James. And so it's traditional for pilgrims to kneel here facing St. James' homeland and to plant their own crosses. You might find a thousand crosses here, the first station of prayer on the Camino de Santiago.

Near the mountain, to the north, is the valley where it is said Charlemagne camped with his army after his soldiers had been killed at Roncesvalles. This route is taken by many pilgrims who don't want to climb the mountain. Coming down from the summit, you'll come to the hostel and church with the rock that the great hero Roland split with a triple stroke. Next up is the town of Roncesvalles, where the battle took place in which King Marsile, Roland, Oliver and another 40,000 Christian and Saracen soldiers were killed.[76]

Key Terms

- **Santiago**—reference to the pilgrimage shrine of St. James in the Cathedral of Santiago de Compostela northwestern Spain.
- **Cross of God**—a relic, a piece of the cross on which Jesus was crucified.
- **Roncesvalles** is the Spanish spelling, Roncevaux is the French spelling; both are often used.
- **Camino**—Camino de Santiago is the Spanish phrase for the pilgrimage route to the Shrine of St. James in the Cathedral of Santiago de Compostela.

Source F
William in the Monastery (twelfth century)[77]

> Listen to a verse that's widely praised, About William, the marquis of the short nose . . .
> [*scenes in which his beloved wife, Guiborc, dies and William mourns*]
> **William Fierebrace** enters the church, he lifts his hand to make the sign of the cross,
> Then he kneels down and bows before the saint. "St. Julien, I am now in your care;
> For God, I have left my castles and marches and my cities and all my kingdom.
> St. Julien, I commend my shield to your care . . .
> The marquis remounts his good battle-horse, he leaves the city and resumes his journey.
> Count William makes his way to the abbey which the angel had shown him;
> He wears his good **hauberk** and his helmet, his sword of steel and the spear that cut well . . .
> He makes his way directly to the church, approaches the altar and presents his arms;
> He has no desire to fight anymore, unless Louis [son of Charlemagne] has great need of him against Saracens.
> He reaches the cloister, afraid of nothing, finds the abbot and greets him courteously.

The abbot asks "Sir William, what are you seeking here?"
The count answers: "An angel came, God sent him to me, so that I would come here and become a monk."
"Sir William," says the abbot, "good, sweet lord, you have caused the death of many men;
Penance for that I cannot keep from you for your sins, there have been twenty thousand.
You will be a monk and accept suffering, but tell me, do you know how to chant and read?"
[*William answers that he can recite things from memory but not read or write*]
The abbot and all of the monks in the chapter house listen and begin to laugh.
"Sir William, you are a noble man and a lord, if God helps me, we will teach you to read in your psalter
and to sing matins too.... When you're a priest you will read the gospel and you will sing mass."...
The abbot takes scissors and cuts the **tonsure** ... [*William is given a black monk's robe, cape, hood, tunic, and cowl to wear*]
The count dons the clothing of a monk, he looks for no excuse. The robe is large but it is not too long;
It is short by more than a half yard ... and the abbot laughs at him and all the monks as well.

Key Terms

- **William Fierebrace**—William Strongarms—one of his nicknames, he was also called Short Nose because his nose had been cut or broken in battle.
- **Hauberk**—a shirt of chain mail.
- **Tonsure**—monks and priests shaved off the hair on the top of their head as a sign of religious dedication.

The Primary Sources: The "Rules" of Vacationing in America

The promoters of tourism and travel create impressions that everyone can and should take a vacation and convey powerful messages about ideal vacations. But in reality, gender, social and economic status, race, and ethnicity shape conceptions about and access to vacation. People within a status, ethnic, or cultural group define the customs of that group and exclude others by making judgments on what is "good" or "bad" behavior. As more people could afford a vacation in the nineteenth and twentieth centuries, upper- and middle-class status groups defined and enforced the "rules" of vacationing by attempting to limit acceptable behavior while on vacation, prescribing appropriate vacations for lower social classes, and excluding entire groups from popular vacation destinations.

The following sources span almost one hundred and fifty years of American vacationing. Students can analyze this set of texts and images as a whole, as they represent both change and continuity over time. Or the sources can be divided into the time periods typically taught in US History and introduced in smaller sets relevant to the individual teaching units.

For example, sources 5 and 9–12 are associated with the reform movements of the late nineteenth and early twentieth centuries. Sources 3 and 7 and figures 2.7 and 2.8 work well with units related to the struggle for civil rights. Sources 4 and 6 are relevant to the etiquette theme described in chapter 3. If all of the primary sources below are analyzed as a whole, students should be asked to consider how changing forms of transportation, the development of advertising and new forms of media, and government policies (for example, the Interstate Highway Act of 1956 and the Civil Rights Act of 1964) impacted vacation over time.

In the Classroom
Ask students to construct a definition for "tourist" and "traveler." Suggest that they conduct an Internet search for the phrases "traveler or tourist." Students will find a wide range of advice about how to be a traveler and avoid being a tourist. Ask students to consider and discuss the differences in the two concepts and how those differences have originated.

Introduce the following information from Daniel Boorstin's *The Image: A Guide to Pseudo-Events in America* (1961). It difficult to illustrate this key theme through excerpts, so it is summarized here, but advanced readers could be encouraged to read chapter 3, "From Traveler to Tourist: The Lost Art of Travel."

Boorstin argued that what used to be "travel" had declined into "tourism." He maintained that men (Boorstin's choice of noun) wanted to go to new places because they wanted to learn and see new things even though it was uncomfortable, difficult, and expensive. "Travelers" did not go for fun, they went with a serious attitude for sophisticated pleasures—to see paintings, sculpture, architecture, the birthplaces of poets.

Boorstin did admit that travel was only for a privileged few, requiring a lot of money and time. He noted several historical developments that enabled more people to travel—rapid development of cheaper, faster, and more comfortable transportation; development of the packaged tour industry pioneered by Thomas Cook; growth of national and international motel and hotel chains; establishment of attractions specifically for tourists; and publication of "modern" tourist guidebooks that recommended and rated attractions. He stated that "this change can be described in a word. It was the decline of the traveler and the rise of the tourist."[78]

According to Boorstin, the "tourist" was passive, a pleasure-seeker who expected things to be easy and packaged and to have pleasant and interesting things happen *to* him. Tourists were portrayed as mindlessly rushing to various advertised attractions, snapping photographs, and buying souvenirs, without truly appreciating the experience or seeing the authentic beauty or culture. The following quotes can be provided to students to sum up Boorstin's views:

- "The tourist seldom likes the authentic (to him often unintelligible) product of the foreign culture; he prefers his own provincial expectations."[79]
- "The democratizing of travel, the lowering cost, increased organization, and improved means of long-distance transportation within our country . . . helped to dilute the experience."[80]

The larger focus of Boorstin's book was a contrast between "the authentic" experience and the "pseudo-event." A pseudo-event was defined as an event or activity that existed for the sole purpose of media publicity. When applied to tourism, a pseudo-event was an attraction that was commercialized, promoted, and packaged just for tourists. In summary, according to Boorstin, upper-class travel was an authentic experience of much more value than the cheaper tourism of the pseudo-events accessible to the middle and working classes. This stratification of vacationing along a spectrum of more or less value was a pervasive theme before Boorstin's time, and continues to be used today.

The most suitable strategy for students reading and analyzing the following sources will depend upon whether the sources are used together or divided into smaller groups for separate teaching units. The reading guide (figure 2.10) is suitable for each individual source, but you may wish to add additional questions related to the specific content of the unit you are teaching. In either situation, be sure to introduce the essential question and require that students address it in an appropriate culminating, formative, or summative assessment.

- *How did cultural expectations and economic realities impact vacation in the past? Are those factors still present today?*

Source #	Year of Source:	Name of Source:
1. What groups/viewpoints does the author represent?		
2. What attitudes/views/actions are being criticized by the author? *Cite or mark key phrases to support your answer.*		
3. According to the author, how should a person act when on vacation? *Cite or mark key phrases to support your answer.*		
4. What groups/viewpoints do the people being criticized represent?		
5. How might the people being criticized respond to the author? In other words, how might they explain, defend or justify their behavior?		

Figure 2.10.   **Reading Guide—American Vacations.**

You may wish to use current news stories about vacations to introduce the activity. At the publication of this book, one can quickly locate articles about jobs that do not offer paid vacation, why some Americans do not use vacation time included in their employment benefit plans, and comparisons of American vacation benefits to those offered in other nations.

Prior to reading, brainstorm a list of different groups of people that might view vacations differently or be treated differently while on vacation and speculate about the origins of those viewpoints. Or you may want to provide a list similar to the one below for students.

Upper Class, Middle Class, Working Class/Poor, Intellectual/Academic, Male, Female, Masculine, Feminine, Ethnicity, Race, Immigrant or Native Born, Religion

Provide the primary sources and the reading guide (figure 2.10) to students.

Photographs, advertisements, postcards, travel brochures, and websites can also be analyzed for messages about who should or should not take vacations. A few examples are provided in this chapter. The Image Analysis Guide (figure 2.11) should be provided to students.

Source 1

Excerpt from *The Travellers: A Tale Designed for Young People* (1825) by Catharine Maria Sedgwick[81]

Niagara Falls was a popular destination for upper-class tourists prior to the Civil War. Before the opening of the Erie Canal in 1825, only the wealthiest tourists could afford the time and cost to visit this remote destination. The Eric Canal made this destination accessible to more tourists and a wide range of attractions and hotels were built around the falls to accommodate the growing number of visitors. It became a New York state park in 1885, the first state park in the United States. The following excerpts are from a novel about the travels of a family, Mr. and Mrs. Sackville and their two children, Edward and Julia, on a tour of Niagara, the Great Lakes, Montreal, and Quebec. Mr. Sackville is a successful lawyer, his wife was "accomplished," and the family lived on a beautiful country estate. The author, Catharine Maria Sedgwick (1789–1867), published novels, short stories, and poems for both adults and children and often promoted the ideal of Republican motherhood.

After visiting Niagara Falls, the children are discussing their experience with their parents. In this excerpt, Edward is describing conversations with other tourists.

"Well, papa, what do you think of that party of city shop-keepers who dined at the inn with us today? I heard one of the ladies say, 'I have been so disappointed in my journey.' When I heard her say that, I dropped my knife and fork and exclaimed,

Source #	Name of Source:
Creator:	Date Created:
1. What groups of people, or viewpoints are represented in the image? *Cite evidence to support your answer.*	
2. What type of tourism, vacations, or travel is represented? *Cite evidence to support your answer.*	
3. What was the original purpose of this image?	
4. What groups of people or views about vacation are not represented?	
5. What messages does this image send about the tourism and vacation? *Positive? Negative? Exclusive? Inclusive? For wealthy people? For everyone? Educational? Historical? Relaxation? Nature? Entertainment?*	

Figure 2.11. Image Analysis Guide.

'Disappointed, madam! Does not the fall [Niagara Falls] look as high as you expected?' She replied laughing, 'Oh, child, I was not speaking of the fall; but I find it is quite too early in the season to travel in the country. I have not seen a roast pig or a broiled chicken since I left the city.' What do you think of that, papa?"

The father replied "Why I think, my dear, she is a **vulgar** woman, who travels because others do; and is naturally disappointed in not finding the dishes she prefers to eat when at home."

Edward said, "What about Mrs. Hilton, papa, who I am sure, is not vulgar—at least she is very rich—and I heard her say to a gentleman, that if she could have remained at **the *Springs***, and then could have gone home and said she had been to Niagara Falls, she would have been glad to do it; for she was sure that no one actually visited the Falls except to say they had been there."

The father answered, "Mrs. Hilton is of the class of the vulgar rich, among whom vulgarity is quite obvious, and much more disgusting, than with the vulgar poor. But let's forget them dear Edward. Talking about the faults and follies of others is not worthy of this beautiful scenery. Thank God that you are not like these people."

Key Terms

- **Vulgar**—not having or showing good manners, good taste, or politeness *or* an adjective used to refer to common people of a lower social class.
- **The Springs**—Saratoga Springs, a popular mineral springs resort in New York.

Source 2
Excerpt from *A Book of Vagaries Comprising the New Mirror for Travellers and Other Whim-Whams*[82]
This book was written as a parody of tourist guides to the popular sites in the northeastern United States in the first half of the nineteenth century. It was originally published in 1828; this excerpt is from an 1868 edition.

As Albany [New York] is a sort of depot, where the fashionable are warehoused a night or two for exportation to Saratoga, Niagara, Montreal, Quebec, and Boston, we shall here present to our readers a short system of rules and regulations for detecting good inns, and generally, for travelling with dignity and refinement.

Never go where the stage-drivers or steam-boat men advise you to go.

Never go to a newly-painted house—those are traps for greenhorns. . . .

Never go to a hotel that has a fine gilt-framed picture of itself hung up in the steam-boat . . . a good hotel speaks for itself, and will be found out without a picture.

Always believe puff in the newspapers in praise of any hotel. It is a proof that the landlord has been over-civil to one guest at the expense of all others . . . Perhaps you may be equally favored, particularly if you hint that you mean to publish your travels. . . .

If you have no servant, always hire one of the smartest-dressed fellows of the steam-boat to carry your baggage, and pass him off as your servant, if possible, till you are snugly housed at the hotel . . .

Grumble at your accommodations every morning. It will make you appear of consequence, and, if there are better rooms in the hotel, in time you will get moved to them . . .

Lastly, never go away from a place without paying your bill, unless you have nothing to pay it with. . . . A man must travel nowadays, or he is absolutely nobody; and if he has no money, it must be at the expense of other people. . . . Be sure to talk "big" about having married a rich wife as ugly as sin, for the sake of her money; about your great relations; and if your modesty won't permit you to pass for a lord, then claim to be a second cousin to one.

Source 3
Excerpt from *New York Times*, June 19, 1877[83]
The Grand Union Hotel at Saratoga Springs was claimed to be the world's largest hotel, with guestrooms for 2,000 guests, and attracted wealthy patrons. Judge Henry Hilton (1824–1899) was an American jurist and businessman. The incident described below came to be known as the "Hilton-Seligman Affair." Henry Hilton was not related to Conrad Hilton (1887–1979), the founder of the Hilton Hotel chain.

Headline: A Sensation at Saratoga. New Rule for the Grand Union. No Jews to Be Admitted.

On Wednesday last Joseph Seligman, the well-known banker of this City . . . visited Saratoga with his wife and family. For 10 years past he has spent the summer at the Grand Union Hotel. His family entered the parlors, and Mr. Seligman went to the manager to make arrangements for rooms. That gentleman seemed somewhat confused, and said: "Mr. Seligman, I am required to inform you that Mr. Hilton has given instructions that no Israelites shall be permitted in future to stop at this hotel."

Mr. Seligman was so astonished that for some time he could make no reply. Then he said: "Do you mean to tell me that you will not entertain Jewish people?" "That is our orders, Sir," was the reply.

Before leaving the banker asked the reason why Jews were thus persecuted. Said he, "Are they dirty, do they misbehave themselves, or have they refused to pay their bills?"

"On, no," replied the manager, "there is no fault to be found in that respect. The reason is simply this: Business at the hotel was not good last season, and we had a large number of Jews here. Mr. Hilton came to the conclusion that Christians did not like their company, for that reason shunned the hotel. He resolved to run the Union on a different principle this season, and gave us instructions to admit no Jew."

Source 4
Excerpt from "Promiscuous Bathing" in *Ladies' Home Journal*, August 1890[84]

Ladies' Home Journal began publication in 1882 and by the early twentieth century became the first American magazine to reach one million subscribers. The magazine provided a wide range of articles and advice to its mostly female, middle-class readers.

When I see a young man and woman, who have only met at their hotel, emerge from their bathing houses, the man looking like a harlequin in his red and white jersey and short blue trousers, legs and arms perfectly bare; the girl in her **costume de bain**, made tight, showing every curve, I feel that a protest is in order. A little innocent girl witnessing this asked her mother "If she might take off her dress and play in her underclothes like the ladies did on the beach." After the swim, these young people settle themselves on the sand, rarely having any chaperon or older person with them.

Our daughters are well bred in virtue, but what about the tired little shop-girl without father or mother or advisor? Can we expect that she will behave as our own tenderly-nurtured children? She is tired and wore out with hard labor and poor food; a day and a night are all she can get of rest from the tread-mill of work. Sick in body, and alas! too often sick in heart, let us give her all the happiness and relaxation we can; but let us hinder, not help her to think that familiarity and license mean recreation. . . . The freedom the morning swim introduces grows as the day speeds on. The companions of these girls, "gentlemen friends" as they are called, are generous. They ride, they dance, they flirt, and when night comes, he has his arm around her slim waist, so careless that they do not even care that they are seen.

Key Term

- **Costume de bain**—swimsuit.

Source 5
Excerpt from "Open Letters: Camping out for the Poor" in *The Century Magazine*, August 1892[85]

The author began the article by reflecting on his own middle-class summer vacations on the ocean shore. He then proposed methods for allowing working-class families to also escape the city heat for their own summer vacation, and concluded the article by advising the working classes of "better use of time that is now nearly or wholly wasted."

One of the benevolent societies connected with Mr. Adler's Society for Ethical Culture subscribed enough money to build a dozen comfortable cottages in a pleasant spot some twenty miles out on Long Island, and induced some poor families of Polish Jews who worked on cheap clothing to make the experiment of living there. Their charitable society made the rent very low and also paying the express mail charges upon the packages of clothing sent in and out from the large shops which gave these people employment. It was hoped that the advantages of a country life of pure air for the children, of lower rents than in their dirty, miserable tenements, of the possibility of a garden, chickens, etc. would encourage others to join such a colony. The result was disappointment, and after a year the experiment was abandoned. The people, especially the women, wanted to get back to the city; they complained that it was lonely. They wanted society—the noise and squabbles, the fights, the dirt, and the crowds of the tenements. This result showed that if these people were to be taught the value of fresh air and quiet, the process must begin with the children. . . .

In the experiment I propose, I wish simply to get such people out of New York during the heat of the summer, when the death rate is largely made up of infants and small children. Such people give up their few rooms in their small tenements at a week's notice. They can store their goods at a small expense, and save enough on the rent to pay for their food during the weeks they are away. . . . What is to prevent such a family from pitching its tent on some of the beaches which stretch out for more than one hundred miles along the south shore of Long Island, or in the Jersey pines? . . .

What might be done by a Camping-out Society would be to tell poor people where and how they might camp out, the advantages and disadvantages of the life, its cost, its ways and means. I should like to hear camping-out lectures in which people who had camped out would give their experiences for and against the life. . . . One poor man whom I urged to make the experiment and take his sickly children to a bit of beach I knew, told me that the noise of the "blooming" ocean made him "blasted" tired. There are too many people who cannot see the trees for the forest.

Source 6
Excerpt from "Asbury Park," New York Times, July 15, 1900[86]

James Bradley (1830–1921) was a wealthy Manhattan brush manufacturer who designed and developed the resort destination of Asbury Park on the New Jersey Shore. The residential resort was named after American Methodist founder Francis Asbury and located next to Ocean Grove, a camp-meeting resort founded by Methodist ministers in 1869. Asbury Park was promoted to the middle class as a moral community that did not allow alcohol and on Sundays restricted beach access and required businesses to close. Working class and black people, many of whom worked within the resort, were not allowed access to the beach or resort amusements.[87]

"Founder" Bradley, the sensor of morals for the town he created, has begun a crusade against the revolting practice of parading through the streets of Asbury Park in bathing suits. Hundreds of women—and not a few men—adopt this method of saving the price of a private bathhouse (in which to change their clothes on the beach), much to the disgust of hotel guests and cottagers. . . . Every day the streets are alive with scantily attired females, many of who seem to take pride in displaying their anatomy. This week, Mr. Bradley, who is a Councilman, and Chairman of the Police Committee, inserted the following advertisement in the local papers: BATHING COSTUME NOTICE!—Do not go through the streets in bathing costumes. It is coarse and vulgar, and is in violation of the city ordnance.

Chairman Bradley said "No woman who has any respect for herself or her sex will make a show of her form in the public streets. Sometimes the show is one of beauty, but more often of beef."

Figure 2.12.   Beachgoers in swimsuits at Long Beach, Los Angeles, California around 1910.
(Courtesy of University of Southern California Libraries and California Historical Society.)

Source 7
Excerpt from "Crum Refused a Chair," *New York Times*, August 15, 1905[88]

West Park, New Jersey, was a working-class district where many immigrant and black employees of Asbury Park lived and where amusements were open to working-class vacationers. It was located across the railroad tracks from Asbury Park.

Dr. William D. Crum, the negro Collector of Customs at Charleston, S.C., who is a summer visitor with his wife at West Park, tried today to hire a **wheel chair** for his wife for a ride on the boardwalk.

Proprietor J. L. Schneider refused to order any of his white lads to push the chair, but said that Dr. Crum might have it if he would wheel his wife himself. Dr. Crum refused in a gentlemanly manner and left.

Key Term

- **Wheel chairs**—rolling chairs rented on a boardwalk by tourists.

Source 8
Excerpt from "Boredom" by Maxim Gorky in *The Independent*, August 8, 1907[89]

Maxim Gorky (1868–1936) was a Russian writer and active in the Marxist movement.

Editor's introduction to the article:

> The following article is a remarkable proof of the trite saying that what is seen depends upon the eye which sees it. To most people, Coney Island, the playground of the metropolis, seems a place of gaiety and comparatively innocent of those somewhat vulgar amusements. But to the man who has assumed the name of "Gorky," "The Bitter One," it only affords further evidence of the stupidity and depravity of the human race and of the tyranny of capital.

Figure 2.13. Wheel chairs or rolling chairs on the boardwalk, Atlantic City, New Jersey, between 1905 and 1920.
Photo by Detroit Publishing Co., Publisher. (Courtesy of the Library of Congress.)

Excerpt from Gorky's essay:

> People go forth to the shore of the sea, where the beautiful white buildings stand and promise respite and tranquility. . . . The sand glitters in the sun with a warm, yellow gleam, and the transparent buildings stand out on its velvety expanse like thin white silk embroidery. . . . I turn my gaze wistfully upon this island. . . . I would recline on its luxurious folds [of the beach], and from there look out into the wide spaces where white birds dart swiftly and noiselessly where ocean and sky lie drowsing in the scorching gleam of the sun [then the author enters the amusement park] . . .
>
> The city, magic and fantastic from afar, now appears an absurd jumble of straight lines of wood, a cheap, hastily constructed toy house for the amusement of children. . . . They are built of wood, and smeared over with peeling white pain, which gives them the appearance of suffering with skin disease. . . . The people huddled together in this city actually number hundreds of thousands. They swarm into the cages like black flies. . . .
>
> But it is necessary to make money . . . and depravity laughs disdainfully at hypocrisy and falsehood . . . it's a wearying, tiresome depravity, but it also is "for the people." It is organized as a paying business, as a means to extract their earnings from the pockets of the people. Fed by a passion for gold it appears in a form vile and despicable indeed in this marsh of glittering boredom. . . . But the precaution has been taken to blind the people, and they drink in the vile poison with silent rapture. The poison contaminates their souls. Boredom whirls about in an idle dance, expiring in the agony of its inanition.

Source 9
Excerpt from *New York Times*, July 31, 1910.[90]

Headline: *"How Long Should a Man's Vacation Be?* President Taft Says Every One Should Have Three Months—What Big Employers of Labor and Men of Affairs Think on the Subject"

According to President Taft, "the American people have found out that there is such a thing as exhausting . . . one's health . . . and that two or three months' vacation . . . are necessary in order to enable one to continue his work the next year with that energy and effectiveness which it ought to have. The American people have come to the conclusion that the women and children especially ought to have a change of air where they can expand their lungs and get exercise in the open. The men can go when they can.

A Times reporter endeavored to ascertain the views of some of the prominent men of New York, especially employers of large numbers of workers, on the vacation proposition.

John Wanamaker
  As to employees in stores, he stated that they certainly should have vacations, and in his opinion, the time should vary. "No, I cannot see the president's two or three months idea at all, except to repeat that it should not be taken too seriously."

Frank Hedley, Vice President Interborough Rapid Transit Railroad
  "It is different with the man whose work is merely physical effort. Take, for example, the man who works in the earth or performs some such simple normal labor. In his case, the Saturday half holiday and Sunday brings much greater relief than to the man who works with his brain. The laborer has a much better chance, it seems to me, to live longer and enjoy good health than the man who is subjected to great mental strain. The man who works at a bench for example, drops his tools and all the cares of his work the moment the whistle sounds. The man above him cannot do this. Responsibility is always on his mind. . . . The manager undoubtedly needs a vacation and a good one."

Henry Clews, Banker
  "The average clerk would be spoiled if the rule for vacation was to extend beyond two weeks, although I do think they should have two weeks' rest."

Colgate Hoyt, Banker
  "Every clerical employee should have two weeks, and as far as the laboring man is concerned he apparently gets his in what is called 'forced vacations';—yet he is entitled by no means to the same amount of rest as one who uses the brain in such an active way."

Joseph Davis, Controller of the American Locomotive Works
  "The laboring man seems to be in a class by himself. Many corporations now hire this force under an hourly wage agreement, and it is rare that the man has a full year's work. The result is that the time 'off,' owing to changing conditions, take the

place of a vacation, but of course it is at their own expense." Mr. Davis stated that it would be extremely difficult to arrange any vacation proposition, with this class of labor, owing to just this hourly wage basis, and because about 40 per cent of the workers change in the course of a year.

Gustav Straubenmuller, Acting Superintendent of New York's Public Schools
"Of course, I believe that the youngsters should have a real out-and-out vacation if it is possible—preferably in the country, where they can obtain good food and fresh air, but it is impossible for us to do this for them."

Supreme Court Justice Henry Bischoff, Jr.
"As to the length of time of vacations it is difficult indeed to fix a time that could apply to all classes, but I am inclined to think that one month for the business man is quite sufficient and that the professional man should have a least two months. Clerical employees should be compensated by two week's rest in a year. Then, too, I believe that the laboring man ought to get a vacation, but unfortunately he cannot unless he takes it—and then it is without pay, which means a lot to him, you know."

Oren Root, General Manager of the Metropolitan Railway
"I cannot see the philosophy in Mr. Taft's statement. I worked ten years at one stretch without a vacation. This year? No, I'm not going to take one, not for two weeks or two months."

Source 10
Excerpt from Hugh Thompson, "The Vacation Savings Movement," *Munsey's Magazine*, May 1913[91]
In this article, the author describes various efforts to help young, unmarried women with jobs find safe, affordable vacation boardinghouses, and describes a plan created to help save money for vacation. In this era, these women are usually referred to as girls or working girls.

An investigation made of the vacation resources of New York [for unmarried women with jobs] showed that vacation homes had been established by a few churches, settlement houses, and philanthropic societies. Three department-stores had such institutions for benefit of their own employees. The church cottages, as a rule, were open to parishioners only. In all, about seven thousand working girls out of the four hundred thousand in the city, or less than two percent of the total, could be accommodated in this way.

While good was accomplished by these different vacation homes, it was found, on inquiry among the girls, that they were unpopular because of the restrictions imposed on the inmates. In most of them the girls had to live by rigid rule; there was no freedom of action. The situation was summed up by a saleswoman who told an investigator: "Why, you can't even look at a man if you go there! I do not want to be bound to go to prayers twice a day."

The general feeling among these self-supporting women, who toiled so hard for the greater part of the year, was that when they did have a chance to get away from the irksome routine of shop and shelf, they wanted to feel absolutely free to rest or to seek innocent amusement.

Source 11
Excerpt from *Christianity and Amusements* (1915) by Richard Henry Edwards[92]
The following rating of the different kinds of amusement in proportion to their moral worth is submitted as representing an opinion based on very careful study:

Motion picture shows—79% good
Theaters—72% good
Dance halls—23.1 % good
River excursion boats—7.7 % good
Pool halls—46.2 % good
Skating rinks—74.1% good
Penny arcades—38.5% good
Shows—"Men only"—0 % good

Shooting galleries—84.7% good
Bowling alleys—77.1 % good
Amusement parks—71.1% good

Medical museums. Social clubs, wine gardens, chop-suey restaurants, and saloons were not graded. They would undoubtedly lower the average of good, wholesome recreation. The totals show 68% are wholesome amusements and 32% are bad. The 32% consists of intemperance, obscenity, suggestions of crime, dissipation, late hours, representing an expenditure of $1,923,211.99.

Source 12
Excerpt from Anzia Yezierska, "The Free Vacation House," *The Forum*, December 1915[93]

In this article, the author, a Jewish immigrant, describes her experiences at a free vacation house sponsored by a charitable group called the Social Betterment Society that is open to poor mothers and children from New York City. In order to go to the vacation house, she must first apply to the charity, report to their office with her children, provide information about her family's earnings, and be examined by a doctor before boarding the train. At the vacation home, she is confronted with many rules and observed by visiting wealthy women who donated to the charity. In the following excerpt, the author sums up her experience.

The reason why I stay out the whole two weeks, is this: I think to myself, so much shame in the face I suffered to come here, let me at least make the best from it already. Let me at least save up for two weeks what I got to spend out for grocery and butcher for my bills back home. And then also think I to myself, if I go back on Monday, I got to do the big washing; on Tuesday waits for me the ironing; on Wednesday, the scrubbing and cleaning, and so goes it on. How bad it is already in this place, it's a change from the very same sameness of what I'm having day in and day out at home. And so I stayed out this vacation to the bitter end.

But at last the day for going out from this prison [the vacation house] came. On the way riding back, I kept thinking to myself: this is such a beautiful vacation house. For why do they make it so hard for us? When a mother needs a vacation, why must they tear the insides out from her first, by making her come down to the charity office. Why drag us from the charity office through the streets? And when we live through the shame of the charities and when we come already to the vacation house, for why do they boss the life out of us with so many rules and bells? For why don't they let us lay down our heads on the bed, when we are tired? For why must we always stick in the back room, like dogs what have to be chained in one spot? If they would let us walk around free, would we bite off something from the front part of the house?

If the best part of the house what is comfortable is made up for a show for visitors, why ain't they keeping the whole business for a show for visitors. For why do they have to fool in worn-out mothers, to make them think they'll give them a rest? Do they need the worn-out mothers as part of the show? I guess that is it, already.

Extending the Theme

Explore tourism in your own community. Often we are the least familiar with the tourist attractions in our own communities. Ask students to research what vacation and tourism sites and experiences are promoted in your community. Who promotes tourism in your state and community, how, and to what groups of people? Analyze the imagery used to market your state and community to tourists and consider how advertising and travel writing about your area impact the collective memories about your area. Can tourism advertising contribute to common stereotypes about a culture or region? Students may develop new advertising campaigns that echo past conceptions or create a new image of the community for future tourists.

Students can also explore the history of tourism in their community. The New Deal American Guide series[94] is an excellent starting point. Did popular vacation destinations exist that declined due to changing transportation or changes in vacation habits? Are there remainders of old tourist sites, motels, or resorts still present in the local landscape? For example, before the Interstate Highway System bypassed towns and realigned major transportation routes, many towns had a major thoroughfare with motels, restaurants, and tourist attractions. The old Route 66 between Chicago and California is an example. What has happened to that thoroughfare in your town?

Figure 2.14. Motel for tourists along state route before construction of federal interstate highways, 1940. Wigwam Village Inn #2 in Cave City, Kentucky, near Mammoth Cave National Park. The motel is located on the Dixie Highway, a highway constructed for automobiles between 1915 and 1927, before the Federal-Aid Highway Act of 1956 authorized the construction of limited-access highways that bypassed many towns and tourist attractions. This motel is still open to visitors. There were seven original Wigwam Villages along tourist routes in Alabama, Florida, Louisiana, Arizona, and California; the other two operating motels are located on US Route 66.
Photo by Marion Post Walcott. July 1940. Farm Security Administration—Office of War Information Photograph Collection. (Courtesy of the Library of Congress.)

Heritage Tourism

Heritage tourism, as defined by the National Trust for Historic Preservation, is "traveling to experience the places, artifacts, and activities that authentically represent the stories and people of the past and present. It includes visitation to cultural, historic, and natural resources."[95] Ask students to identify, research, and visit heritage tourist sites in their area. Heritage tourism is often criticized for presenting more myth than historic reality; students can analyze the accuracy of the history recounted at the site through the signs, exhibits, and tours.

Students can be encouraged to identify potential heritage sites in their communities, especially ones that tell the story of regular or forgotten people of the past. Your state may have a program for historical highway markers. Students may be able to propose new sites for these programs or get involved in the promotion, interpretation, or restoration efforts of local heritage tourism sites.

Who Can Take a Vacation in the Twenty-First Century?

The unwillingness, or inability, of modern Americans to take a vacation is a consistent theme in the media. Various surveys find that people who receive paid vacation time do not use it, a fact that is often attributed to the uncertain economy and job markets. Many nations have labor laws that require that employers provide a minimum number of paid vacation days; laws in the United States do not require employers to allow paid vacation time or holidays. Many American workers do get paid vacation days, but access to paid vacation and the number of days varies greatly by occupation.

The Bureau of Labor Statistics provides data on time-off benefits; students can analyze the national statistics for civilian, private, and government employees and compare American vacation policy trends to the vacation policies of other nations and to employers in their own communities. Encourage students to propose plans for improvement.

Vacations in Government or Economics Classes
Tourism is a worldwide, multibillion dollar industry, and almost every aspect of travel is regulated or supported by government. *Overbooked: The Exploding Business of Travel and Tourism* (2013) by Elizabeth Becker is an excellent source for the study of vacation as a theme in a government or economics course. The author examines how the modern-day policies by the governments of the United States, France, Venice, Cambodia, the Middle East, Zambia, Costa Rica, Sri Lanka, and China promote, protect, or prohibit the business of tourism.

Environmental Conservation
The popularity of vacationing in nature and tours of scenic sites such as Niagara Falls and Yosemite helped to inspire the conservation movement and creation of the state and national park systems in the late 1800s and early 1900s. The study of the history of these movements is interesting in itself, and interdisciplinary lessons and units can be developed in cooperation with science teachers.

In the twenty-first century, the popularity of these parks threatens to destroy the natural environment of the parks and state and national funding for parks is continually questioned. Students can consider how state and federal government should balance the responsibilities for parks, the natural environment, and the promotion of the business of tourism and become involved in local initiatives to protect and preserve the natural environment or promote tourism at a local natural attraction.

Vacations and Geography
All five themes of geography—location, place, human-environment interaction, movement, and region—can be studied in the context of vacation and travel. Students can learn map skills planning a vacation (and analyze the impact of GPS devices on travel); examine the cultures of the proposed travel destination; evaluate how the environment affects travel and is modified by travel; consider how past and present transportation methods and routes impact vacation decisions, and study the unique human and physical characteristics of regions that are popular vacation destinations.

Mental mapping, the objective and subjective perception of a location by individuals, is especially applicable to geography concepts, collective memory, and vacation destinations. Ask students to draw from memory an illustrated map of a popular vacation destination that they may have visited or would like to visit. Then ask students to compare their mental maps to the maps of other students or to actual maps of the location and analyze what elements were omitted from their mental maps, the significance of the items they did include, and the sources upon which they drew for their mental map.

Travel and Literature
Travel and vacation narratives survive from all eras of history and are worthy of study in English and language arts classes as literature, as well as in social studies as primary sources. Many guidebooks, travel journals by unknown and famous people, blogs, and works of fiction use a journey as the setting. Jack Kerouac's *On the Road* or the quest in *Lord of the Rings* are just two examples of travel narratives that can be used to explore setting, character, theme, plot, point of view, and conflict.

Notes

1. Sarah Barber and Corinna Peniston-Bird, "Introduction," in *History Beyond the Text: A Student's Guide to Approaching Alternative Sources* (Abingdon, UK: Routledge, 2009). The authors define cultural circuit as the process in which "a continuous interrelationship between memories of events and cultural representations of events, and thus between past and present, is set up." In this work, cultural circuit describes interaction between historical events; how film, fiction, and living history interpretations portray those events; what oral history interviewees recall about the events; and how all of those factors continue to interact and influence the impressions of future generations.

2. E. D. Hunt, "Travel, Tourism and Piety in the Roman Empire: A Context for the Beginnings of Christian Pilgrimage," *Echos De Monde Classique* 28, no. 3 (1984): 394.

3. Pausanias, *Description of Greece*. Full text available at http://www.perseus.tufts.edu/hopper/text?doc=Perseus%3Atext%3A1999.01.0160.

4. Cindy S. Aron, *Working at Play: A History of Vacations in the United States* (Oxford/New York: Oxford University Press, 1999), 32–33.

5. "Vacations for Business Men," *New York Daily Times* (July 6, 1855). Retrieved from http://libproxy.eku.edu/login?url=http://search.proquest.com.libproxy.eku.edu/docview/95893764?accountid=10628.

6. Richard Gassan, *The Birth of American Tourism: New York, the Hudson Valley, and American Culture, 1790–1835* (Amherst: University of Massachusetts Press, 2008), 4–5.

7. Ibid., 4–6.

8. Linda Kay Davidson and Maryjane Dunn-Wood, *Pilgrimage in the Middle Ages: A Research Guide* (New York: Garland Publishing, 1993), 13.

9. David Herlihy, *Medieval Households* (Cambridge, MA/London: Harvard University Press, 1985), 113. Herlihy counted 3,276 saints that died before the year 1500 whose lives were recorded in the *Acta Sanctorum*, a collection of saints' lives.

10. Jacques De Vitry, *The History of Jerusalem A.D. 1190*, trans. Aubrey Stewart (London, UK: Palestine Pilgrims' Text Society, 1885), 90. https://archive.org/details/cu31924028534422.

11. Jonathan Sumption, *Pilgrimage, An Image of Mediaeval Religion* (Totowa, NJ: Rowman and Littlefield, 1975), 13.

12. Cynthia W. Resor, "Richard I Takes the Cross: The Twelfth-Century Culture of Crusade." PhD diss., University of Kentucky, 2002. ProQuest (ProQuest document ID 251650215). Retrieved from http://libproxy.eku.edu/login?url=http://search.proquest.com.libproxy.eku.edu/docview/251650215?accountid=10628.

13. John Theilmann, "Medieval Pilgrims and the Origins of Tourism," *Journal of Popular Culture* 20, no. 4 (Spring 1987): 94.

14. Peter Jan Margry, *Shrines and Pilgrimage in the Modern World: New Itineraries into the Sacred* (Amsterdam, Netherlands: Amsterdam University Press, 2008), 29.

15. Gassan, *The Birth of American Tourism*, 4–5.

16. Peter Brown, *The Cult of the Saints: Its Rise and Function in Latin Christianity* (Chicago: University of Chicago Press, 1982).

17. Full text available online: *Itinerary from Bordeaux to Jerusalem*, https://archive.org/details/cu31924028534158.

18. Sumption, *Pilgrimage*, 173–74.

19. Ibid., 188–89.

20. Ibid., 257–58.

21. David E. Kyvig and Myron A. Marty, *Nearby History, Exploring the Past around You*. 3rd ed. (Lanham, MD: Altamira Press/Rowman & Littlefield, 2010), 6–7.

22. Http://www.snopes.com/ is a helpful resource for current urban legends.

23. Eugene Hoade, trans., "The Itineraries of Fr. Simon Fitzsimons (1322–23)," in *Western Pilgrims* (Jerusalem: Franciscan Printing Press, 1970), 21.

24. Maurice Halbwachs, "Conclusions of the Legendary Topography of the Gospels in the Holy Land," in *On Collective Memory*, ed. and trans. Lewis A. Coser (Chicago: University of Chicago Press, 1992), 206–9, originally published in 1941. Full text available online: Torquato Tasso, *Jerusalem Delivered* at http://omacl.org/Tasso/. Full text available online: François-René de Chateaubriand, *Of Travels in Greece, Palestine, Egypt, and Barbary, during the years 1806 and 1807* at https://archive.org/details/travelsingreece00chatgoog.

25. Jack Larkin, *The Reshaping of Everyday Life, 1790–1840* (New York: Harper Collins, 1988), 205.

26. J. Winston Coleman, "Old Kentucky Watering Places," *The Filson Club History Quarterly* 16 (January 1942): 1–26; Aron, *Working at Play*, chapter 1.

27. John F. Sears, *Sacred Places, American Tourist Attractions in the Nineteenth Century* (New York/Oxford: Oxford University Press, 1989), chapter 5.

28. Aron, *Working at Play*, 30–32.

29. Thomas J. Schlereth, *Victorian America: Transformations in Everyday Life, 1879–1915* (New York: Harper Collins, 1991), xiii; Daniel E. Sutherland, *The Expansion of Everyday Life, 1860–1879* (New York: Harper Collins, 1989), xii.

30. Schlereth, *Victorian America*, 216.

31. Aron, *Working at Play*, chapter 4.

32. Marguerite S. Shaffer, *See America First, Tourism and National Identity, 1880–1940* (Washington, DC: Smithsonian Books, 2001), 4, 128.

33. Warren James Belasco, *Americans on the Road, From Autocamp to Motel, 1910–1945* (Baltimore: Johns Hopkins University Press, 1979); Aron, *Working at Play*, chapter 6.

34. Stephen Fried, *Appetite for America: Fred Harvey and the Business of Civilizing the Wild West—One Meal at a Time* (New York: Bantam, 2011), prologue, Kindle.

35. Sutherland, *The Expansion of Everyday Life*, 159–63.

36. Schlereth, *Victorian America*, chapter 6.

37. "Amusement Parks and Theme Parks," in *Oxford Encyclopedia of American Social History*, ed. Lynn Dumenil (Oxford, UK/New York: Oxford University Press, 2012), 1:37.

38. Ibid., 39.

39. Kathy Peiss, *Cheap Amusements: Working Women and Leisure in Turn-of-the-Century New York* (Philadelphia: Temple University Press, 1986), 164–87.

40. Aron, *Working at Play*, 214–16.

41. "Amusement Parks and Theme Parks," 38.

42. Aron, *Working at Play*, 238; Michael Berkowitz, "A 'New Deal' for Leisure: Making Mass Tourism During the Great Depression," in *Being Elsewhere: Tourism, Consumer Culture, and Identity in Modern Europe and North America*, ed. Shelley Osmun Baranowski and Ellen Furlough (Ann Arbor: University of Michigan Press, 2001), 191.

43. Berkowitz, "A 'New Deal' for Leisure," 185–212.

44. Richard K. Popp, *The Holiday Makers, Magazines, Advertising, and Mass Tourism in Postwar America* (Baton Rouge: Louisiana State University Press, 2012), 21; Berkowitz, "A 'New Deal' for Leisure," 185–212.

45. Susan Sessions Rugh, *The Golden Age of American Family Vacations: Are We There Yet?* (Lawrence: University of Kansas Press, 2008), 17–18.

46. Stephanie Coontz, *The Way We Never Were: American Families and the Nostalgia Trap* (New York: Basic Books, 1992, 2002), 29. Poverty data was not collected for Hispanics until 1972.

47. Ibid., 26–28.

48. Gary S. Cross and John K. Walton, *The Playful Crowd: Pleasure Places in the Twentieth Century* (New York: Columbia University Press, 2005), 167–68; Rugh, *The Golden Age of American Family Vacation*, 97–106.

49. Rugh, *The Golden Age of American Family Vacations*, 42.

50. Ibid., 18–24, 43–54, 33–40.

51. Aron, *Working at Play*, 77.

52. Cross and Walton, *The Playful Crowd*, 59.

53. Jim Butcher, *The Moralisation of Tourism: Sun, Sand . . . and Saving the World?* (London/New York: Routledge, 2003), chapter 1.

54. The Right Question Institute, "Right Question Strategy," accessed July 15, 2016, http://rightquestion.org/about/strategy/.

55. Resor, "Richard I Takes the Cross: The Twelfth-Century Culture of Crusade," chapter 5.

56. Full text available online: *The Song of Roland*, http://legacy.fordham.edu/halsall/basis/roland-ohag.asp.

57. Epics and romances related to King Arthur and his knights also originated in this era and were promoted by the Angevin kings of England to legitimize their rule.

58. John L. Grigsby, *The Gab as a Latent Genre in Medieval French Literature, Drinking and Boasting in the Middle Ages* (Cambridge: Medieval Academy of America, 2000), 1–5.

59. Glyn S. Burgess, ed. and trans., *The Pilgrimage of Charlemagne (Le Pèlerinage de Charlemagne)*, introduction by Anne Elizabeth Cobby, vol. 47, series A of the Garland Library of Medieval Literature (New York: Garland Publishing, Inc., 1988).

60. Matthew Gabriele, *An Empire of Memory: The Legend of Charlemagne, The Franks, and Jerusalem before the First Crusade* (Oxford, UK: Oxford University Press, 2011), 139–40.

61. Rosalind Hill, trans., *Gesta Francorum et Aliorum Hierosolimitanorum—The Deeds of the Franks and the Other Pilgrims to Jerusalem* (London: Thomas Nelson and Sons Ltd., 1962), 2.

62. Ronald N. Walpole, "The Pèlerinage de Charlemagne, Poem, Legend, and Problem," *Romance Philology* 8 (1954–55): 180–182.

63. Joan M. Ferrante, trans., *Guillaume d'Orange: Four Twelfth-Century Epics* (New York/London, Columbia University Press, 1974), 6–8.

64. Thomas F. Coffey, Linda Kay Davidson, and Maryjane Dunn, eds. and trans. *The Miracles of Saint James* (New York: Italica Press, 1996), xxxv; Kevin R. Pool, ed. and trans., *The Chronicle of Pseudo-Turpin—Part IV of the Liber Sancti Jacobi (Codex Calixtinus)* (New York: Italica Press, 2014), xiii.

65. Coffey, Davidson, and Dunn, *The Miracles of Saint James*, xxxiv.

66. Walter Starkie, *The Road to Santiago, Pilgrims of St. James* (New York: E. P. Dutton & Co., 1957), 22–31.

67. Pool, *The Chronicle of Pseudo-Turpin*, xviii–xix.

68. Einhard, *The Life of Charlemagne*, trans. Lewis Thorpe (London/New York: Penguin Books, 1969), 64–65. Full text of a different translation available online at http://legacy.fordham.edu/halsall/basis/einhard.asp.

69. Pool, *The Chronicle of Pseudo-Turpin*, 5–6, 58.

70. Coffey, Davidson, and Dunn, *The Miracles of Saint James*, 76–78.

71. Burgess, *The Pilgrimage of Charlemagne*, 31–33.
72. Denis Murphy, trans., *Pilgrim's Guide*, 2011, https://sites.google.com/site/caminodesantiagoproject/home. A critical edition and translation has also been published by William Melczer, ed. and trans., *The Pilgrim's Guide to Santiago de Compostela* (New York: Italica Press, 1993).
73. *Pilgrim's Guide*, https://sites.google.com/site/caminodesantiagoproject/chapter-viii-saints-tombs-to-be-visited.
74. Ibid.
75. Ibid.
76. *Pilgrim's Guide*, https://sites.google.com/site/caminodesantiagoproject/chapter-vii.
77. Ferrante, *Guillaume d'Orange*, 281–86. An 1892 translation is available online at http://www.maryjones.us/ctexts/charlemagne2.html.
78. Daniel Boorstin, *The Image: A Guide to Pseudo-Events in America* (New York: Harper & Row, 1964, 1961), 85.
79. Ibid., 106.
80. Ibid., 109.
81. Catharine Maria Sedgwick, *The Travellers: A Tale Designed for Young People* (New York: E. Bliss and E. White, 1825), 82–83. https://archive.org/details/travellersatale00sedggoog.
82. James Kirke Paulding, *A Book of Vagaries Comprising the New Mirror for Travellers and Other Whim-Whams*, ed. William I. Paulding (New York: C. Scribner, 1868), 166–67, https://archive.org/details/bookvagaries00paulrich.
83. "A Sensation at Saratoga," *New York Times*, June 19, 1877, 1. Retrieved from http://libproxy.eku.edu/login?url=http://search.proquest.com.libproxy.eku.edu/docview/93604810?accountid=10628.
84. Felicia Holt, "Promiscuous Bathing," *Ladies' Home Journal* (August 1890): 6. https://babel.hathitrust.org/cgi/pt?id=mdp.39015012341569;view=1up;seq=280.
85. Philip G. Hubert, Jr. "Open Letters: Camping Out for the Poor," *The Century* 44, no. 4 (August 1892): 632–34, http://ebooks.library.cornell.edu/cgi/t/text/pageviewer-idx?c=cent;cc=cent;rgn=full%20text;idno=cent0044-4;didno=cent0044-4;view=image;seq=643;node=cent0044-4%3A30;page=root;size=100.
86. "Asbury Park," *New York Times*, July 15, 1900, 15. Retrieved from http://libproxy.eku.edu/login?url=http://search.proquest.com.libproxy.eku.edu/docview/95996726?accountid=10628.
87. Glenn Uminowicz, "Sport in a Middle-Class Utopia: Asbury Park, New Jersey, 1871–1895," *Journal of Sport History* 11, no. 1 (Spring 1984): 51–73.
88. "Crum Refused a Chair," *New York Times*, August 15, 1905, 1. http://libproxy.eku.edu/login?url=http://search.proquest.com.libproxy.eku.edu/docview/96521132?accountid=10628.
89. Maxim Gorky, "Boredom," *The Independent* 63, no. 3062 (August 8, 1907): 309–317, https://babel.hathitrust.org/cgi/pt?id=pst.000020207205;view=1up;seq=331.
90. "How Long Should a Man's Vacation Be?" *New York Times*, July 31, 1910, SM3. http://libproxy.eku.edu/login?url=http://search.proquest.com.libproxy.eku.edu/docview/97036455?accountid=10628.
91. Hugh Thompson, "The Vacation Savings Movement," *Munsey's Magazine* 49 (May 1913): 257–59. https://babel.hathitrust.org/cgi/pt?id=uc1.b2870653;view=1up;seq=259.
92. Richard Henry Edwards, *Christianity and Amusements* (New York: Association Press, 1915), 19. https://play.google.com/store/books/details?id=Zy83AAAAMAAJ&rdid=book-Zy83AAAAMAAJ&rdot=1.
93. Anzia Yezierska, "The Free Vacation House," *The Forum* (December 1915): 706–741, http://www.unz.org/Pub/Forum-1915dec-00706.
94. For a complete list see "The American Guide Series," http://www.senate.gov/reference/resources/pdf/WPAStateGuides.pdf.
95. Jamesha Gibson, "Preservation Glossary. Today's Word: Heritage Tourism," last modified June 17, 2015, accessed July 22, 2016, https://savingplaces.org/stories/preservation-glossary-todays-word-heritage-tourism#.V5ImQ6K1Zlc.

Additional Resources

Ashby, LeRoy. *With Amusement for All: A History of American Popular Culture since 1830*. Lexington, KY: University Press of Kentucky, 2006.

Entertainment and leisure are closely related to the vacation. This book provides a detailed, chronological approach to all types of popular entertainment. Popular culture entertainment is defined as entertainment that has been created and disseminated for the purposes of profit. The author argues that even though it has been created for profit, it is also influenced by groups of people from all levels of society, including immigrants, ethnic and racial minorities, women, and other marginalized people. The endnotes and bibliography, divided by journal articles and books, are a treasure trove for anyone interested in exploring entertainment and leisure as a theme.

Aron, Cindy S. *Working at Play: A History of Vacations in the United States.* Oxford/New York: Oxford University Press, 1999.
  A scholarly history of vacationing from the early nineteenth century through the Depression that stresses how Americans often struggled with a perceived conflict between the value of hard work and the benefits of vacation. Excellent endnotes and bibliography with references to many primary sources.

Newman, Paul B. *Travel and Trade in the Middle Ages.* Jefferson, NC: McFarland & Company, Inc., 2011.
  An overview of all aspects of travel by land and water in the Middle Ages, with bibliography of additional secondary sources, but no primary sources are included.

Rugh, Susan Sessions. *The Golden Age of American Family Vacations: Are We There Yet?* Lawrence, KS: University of Kansas Press, 2008.
  A history of the American middle-class family vacation, including the experiences of middle-class African American and Jewish families, between 1945 and the early 1970s when the Oil Embargo changed the American economy. Extensive endnotes and bibliography and several images that can provide additional ideas for locally available primary source images appropriate for the vacation theme.

Sumption, Jonathan. *The Age of Pilgrimage: The Medieval Journey to God* (2003), originally published as *Pilgrimage, An Image of Mediaeval Religion.* Totowa, NJ: Rowman and Littlefield, 1975.
  An overview of medieval pilgrimage by a historian, including chapters on the relics, saints, the crusades, the journey, Rome, and the development of pilgrimage over one thousand years. Many quotes of and references to primary sources.

Whalen, Brett E. *Pilgrimage in the Middle Ages: A Reader.* Book 16, Readings in Medieval Civilizations and Cultures Series. Toronto: University of Toronto Press, 2011.
  A collection of translated primary sources relating to medieval pilgrimage. This series is just one example of primary source collections published to be used as college textbooks, but very helpful to middle and high school teachers searching for primary sources.

Yorke, Douglas A., and John Margolies. *Hitting the Road: The Art of the American Road Map.* San Francisco: Chronicle Books, 1996.
  This short book features numerous color reproductions of road maps and is a good resource for primary source images. This book is one of several by John Margolies that features images of travel brochures, motels, attractions, and road signs related to American vacations.

CHAPTER THREE

Manners and Etiquette

I am always saying "Glad to've met you" to somebody I'm not at all glad I met. If you want to stay alive, you have to say that stuff, though.

—J. D. Salinger, *The Catcher in the Rye*[1]

Should outward behavior (manners) always reflect inner beliefs or morals? Why or why not?

- Do situations exist in which polite manners are required in order to interact with other people in a positive way, despite how a person may really believe or feel?
- Can a person's morals and beliefs be accurately judged by her or his manners and behavior?
- When the manners of a society change, do these changes reflect a decline or change in the morality of the whole society?

A whistling girl and a crowing hen will both come to some bad end.

—English, Scottish, or American proverb—origin unknown

Why are men and women expected to follow different codes of etiquette?

- How do different expectations of behavior for men and women impact the lives of individuals?
- How are individuals who do not conform to societal gender expectations treated?
- Why do different groups of people (different cultures, social classes) have different codes of etiquette?

Throughout history, advice on appropriate behavior has been provided by a wide range of authors. The experts giving the advice, the intended audience for the advice, the advice itself, and the culture in which the advice is followed or not followed vary over time and place; however, advice literature has yet to go out of style. The most modern version of advice—self-improvement books, seminars, audio and video products—is a booming business. One-third to one-half of modern Americans have purchased a self-help book, and between 1972 and 2000 the number of self-help books published has doubled.[2]

This chapter examines the evolution of advice literature using two specific themes and time periods: The Enlightenment ideals reflected in eighteenth-century English and colonial American advice literature, and the prescribed roles of men and women in the late-nineteenth and twentieth centuries are the focus areas. Advice on conduct during these years was published in books as well as in growing numbers of newspapers and magazines.

What is advice literature, also referred to as etiquette or conduct manuals? This type of literature includes manuscripts, books, or articles within larger works, such as newspapers or magazines, that provide advice on how to behave according to the expectations of a particular society. Common examples are advice on the proper and improper way to eat, dress, speak, and interact with others. The advice in conduct manuals often overlaps with religious instruction, but the focus is usually upon outward behavior rather than on religious belief or the salvation of the soul.

One historian has characterized the difference as the "big rules" of social life, which include law, morality, and religion, and the "little rules" of advice literature that are necessary to interact with other people on a daily basis.[3] But often the distinction between religious instruction and outward behavior is not made because the author assumes that proper outward behavior is a necessary element of a religious life; in other words, that manners and morals are fused together and must reflect one another. This belief that outward behavior must reflect inner morality was especially prominent in the eighteenth century and, although less prominent today, is still present in some modern self-help and advice literature.

Advice literature does not always describe the actual behavior of an era, but instead, the dominant code of behavior that was expected. It falls into a wider category called prescriptive literature, writing that instructs the reader how life should be conducted, a "how-to" book. This type of writing can reflect actual behavior but usually the advice is representative of the reality of a particular group of people and may have very little relationship to the lives of people of different social classes, sexes, races, regions, or age groups.

For example, advice to middle-class women in the nineteenth century often included information on how to manage household servants. Not all middle-class women employed household servants, but the advice in the book may have made the reader believe that to be in the middle class, one should have servants. And this advice certainly did not apply to working-class women, who couldn't afford to employ servants and may have worked as servants themselves.

The vast majority of advice literature from the eighteenth century to present represents expectations for the behavior of the middle class. But one must be careful to not assume that everyone *was* middle class, or that everyone *wanted to be* middle class. Furthermore, middle class is a very general term for a group of people that has changed in size and composition over the last four hundred years. For example, the phrases "middle sort of people" or "middling sort" began to be used in seventeenth-century England in writings describing social distinctions, but its meaning is the subject of debate among historians.

Modern historians define "middle sort of people" in one of two ways—by defining the wealth or occupation (social class) *or* by defining the group as a status group through their common experiences and social values about property, work, leisure, manners, or fashion.[4] But due to the lack of precise demographic data from the 1600s and 1700s, the use of different types of primary sources by historians, and the distinctive focus of various historical studies, the term remains a vague generalization that refers to the people between the wealthiest and the working classes.

The advice on behavior given in prescriptive literature creates a cultural expectation of how one should act, a framework that can be used to measure one's self by what is perceived to be the appropriate behavior of others. Over time, individuals accept (or reject) the "rules" of the etiquette of the era and assume that those rules are the norm without question. In other words, assumptions about behavior, learned from one's culture, become the reality of what people see and do.

For example, cheerfulness was behavior that was prescribed in advice books starting in the eighteenth century. English visitors to America in the nineteenth century grew up in a society in which cheerfulness had been stressed in advice literature for several generations and knew that cheerfulness was expected in social situations (a cultural meta-message). They saw cheerfulness in the American personality, describing it in their published travel accounts.

Likewise, they may have failed to note non-cheerful behavior, because they were expecting to see cheerful people. So subsequent visitors to America expected cheerfulness, looked for cheerfulness, and found examples of it because they learned that Americans were cheerful in the travel accounts they had read. They were looking for it, and they found it, confirming what they already believed.

Furthermore, American advice books recommended cheerfulness; individuals worked to be cheerful, believing society as a whole expected it. By the twentieth century, cheerfulness was ingrained as an expected norm for behavior, especially in professional settings.[5]

The rules in advice literature are not copyrighted. People have always felt free to recycle the work of previous advisors, rarely attributing the original author because the knowledge is considered property of the wider culture. At the same time, the types of advice from the same time period can vary greatly, prescribing very different behaviors, which represented the conflicting views within a culture.

Historians studying advice literature must give special attention to the beliefs and affiliations of the author and the intended audience in order to determine whether the advice upholds the conservative traditions of the past or promotes new manners for a new age. Modern readers must be careful not to assume that every reader of a conduct manual followed or agreed with the advice provided. Students ask critical questions about the author, the intended audience, whether the work actually reflects behavior that was occurring in the time the book was published, and if the intention of the author was to uphold the traditions of the past or to initiate changes in behavior.

Advice for behavior may be repeated and reused for decades or even centuries after its origin. When advice does become outdated, it is attributed to a number of different causes. Often, specific changes in technology precipitate changes in etiquette; the introduction of the telephone and automobile changed manners. But the historian must be very careful when attributing the cause of change.

For example, rapid advances in technology, and thus manners, are often perceived in terms of generational change and framed in nostalgia. Parents or grandparents may disapprove of the new rules of etiquette of the younger generation and wish for a return to the "good old days" of their youth. Nostalgia is the wistful longing for an ideal period from the past, often framing the present as a period of decline in human morality.

In every historical era, social conservatives lament the passing of the old, proper, and better ways of doing things. For example, at the beginning of the twentieth century, changes in manners were blamed on the surge of immigration, the corruption of the very rich, the insolence of the working classes, the decline of respect for women, the aggressive women entering the work force, or the squalid conditions of urban life.

As the decades progressed, the perceived decline in polite public behavior was blamed on World War I, Prohibition, jazz music, movies, automobiles, the radio, the Depression, World War II, television, permissive child rearing techniques, rock music, birth control pills, the Vietnam War, the women's movement, psychological therapies, and fast food.[6] Each of these innovations or events may have indeed caused shifts in behavior, but one must not fall victim to nostalgia and assume that the past was as wonderful as the author suggests or that the present is really that bad.

The Vocabulary of Proper Behavior

In order to study the history of manners, or any theme throughout history, one must take time to define the key terms and concepts related to the theme. Several modern words are used to describe or are related to what is often called manners today, and the different words may have slightly different meanings that have shifted over time. An analysis of shifts in terms was used by the sociologist Elias Norbert and successive historians as evidence for their theories that changes in the language related to manners are evidence of changes in the power of government.

These scholars argued that the word courtesy was representative of the power of monarchs in the medieval age. The use of the word civility demonstrated a shift to powerful national governments, and the introduction of the word etiquette in eighteenth century represented an era when power began to be spread out among various groups of people in England and America.[7]

Ask students to brainstorm synonyms for manners and discuss how these words differ. Then, highlight the following key terms that historians have singled out as important in the history of manners—courtesy, civility, and etiquette. As discussed in chapter 1, this is an excellent opportunity to demonstrate to students how the *Oxford English Dictionary* can be a historian's tool.

- *Manners*—This is one of the most general terms used to describe expected behavior; the way the word is used denotes whether that behavior is good or bad, socially correct or incorrect, polite or impolite.
- *Courtesy* is defined as "courteous behavior; courtly elegance and politeness of manners; graceful politeness or considerateness in intercourse with others." The word originated in France and Italy, the centers of court culture in the Middle Ages and Renaissance that was described in Castiglione's sixteenth-century *The Book of the Courtier*. In fact, several of the historical quotes in the *Oxford English Dictionary* reference the court where the nobility worked for and waited upon a monarch.[8]
- *Civility*, defined as "observance of the principles of civil order; orderly behavior; good citizenship," has a slightly different association. Instead of associating good manners with the court of a monarch, civility connects manners

to good citizenship in a nation-state and with fellow citizens. Civility also came to be understood as "culture, refinement, good breeding; cultured, refined, or scholarly education." The first example of the use of "courtesy" in the English language was in the thirteenth century; the first uses of "civility" as defined here was in the sixteenth century.[9]

- *Etiquette*, "the customary code of polite behavior in society; good manners," is French in origin and was first used in English in the eighteenth century. The term was used in an influential book of advice by Lord Chesterfield in 1750 in a way that still associated manners with ceremonies required in a monarch's court, but just seven years later, the term began to be used to describe rules of good manners in general.[10]

Relationships to Sociology, Psychology, Anthropology

The history of manners has not been studied extensively by historians. This area of study has more often been the focus of sociologists, who study the interactions between people; psychologists, who study the thoughts and actions of individuals; and anthropologists, who study social relations and culture over time. Scholars of manners consistently credit Norbert Elias, a sociologist, as the first to study the history of manners. Elias's famous work, the two-volume *The Civilizing Process*, was published in 1939 in German.

The first volume, *The History of Manners*, was translated into English in 1969. Elias used European books on manners from the medieval to modern period to argue that manners regarding violence, sexual behavior, bodily functions, and eating changed over time, in part in response to the consolidation of power by government. He also associated changes in the social structure with changes in individual personality, arguing that over time, individuals exhibited more self-control of emotion and made bodily functions more private.

For example, slurping, chewing with the mouth open, and farting at the table became less and less acceptable over time.[11] Today, his theories have critics, but his work is still considered important because it was the first to use books of manners to study wider historical themes. Much of the work of subsequent historians who use manners books and advice literature as primary sources relies upon research methods and theories of sociology, psychology, or anthropology.

The History of Advice Manuals

Advice on various daily matters and personal conduct has survived in manuscripts from throughout Western civilization from the cultures of the ancient Egyptians, Jews, Greeks, and Romans and from the Middle Ages. This advice was largely produced by and for the upper classes, the wealthy and powerful of the era. Prior to the Early Modern Period (c. 1450–1700), these upper classes are generally referred to as the nobility or aristocracy, and birth usually determined one's rank in the social hierarchy.

Different levels of status did exist within these highest ranks, and proper conduct could assist in moving up within the upper ranks, but rarely could one move from the poorest classes to the upper ranks of society. For example, in the European Middle Ages, a knight could be poor and at the lowest level of the nobility or he could be wealthy and powerful and ranked highly within the noble class. Improving manners might improve the prospects of the poor knight who hoped to be promoted and endowed with lands by his lord, but a peasant who learned all of the correct manners still had little chance of advancement.

Prior to the 1700s, the majority of advice on daily conduct was written by men and for men. The exceptions were generally advice provided by a man about the proper conduct of a dutiful wife that reinforced expectations of female behavior to both men and women. Texts from these early periods are available and can be analyzed by students. But because only a small minority of ancient and medieval people could read and because the circulation of handwritten manuscripts was limited when compared to more recent mass-produced books, these eras will not be the focus of this chapter.

Two advice manuals published during the Renaissance influenced centuries of later publications: *The Book of the Courtier* (written in 1508 and published 1528)[12] by Baldassare Castiglione and *Il Galateo: The Rules of Polite Behavior* (1558) by Giovanni della Casa. *The Book of the Courtier*, written as a series of conversations that defined the perfect courtier in a monarch's court, became the model followed by generations of European and American gentlemen. In *Il Galateo: The Rules of Polite Behavior*, the advice was presented in different categories such as how to dress, table manners, and polite conversations.

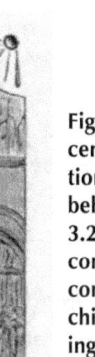

Coarse and Boisterous.

Figure 3.1. Etiquette for Conversation. Nineteenth-century rules of etiquette focused upon class distinctions, but also prescribed different expectations for the behavior of men, women, and children. Figures 3.1 and 3.2 from Hill's *Manual of Social and Business Forms* compare and contrast the improper and proper forms of conversation. What rules of etiquette are the women and children breaking in figure 3.1 and correctly demonstrating in figure 3.2? Are the differences in behavior of the men in the two images as different as the differences in behavior of the women and children?

Thomas Hill. Hill's Manual of Social and Business Forms. Chicago: Hill Standards Book Co., 1888, 152–53. (Image courtesy of Internet Archive and the California Digital Library.)

Both books were translated into French, English, and other European languages within just a few years of their first publication and became some of the most widely distributed books of the sixteenth century.[13] Both the advice provided and the method of organizing the content by topic or as questions and answers were copied over and over again, often word for word, in conduct manuals for the next two hundred years.

The growth of trade and colonialization in the Early Modern Period meant that more people were engaged in commerce. By the eighteenth century, these new sources of wealth opened opportunities for the "middling sort" of people to set themselves apart and possibly even enter the upper status groups. But those seeking advancement needed to improve their manners, and the publication of advice manuals increased, helped by new technology in printing.

At first, colonial Americans imported English advice books, but as the traditional social status group lines were blurred and the proscriptions for deference to one's betters became outdated, Americans began to publish their own rulebooks of conduct. Advice manuals began to be written by both men and women authors; more and more titles were published and republished through nearly every decade of the 1700s and 1800s.

Nineteenth-century etiquette focused upon issues related to social stratification and the competitive struggle for status. Industrialization expanded the middle class and created new ranks of very wealthy elite. These groups sought to learn the "rules" of etiquette in order to establish codes of behavior that defined these new status groups and either

Cultured and Refined.

Figure 3.2.

Thomas Hill. Hill's Manual of Social and Business Forms. Chicago: Hill Standards Book Co., 1888, 152–53. (Image courtesy of Internet Archive and the California Digital Library.)

excluded new members or allowed one to move up into a higher status by mastering the rules. Those in the growing middle classes of salaried and professional workers wanted to demonstrate their respectability and advance socially as their incomes grew.

At the same time, the very wealthy elite worked to make the highest ranks more exclusive. Some groups of people were ignored or excluded because of their race or ethnicity but sought to define proper behavior within their own community. For example, newspapers printed in and for immigrant communities included advice columns in both native languages and English, and African Americans also published etiquette advice books for the African American audience.

While the etiquette of the nineteenth century focused upon class distinctions, the etiquette of a majority of the twentieth century focused on issues related to sex and gender. Continued economic and technological changes that resulted in more and more women leaving the home to enter the workplace threatened the "natural" barriers that had been perceived to exist between the sexes throughout history.

Customs and etiquette related to courtship and dating experienced dramatic changes between the late nineteenth century and the mid-twentieth century, reflecting the shifting economic and social status of men and women. At the same time, references to class or social distinctions, while still occasionally present, decreased and were often discouraged. Everyone came to be perceived as middle class, even though in reality many groups of people in America were excluded by race, ethnicity, or earnings from the middle-class lifestyle.[14]

The Eighteenth-Century Dilemma—Does Outward Behavior Reflect Inner Beliefs?

What is the relationship between inward morality and outward behavior? This was a key question in the eighteenth-century discussion of manners in England and its colonies in America and is a question still considered in the modern era. In other words, do people have good manners because they automatically reflect inherent good morals, thoughts, and intentions? And likewise, does rude behavior signify corrupt morals? Or, on the other hand, are good manners learned and outwardly performed in order to get ahead for selfish reasons—to manipulate others or create good impressions to get ahead socially or in business? Is one's reputation for civility more important than what one really believes or feels inwardly?

The following paragraphs summarize a century of social change and demonstrate two challenges when teaching social history in the classroom—the difficulty of providing specific dates for key transformations and the shifting definitions of important terms. The years between 1700 and 1840 included around six generations in which changes in attitudes about manners and the manners themselves evolved. During this time, words relevant to the discussion came into use or shifted in meaning.

Many of the same words are used in modern English but may not have the same connotations as before. For example, *sensibility* is a word rarely used today and in modern usage means one's ability to physically feel stimuli or emotions. *Sensibility* in the eighteenth century was a philosophy of behavior. Furthermore, when one reads scholarly work by historians and scholars of English literature, it is common to find that the same terms are used differently or imprecisely, partly because the modern disciplines differ in their approaches and partly because the historical sources may use the terms in different ways.

Eighteenth-century English manners were influenced by the philosophers of the Enlightenment who believed humanity, through its use of reason, could progress and improve over time. The English Enlightenment philosopher John Locke (1632–1704) is considered the father of Liberalism, the political philosophy that holds humans have the ability to reason, rule themselves, and with proper education make rational decisions. Locke believed that good manners and morals would result if a child was educated properly.

In *Some Thoughts Concerning Education* (1693), he outlined the key elements of a proper education; the most important element of this education was to instill virtue and teach children to reason why they must act appropriately, rather than require them to just memorize the rules of behavior. The result of Locke's recommended education was a merging of the inner and outer values that would be evident in a mannerly person (see source A).

One should note that Locke did not believe, as previous generations believed, that religious instruction or threats of corporal punishment or religious damnation were needed to produce a moral and mannerly person. Likewise, Locke's definition of politeness was in contrast to the courtiers of Renaissance courts, widely known through English editions of Castiglione's *The Rules of Polite Behavior*.

The courtier was considered a fake by Locke; the courtier had perfect manners in order to impress others and the king, but his friendships were false and his motives were cold and calculating. In other words, using the definitions explored above, a system of rules governing outward behavior enabled a courtier to get ahead. *Courtesy* became *civility* in the seventeen century, a word for behavior that reflected good citizenship and concern for others.[15]

Locke's philosophy became the basis for an eighteenth-century form of refinement labeled *politeness*. Politeness described how humans socialized in a positive manner with others. Politeness wasn't just a set of rules to be memorized—it was innate, like "life, liberty and the pursuit of happiness" referenced by Thomas Jefferson in the Declaration of Independence. Although humans were born with it, politeness had to be cultivated through the kind of education Locke proposed for gentlemen. A polite gentleman did not want to compete with or embarrass others; he wanted to engage in entertaining and informative conversations with others and always showed tolerance when listening to others.

The concept of politeness was disseminated in a wide range of publications—conduct manuals, newspapers, sermons, pamphlets, and novels. The popular newspaper, *The Spectator*, is one example. It was published daily from 1711 to 1712, by Joseph Addison and Richard Steele, and reprinted in bound volumes and sold into the early nineteenth century.[16] The purpose of the publication was to provide quality reading that could be used for informed discussion and to provide models for polite behavior.

The newspaper was widely read in homes and coffeehouses and circulated in both England and the American colonies. Fictional characters that served as models for behavior or demonstrated behavior to be avoided were created. The *fop*, a narcissistic man dedicated to fashionable manners but with no morals, was an especially popular stereotype in literature of the day. New habits were promoted that demonstrated one's politeness. The convention of signing letters with "yours sincerely" or "yours truly" was adopted in the eighteenth century to demonstrate the connection between one's virtue and the contents of the letter.[17]

Conduct manuals written specifically for women began to be published in the seventeenth century, and the genre grew, with numerous titles published and republished throughout the eighteenth and subsequent centuries. This new genre was a combination of the earlier courtesy books intended for men and pious literature giving religious and moral instruction. Just one example is Richard Allestree's *Ladies Calling* (1673)[18] published in twelve editions by 1727 and another eight editions by 1737 when republished as *The Whole Duty of a Woman* (see source B).[19]

Prescribed behavior in the manuals slowly shifted from older views of female character as weak and sinful (a reflection of the biblical sins of Eve) to the Enlightenment view that proper female behavior, centered around virtues of modesty, chastity, and submission, was the spontaneous product of the inner female nature. These "natural" tendencies of women should be developed through proper education and rewarded in a marriage in which the wife assumed her "natural" role of wifely subordination.[20] How to properly attract a suitable husband and conduct oneself in the role of a wife became a main topic of advice for a woman.

But even the most avid proponents of politeness realized the potential for faking inner virtue and disguising it with the proper manners. A *rake* was a term used for a man who seemed to have the proper manners, but only used them to disguise his true purpose of taking advantage of women, and much advice was given on how to avoid these frauds.

On the other hand, one might be a truly moral person who did not display behavior that properly reflected one's inner goodness. Samuel Johnson, famous literary critic and lexicographer, pointed out that many worthy and intelligent men, such as scholars, did not have the time to cultivate polished manners. Mary Wollstonecraft and many others warned women against both of these hazards (see source E).

By the mid-eighteenth century, many questioned whether politeness really portrayed a connection between manners and moral virtue, and a shift occurred into a new system of social refinement called *sensibility*. As with any cultural shift, the change was gradual and not adopted by everyone. The concepts of politeness were used through the remainder of the eighteenth century and were often applicable to the new ideal of sensibility. Sensibility was not completely different from politeness, but rather a new phase in the understanding of the bond between manners and morals.[21]

Sensibility emphasized communicating one's emotions and displaying empathy and appropriate emotion, rather than just emphasizing only formal good manners. Two intellectual theories impacted the development of sensibility. First, the concept of philosopher David Hume (1711–1776) called "mutual sympathy" that described the innate tendency of humans to perform acts of goodness toward others was widely accepted. Second, anatomists formulated theories on the system of nerves in which sensations were conveyed in the human body.

These concepts merged and were popularized in fiction and magazine essays as a system of social interaction rooted in the human tendency to sympathize that was conveyed through the nervous system and displayed by the body through tears and facial expressions. A person with sensibility did not just follow the more formal behavior prescribed by politeness, but instead behaved with expressive actions such as sighing, trembling, or weeping, all emotions that were evidence of refined inner feelings and empathy for others. One's behavior directly mirrored one's emotional and moral state. The lack of manners of a less polished person could be tolerated if that person displayed the proper feelings of sensibility.[22]

The concept of sensibility in behavior became especially common in a new form of fiction in the English language, the novel. Novels, then and today, serve as an example to readers about how to act, as well as mirroring the culture of the time. The "sentimental novel" or "novels of sensibility" are terms used for eighteenth- and nineteenth-century novels that express feeling over reason. Characters expressed deep feelings and emotion toward fellow humans and the beauty of natural settings, art, and music.

Jane Austen's novels, published between 1811 and 1818, are especially good choices to illustrate eighteenth-century politeness and sensibility to modern students. Her novels are well known in modern literature courses, movies, and television series. *Mansfield Park* (1814) explores the relationship between good manners and moral character. The main character, Fanny Price, has both proper manners and morals, but most of the other characters have only the polished manners without a moral anchor. In *Sense and Sensibility* (1811), the two main characters, the sisters Elinor and Marianne Dashwood, represent the manners of politeness and sensibility, respectively (see source G).

In 1774, an advice book was published that shocked those dedicated to politeness and sensibility because it suggested good manners, natural openness, and empathy might be used for personal advancement, instead of being a reflection of good inner morality. *Letters to His Son on the Art of Becoming a Man of the World and a Gentleman*, by the fourth Earl of Chesterfield, was a series of letters written over thirty years (1737–1768) in which Chesterfield provided a wide variety of advice to his illegitimate son, Philip Stanhope (see source C).

While Chesterfield stressed the importance of polished manners, he also understood that in many situations, it was outward appearances that really mattered and that inward thoughts and motives must be concealed. The book was very popular, partly due to the controversy it created. At least thirty-one editions were published between 1775 and the 1800s but with variations of titles and shortened texts, such as *Principles of Politeness*, that had the more scandalous advice removed.[23] One of the first uses of the word *etiquette* appeared in Lord Chesterfield's book and by 1857 came to mean "the customary code of polite behavior in society; good manners."[24] By the nineteenth century, the word *etiquette* was widely used in articles and books of advice.

Colonial Americans read English conduct advice in editions imported from England or reprinted in the colonies. Americans such as John Adams and Benjamin Franklin also subscribed to Enlightenment views on human behavior, the codes of politeness and sensibility, and an acknowledgment that manners and morals were not always unified.

For example, Benjamin Franklin, in his autobiography (written 1771–1790), echoed Lord Chesterfield's views on how to get ahead. Franklin realized that people were judged by appearances and that bad behavior could be hidden, especially in colonial American society where people were mobile and it was impossible to be familiar with the character of everyone that a person might meet. In his description of his early years in Philadelphia, Franklin stressed the efforts he took to both be successful and appear successful. But Franklin also noted the importance of polite, or civil, behavior in conversations with others (see source D).

Americans began to differ from the English in their views of proper behavior among people of different social ranks. In the colonies, traditional ranks of English society were harder to identify, and new social and economic systems were developing for which English advice might not be acceptable or appropriate. The British settlers came from a highly rank-ordered society and, as a whole, accepted the traditional hierarchy, while new Americans ignored many of those customs.

Those accustomed to the traditional manners of paying respect to gentlemen of the upper classes in England were often shocked by what appeared to be American classlessness. Alexander Hamilton (1712–1756) was a Scottish-born and -educated doctor who immigrated to Maryland to set up his own medical practice. In 1774, he traveled from Maryland to Maine, recording his impressions of life in the American colonies in his travel journal, *Itinerareum*. Hamilton was himself a part of the upper middling sort and accustomed to the manners of the English gentry. Throughout the account, his comments reveal the growing differences in American behavior.

> I knew here several men of sense, ingenuity, and learning, and a much greater number of fops, whom I chuse [sic] not to name, not so much for fear of giving offence as because I think their names are not worthy to be recorded either in manuscript or

printed journals. These dons commonly held their heads higher than the rest of mankind, and imagined few or none were their equals. But this I found always proceeded from their narrow notions, ignorance of the world, and low extraction, which indeed is the case with most of our aggrandized upstarts in these infant countries of America, who never had an opportunity to see, or (if they had) the capacity to observe the different ranks of men in polite nations, or to know what it is that really constitutes that difference of degrees.[25]

The cultures of politeness and sensibility were declining by the early nineteenth century in both England and the United States. The liberal Enlightenment belief in the natural goodness of humans was challenged by the violence of the French Revolution and religious conservatism. People generally accepted that they were vulnerable to deceit and exploited by cynics if they assumed that a good manner reflected inner goodness and that many people around them practiced correct manners or displayed excess emotion for personal gain.

American manners became more distinct over time and were often commented upon by European visitors such as Alexis de Tocqueville (1805–1859)[26] and Frances Trollope (1780–1863).[27] Distinctly American manuals by American authors began to be published. Americans in the northern states tended to prefer conduct advice with a moral and religious focus that was somewhat egalitarian and accepting of northern commerce and trade. Southern Americans preferred the models of courtly behavior of the landed gentry of Britain and Europe that stressed chivalry, codes of honor, and hierarchy.[28]

Etiquette in the United States

Advice literature increased in nineteenth-century America, appearing under more titles and in different types of publications. Numerous publications focused on a wider range of behaviors, by male and female authors with different backgrounds, and a variety of audiences. Why did advice literature become so prolific and so popular? Economic and social changes caused by the Industrial Revolution led to the increased potential to move into the growing middle class or into the wealthy elite.

As American population in larger towns and cities grew, it became more difficult to know a person by his or her previous conduct or family connections. Advice literature provided guidelines of conduct for those who aspired to move up and "re-make" themselves. At the same time, advice literature reinforced the rules so that the "undeserving" working and poor could be excluded from the middle- or upper-class status group and new people could be judged according to a set of established social conventions. Countless rules of etiquette that looked to past models of behavior served as reassuring standards of behavior in an age of social and economic change.

Providing advice was also a money-making business. Advice books were popular sellers for the growing book industry and advice columns and articles became popular features in both newspapers and the developing magazine industry. In every decade of the nineteenth century, old titles were reprinted and more new titles were introduced; at least twenty-eight different conduct manuals were published in the 1830s, thirty-six in the 1840s, and thirty-eight in the 1850s.[29]

The ever-increasing flow did not decline after the Civil War. Publishers employed door-to-door salesmen to sell subscriptions to a variety of books, and etiquette and advice books were popular—on topics such as housekeeping, medical care, letter writing, child raising, and public speaking, as wells as books on general manners. Magazines and newspapers advertised advice books that could be ordered through the mail. Inexpensive editions and pamphlets were even given away in sales promotions by stationery or drug companies.[30]

The authors and audiences of this deluge of advice varied, but they were largely middle class. About half of the works were published anonymously or pseudonymously under names such as "an American lady" or "a woman of fashion." Of the signed works, some of the authors were actually people of wealth and influence, while others were professional writers or magazine contributors who saw the potential of such a popular genre.

Advice literature related to specific areas or general conduct was also produced by clergymen and reformers; professors, teachers and school leaders; and businessmen. Textbooks were published for public schools to teach morals and deportment to children, especially those of the working classes and immigrants.

It is difficult to assess exactly who read advice literature. The intended audiences for conduct literature varied by sex, profession, or even race, but the majority were aimed at a middle-class readership. Advice was published for children of both sexes, or specifically for boys or girls. A few publications addressed an African American audience, such as *The Negro in Etiquette: A Novelty* (1899) and Mary Frances Armstrong's *On Habits and Manners* (1888).[31]

FIG. 11. BAD MANNERS AT THE TABLE.

No. 1. Tips back his chair.
" 2. Eats with his mouth too full.
" 3. Feeds a dog at the table.
" 4. Holds his knife improperly.
" 5. Engages in violent argument at the meal-time.
" 6. Lounges upon the table.
" 7. Brings a cross child to the table.
No. 8. Drinks from the saucer, and laps with his tongue the last drop from the plate.
" 9. Comes to the table in his shirt-sleeves, and puts his feet beside his chair.
" 10. Picks his teeth with his fingers.
" 11. Scratches her head and is frequently unnecessarily getting up from the table.

Figure 3.3. Etiquette in the Dining Room. Thomas Hill began publishing *Manual of Social and Business Forms* in 1873 and republished it regularly with revisions and additions until 1911. Hill also published companion books such as the *Album of Biography and Art*. These comprehensive volumes provided advice on everything from letter-writing to appropriate inscriptions for tombstones. Figures 3.3 and 3.4 are from the 1888 edition and provide an annotated illustration of good and bad table manners. Note the differences in the clothing and dining room furnishings. Hill's images suggested that good manners were something practiced by the middle and upper classes, but unknown to working-class people.

Thomas Hill. Hill's Manual of Social and Business Forms. *Chicago: Hill Standards Book Co., 1888, 158–59. (Image courtesy of Internet Archive and the California Digital Library.)*

Historian C. Dallett Hemphill provided an excellent example of how a social historian can use statistical analysis to analyze trends over time. For example, between 1821 and 1860, of the 107 books analyzed by Hemphill, 48 percent had middle-class authors, 1 percent had a lower-class author, and the authors of 51 percent of the books are unknown. The known occupations of the authors of these books were professional writers (19 percent), clergy (18 percent), and educators (10 percent), but the occupation of about half is unknown (49 percent). More women were authoring advice books over time; during the seventeenth century, there were no female authors, but by the nineteenth-century period (1821–1860), 19 percent of the authors were female, 52 percent of the authors were male, and the sex of 29 percent of the authors was unknown.[32] It is likely that many in the unknown category were women.

As in the previous century, much of the advice provided was conventional, often recycled and reprinted from previous publications, and most tended to uphold tradition. Like their eighteenth-century predecessors, Americans still often

Figure 3.4.
Thomas Hill. Hill's Manual of Social and Business Forms. *Chicago: Hill Standards Book Co., 1888, 158–59. (Image courtesy of Internet Archive and the California Digital Library.)*

used manners to evaluate the sincerity and morality of a person. In the etiquette of nineteenth-century mourning, the clothing and behavior of a mourner was believed to represent the sincerity of the mourner's grief.

But by the mid and late nineteenth century, the belief that outward manners reflected inward morality receded, leaving in its place complicated rules of etiquette that were used to define one's class status instead of one's moral uprightness and sincerity.[33] This shift can be seen in the comparison of the novels of Louisa May Alcott's *Little Women* (1868–1869) and William Dean Howells's late-Victorian novel *The Rise of Silas Lapham* (1885). The March family values piety, sacrifice for others, and integrity. The Lapham family seeks tangible items to prove their status—a new house, fashionable clothing, and association with the right people.[34]

Historians have noted two important shifts in the focus of proper behavior in nineteenth-century American advice literature. First, the advice given stressed American ideals of equality and democracy. In the absence of inherited social hierarchies, correct behavior was used to distinguish between the successful individual and the lower classes of people. After the Civil War, the fast pace of industrial change, growing wealth inequality, and a surge in immigration forced Americans to recognize that social inequality did exist, and the recognition of these distinctions in everyday behavior became more permissible.

Finding a balance between the requirements of democracy and the demands of social distinctions became difficult. Economic and social inequality became impossible to ignore. New ways of viewing the poor in the work of Herbert

Spencer and the philosophy of Social Darwinism helped to justify a declining attention to the ideal of American classlessness.[35] Social Darwinism applied the biological concepts of natural selection and survival of the fittest to human society; its followers argued that the wealthy were wealthy because of their natural superiority, while the poor and working classes were deficient.

America's ultra-wealthy elite codified behavior that distinguished them from the middle class, and adopted an elaborate system of etiquette modeled on European aristocracy. This urge to define the "best" ranks from families of old money and the nouveau riche of the Gilded Age drove the creation of Ward McAllister's (1827–1895) and his patroness Caroline Astor's (1830–1908) identification of "The Four Hundred" high society New Yorkers.

Other cities created Social Register "Blue Books" that listed the top ranks of people chosen by committees of social leaders. Wealthy American debutantes sought aristocratic husbands in Europe. This struggle to enter or stay in the highest circles is the basis of many of Edith Wharton's short stories and novels such as the *The House of Mirth* (1925) and *The Age of Innocence* (1920). Her final novel, *The Buccaneers* (1938), is about five wealthy American girls in search of aristocratic English husbands. In the television series *Downton Abbey* (2010–2016), the character of Cora, Lady Grantham, is an American heiress whose money helped to save the Grantham family estate.

The second prominent theme in nineteenth-century advice literature reflected the ideal models of female behavior labeled "republican motherhood" and the "cult of true womanhood" or "cult of domesticity." Republican motherhood is a modern phrase coined by historian Linda Kerber to describe the Enlightenment influence on the role of the ideal American women of the 1790s. The civic duty of American women was to become educated and virtuous mothers who trained their sons to be model citizens in the new nation.[36]

Throughout most of Western history, women were believed to be morally inferior and naturally sinful, in the image of the biblical Eve who tempted Adam to sin in the Garden of Eden. But during the Enlightenment women began to be viewed as morally superior and free of the worldly urges of men to indulge in sexual behavior, govern, and earn money in a cutthroat world.

The ideals of republican motherhood merged with what was labeled the "cult of true womanhood" or the "cult of domesticity" in advice literature published between 1820 and 1860. A woman was to be judged by her religious piety, sexual purity, submissiveness to her husband, and domestic accomplishments in the home.[37] Essays, sermons, novels, poems, and manuals offering advice that reflected these ideals began to flood the market beginning in 1820s and 1830s and continued to be published throughout the following century. These publications focused upon the role of the mother, principles for raising children, the role of women in society, the appropriate types of education for women, and specific advice on appropriate manners of men and women.[38]

Catharine Maria Sedgwick (1789–1867) was a popular author who wrote numerous novels, pamphlets, and magazine articles that promoted republican motherhood and the cult of true womanhood. Lydia Maria Child's *The Mother's Book* (1831)[39] and Lydia Sigourney's *Letters to Mothers* (1838)[40] advised women on raising good citizens. The perceived moral superiority of women also enabled women to work within some reform movements outside of the home, such as temperance, because these movements sought the moral reformation of the wider society. Although these nineteenth-century models for women created an illusion of "ladies first," in reality women continued to be economic and political inferiors.[41]

"Relax" in the Twentieth Century

In the words of social historian Arthur Schlesinger, the rules of behavior had relaxed in the early twentieth century.[42] Several factors are thought to have contributed to this shift: a decline in respect for the elite because of exposure of abuses by Progressive muckrakers, the increased economic independence and political voice of women, the change in attitudes after World War I, the passage of Prohibition that encouraged normally law-abiding people to break the law, and the influence of the theories of Sigmund Freud.[43] All of these may have had some influence, but changes in technology and the economy that provided a better living to a wider range of people, the impact of new mass media such as radio and motion pictures, and an increased focus by advertisers on Americans as "consumers" rather than members of a social class may have had a far larger impact.

Ascertaining the specific causes of shifts in behavior are some of the most challenging and elusive tasks of a social historian, and opinions often differ. For example, social historians agree that there was a shift in values and behavior in the years before and during the 1920s, but their interpretations vary.

David Riesman described the twentieth-century character as "other-directed," tuned in to the opinions of others, while the previous century's middle-class character type was "inner-directed" to act in a moral manner. Leo Lowenthal characterized the shift as one from a nineteenth-century focus on the "production" of individuals to a twentieth-century focus on "consuming" products that could be purchased. Jackson Lears attributed the shift to a "therapeutic ethos," a widespread trend in middle-class culture that pervaded religion, self-help literature, and advertising.[44]

Traditional physicians, new types of doctors such as neurologists and psychologists, and social scientists prescribed cures for the perceived ills of the new modern life. Mass culture, advertisers, moviemakers, and popular writers echoed this therapeutic advice and reinforced the message that the frustrations of modern life could be remedied through buying new products (consumption) and leisure activities.

Cultural historian Warren Susman described a shift from a focus on the character of an individual to an obsession with personality. According to Susman, the older culture stressed moral qualities, or "character," as a civic duty, while the new twentieth-century culture insisted on "personality" so that one could be liked and admired. Susman reviewed over two hundred books, pamphlets, and articles produced during the nineteenth century, including character studies that provided models to be followed and manuals that outlined how to develop character and achieve worldly success. He identified the repeated use of key terms related to character, for example, *citizenship*, *duty*, *democracy*, *work*, *honor*, *reputation*, *morals*, and *integrity*.

In the manuals and guides for self-improvement published between 1900 and 1920, the modern key word becomes "personality," a word that had been used occasionally before the twentieth century but by the first part of the twentieth century was an important part of the American vocabulary. The adjectives associated with personality suggest a very different concept from that of character—*fascinating*, *stunning*, *attractive*, *magnetic*, *glowing*, *creative*, and *dominant*.[45]

The best-selling work by Dale Carnegie, *How to Win Friends and Influence People* (1936), a summary of the advice that he had been giving on lecture tours throughout the 1920s, is an often-cited example of the shift in the nature of advice manuals. Carnegie provided advice on how to make people like you and agree with you; in other words, the manipulation of others through the development of one's personality in order to get ahead. According to the advice publications, personality stressed self-fulfillment, self-expression, and self-gratification and could be developed by making the correct choices for leisure time or vacation and buying the right products. Advertising messages confirmed the advice and attempted to convince consumers that their products could create attractive personalities.

Another trend evident in twentieth-century conduct manuals was an acceptance of more democratic ways to interact with people of lower social classes. People were expected to treat others, even those below them in social rank, on more equal terms. Whereas centuries of advice had warned against the dangers of social mixing, and had provided countless rules on how to behave toward one's social inferiors or social betters, now one was advised on how to show mutual respect, but often on how to do it while still maintaining some distance.[46]

The use of the word *snob* is illustrative of this shift.[47] According to the *Oxford English Dictionary*, in the 1850s snob described "a person belonging to the ordinary or lower social class; one having no pretensions to rank or gentility." At the same time, the term could be used for a person who wanted to imitate or associate with those of higher social status. By 1911, the meaning of snob had reversed to a definition that we would recognize today—"a person who despises those whom he or she considers to be inferior in rank, attainment, or taste."[48] Twentieth-century etiquette expert Emily Post noted the following in 1940:

> In the general picture of this modern day the smart and the near-smart, the distinguished and the merely conspicuous, the real and the sham, and the unknown general public are all mixed up together. The walls that used to enclose the world that was fashionable are all down. Even the car tracks that divided cities into smart and not-smart sections are torn up.[49]

During the early decades of the twentieth century, several conduct manuals were published by members of the black elite who presented the rules of proper middle-class behavior to children and young adults. Well-known vocalist E. Azalia Hackley published *The Colored Girl Beautiful* (1916);[50] Silas X. Floyd, a prominent preacher and newspaper editor, published *Floyd's Flowers, or Duty and Beauty for Colored Children* (1905)[51] and *Short Stories for Colored People Both Old and Young* (1920); and Edward S. Green published *National Capital Code of Etiquette* (1920)[52] for adult readers. These publications for an African American audience represented a wide range of views, from the nineteenth-century white, conservative values of female domesticity, to calls for a reinvention of black identity in a new century.[53]

Dating in the Twentieth Century—Etiquette for Men and Women

The focus of twentieth-century etiquette shifted to a focus on the proper roles of men and women. More women began to enter the workplace, threatening the traditional roles prescribed for the sexes. References to social distinctions, while still occasionally present, became impolite. Advertisers encouraged Americans to perceive themselves as middle-class consumers, even though in reality many groups of people in America were excluded by race, ethnicity, or earnings from the middle-class lifestyle.[54]

Proper etiquette for men and women was especially important when seeking a partner in marriage. Dating, a new style of romance between men and women, replaced the older form of American courtship in the early twentieth century. The conventions of courtship, described in advice literature of the nineteenth century, centered upon "calling," in which a man visited a woman in her home. The young woman, or her mother, extended the invitation to the young man to visit and a multitude of rules were to be followed. These rules varied somewhat in urban or rural settings, or by social class, but the general outline of the procedures were followed by all who wanted to be considered "respectable."

In the late nineteenth century, a new form of socializing between men and women was introduced that came to be known as "dating." The word "date" began to appear in print in the 1890s and was lower-class slang in stories about working-class life. By 1914, the term was used in *Ladies' Home Journal*, a respected middle-class magazine. Dating began as an urban necessity for girls who lived in crowded city tenements with no parlors to accept male callers. Instead, these women socialized in urban public places—free or low-cost dance halls, amusement parks, and, later, at the movies.[55]

Figure 3.5. A Couple at Coney Island, c. 1903. In the late 1800s, young urban women began going on unchaperoned dates to dance halls, amusement parks, and other public amusements instead of following the middle- and upper-class rules of courtship.

Detroit Publishing Co. South end of Bowery, Coney Island, NY. *(Courtesy of the Library of Congress.)*

Upper- and middle-class women, many of whom were entering the public world to go to college or take jobs, were attracted to the idea of socializing without adult chaperones and began to "date" instead of court in the traditional manner. The automobile contributed to the trend of dating, especially in rural and suburban areas, but simply accelerated a practice that was already under way. Between 1890 and 1925, courtship did not completely disappear, but dating had become a nearly universal custom in America.

Historian Beth Bailey noted that this shift represented a transfer of power in relationships from female to male control. In courtship, the woman, or her mother, invited the man to her home. The woman's family could screen out men who did not meet their social-class expectations. But in the code of etiquette that developed for dating, men extended the invitations, men paid for the public entertainments on the date, and, by extension, men were assumed to expect a return on their investment.

In the courting system, chaperones were present; physical contact of all forms was nearly impossible prior to marriage if the rules of courtship were properly observed. But because young people on dates were unchaperoned, in public places, and later in the privacy of automobiles, twentieth-century etiquette manuals had to address the etiquette of sexual relationships. Couples were to avoid sexual relations until after marriage, and the woman was almost always expected to be the moral "gatekeeper" who said no. The concept of the morally superior yet physically and mentally inferior women from the eighteenth and nineteenth century had not disappeared.

Defining masculinity and femininity became a key theme in twentieth-century advice manuals. In order to marry, one was expected to develop masculine or feminine qualities that the culture said appealed to the opposite sex. Mid-twentieth-century advice stressed the need for women to demonstrate submissive qualities and a need for protection in order to attract men. Women were advised against displaying any masculine qualities by being too outspoken, too aggressive, or being too "brainy" and appearing to be smarter than men.[56] Women were convinced by the postwar mass media that a shortage of marriageable men, caused by casualties in World War II, necessitated proper feminine behavior in order to obtain a husband from the scarce selection.

The written rules of behavior for teenagers, as well as adult men and women, were reinforced by three new twentieth-century modes of transmission—radio, motion pictures, and television. All three presented programming that offered a common reference for behavior for Americans. Many groups of Americans were not represented in the new media, or were represented in a very negative light—African Americans, Hispanic Americans, the poor—but the national media defined, disseminated, and reinforced a relatively coherent body of acceptable behavior for those who hoped to be considered "middle class."[57]

Popular shows from the 1950s, '60s, and '70s—*Father Knows Best* (1954–1960), *My Three Sons* (1965–1972), and *Happy Days* (1974–1984)—reinforced the etiquette of dating and the conservative expectations of masculine and feminine behavior. *The Brady Bunch*, which originally aired from 1969 to 1974 and continued to air for years in syndicated reruns, was one of my favorite shows when I was in elementary and middle school. (When I watch reruns as an adult, I notice examples of gender polarization and how the "rules" of boy-girl interactions were taught, because I'm reexamining the show through a new set of cultural glasses.) Furthermore, it was assumed natural and unquestionable that the male had the right to initiate the date, both androcentric and supportive of the assumption that men were naturally dominant.

The social rebellions of the late 1950s, 1960s, and 1970s by African Americans, women, American Indians, gays and lesbians, migrant workers, and middle-class white youth, along with the economic insecurity that began with the 1973 Oil Embargo, led to a shift in etiquette advice. New rules of etiquette allowed men and women more freedom in their relationships and in how they defined masculine and feminine behavior. But in the twenty-first century, new rules of behavior constrained people in new ways.

Scholar Margaret Visser argued that in the modern era we excuse our lack of formal manners because we are always expected to be in a hurry and short on time. Today, we feel that we must continually rush to complete all of the daily tasks required at school, work, home, and even during leisure time.

On the other hand, she pointed out that we have created a new system of etiquette around a very modern demand for cleanliness. We spend a lot of that precious time washing ourselves, our clothes, and our homes, and spend vast amounts of money to buy machines and products to keep clean.[58] Ask students to analyze their daily habits and behavior in search of old rules that have not disappeared and new codes of etiquette that have developed in response to the technology, economy, and cultures of modern life.

In the Classroom: Introducing the Theme

Ask students, individually, to write a list of three rules of good behavior for the following scenarios:

- A job interview
- A social occasion with friends
- A family event such as a holiday celebration, reunion, picnic, and the like

After students generate the rules, ask students, in groups of three or four students, to share their rules and to discuss the following.

- List words or phrases that describe rules of behavior for the situations described above.
- The origin of their rules—where they learned this behavior and how they know to follow these rules.
- Similarities and differences between the rules for the three different scenarios.
- Similarities and differences in the rules listed by each individual student in the group.
- Would the parents or grandparents of the students write the same list of rules? Why or why not?

After individual group discussions, ask student groups to report their conclusions to each question. Direct students' attention to key concepts in the study of manners. Provide students with a few modern examples of advice for proper conduct from newspapers, magazines, or the Internet, such as "Dear Abby," available in newspapers, on the Internet, and on social media such as Twitter at #DearAbby.

The Primary Sources: Manners and the Enlightenment

In the Classroom

Post the essential question—*Should outward behavior (manners) always reflect inner beliefs or morals? Why or why not?*—along with the quote from *Catcher in the Rye* at the beginning of this chapter or the poem "I'm Making a List" by Shel Silverstein.[59] If needed, encourage discussion with the additional questions provided at the beginning of the chapter.

Prior to introducing the primary sources, students will need a basic knowledge of the ideals of the Enlightenment and how those ideals were represented in the manners of the eighteenth century. This information is provided in the previous section and can be presented to students in a manner that is most appropriate.

The impact of the Enlightenment is usually addressed in the context of the development of the American government, or in a European history course unit on the Scientific Revolution. Highlighting the impact of an intellectual movement on the daily lives of average people can provide students with a wider insight into the depth and complexity of history.

Language in eighteenth-century sources is often archaic, and unedited primary sources from this era may quickly discourage struggling readers. The excerpts below are short, and in some cases, language has been simplified. Entire advice books from this period, digitally reproduced in their original form, are available online, but the use of the "long s" (it looks like the letter f) in works printed before 1800 can be an additional level of difficulty. Encourage students to review the original sources if possible.

Choose the best reading strategy for your students and provide them with the reading guide (figure 3.6).

Source A
Excerpt from *Some Thoughts Concerning Education* (1693)[60] by John Locke (1632–1704)

> Every man must some time or other be trusted to himself and his own conduct; and he that is a good, a virtuous, and able man, must be made so within. And therefore what he is to receive from education, what is to sway and influence his life, must be something put into him betimes; habits woven into the very principles of his nature, and not a counterfeit demeanor, put on by fear, only to avoid the present anger of a father who perhaps may disinherit him.

Source B
Excerpt from *The Whole Duty of a Woman, or, An Infallible Guide to the Fair Sex: Containing Rules, Directions, and Observations, for Their Conduct and Behavior through All Ages and Circumstances of Life, as Virgins, Wives, or Widows: With . . . Rules and Receipts in Every Kind of Cookery* (1737 edition); no author listed on 1737 edition; reprint of *The Ladies Calling* (1673) by Richard Allestree[61]

	Source A	Source B	Source C	Source D	Source E	Source F	Source G
Date of document							
Social status of author							
Audience							
Type of document *letter, advice book, novel, etc.*							
Prescriptive OR Descriptive?							
Key idea(s) relating to manners							
Does this author agree or disagree with the Enlightenment view that outward behavior reflects inner beliefs/morals? *Cite or circle the sentences or phrases that support your answer.*							

After reading the sources, consider the following questions:

1. The primary sources cover how many years?
   - Within this time period, did all of the authors agree that outward behavior is an accurate reflection of inner beliefs/morals?
   - If not, what might explain these disagreements?

2. What social status group is most represented in the authors and audiences of these sources?
   - What groups of people might not have been familiar with advice books or may not have agreed with the advice in the sources?

3. What were the different expectations for males and females described in these sources?
   - Are men and women expected to have different manners today?
   - Are men and women believed to have different inner beliefs/morals today? For example, in Source B, women were advised to have the inner virtue of modesty, but this was a distinctly female virtue?

4. Many of these sources are prescriptive. Did everyone who read these sources follow the advice provided?
   - What would have been the consequences of not following the established expectations of proper behavior?

5. When Lord Chesterfield's letters were published (Source C), many people were shocked that he seemed more concerned with getting ahead in the world than with being a moral, honest person.
   - Are people shocked today if they learn that a person is just pretending to act mannerly in order to get ahead?
   - Why or why not?

6. These primary sources reflect changing beliefs about manners and morality. Do these changes reflect a decline in the whole society or do they reflect other factors?
   - What other factors might influence changes in manners?

Figure 3.6. Reading Guide—Manners and the Enlightenment.

From Chapter II—Of Modesty

It (modesty) is indeed a virtue of a general influence, that balances the mind with sober and humble thoughts of ourselves, also steers every part of the outward expression. Modesty appears in the face as calm and meek looks . . . certainly there is nothing which gives a greater luster to feminine beauty. Women who refrain from overdressing, and have innocent modesty, and a natural look, and shall eclipse those who dress richly and have artificial beauty. On the other hand, if boldness can be read in a woman's face, it blots all traces of beauty, like a cloud over the sun. . . . But modesty is not only confined to the face, it is in the life of the woman and in her words; modesty banishes all indecency and rudeness, all **insolent** boasts, and **supercilious** disdains. . . . Modesty refines a woman's language so that the modest tongue is like soft, sweet, charming music.

Key Terms

- **Insolent**—rude, not showing respect.
- **Supercilious**—behaving or looking like one believes he or she is superior to other people.

Source C
Excerpts from *Letters to His Son on the Art of Becoming a Man of the World and a Gentleman* (written 1737–1754, published in 1774 after the author's death) by Philip Dormer Stanhope, 4th Earl of Chesterfield (1694–1774)[62]

Letter CLXXXII, BATH, November 16, 1752.
  To men, I said whatever I thought would give them the best opinion of my career and learning; and to women, what I was sure would please them; flattery, gallantry, and love. And, moreover, I will own to you, under the secrecy of confession, that my vanity has very often made me take great pains to make a woman in love with me, if I could, even if I was not interested in her. In company with men, I always endeavored that my manner outshined, or at least, if possible, equal the most shining man in it. . . . With the men I was a **Proteus,** and assumed every shape, in order to please them all: among the gay, I was the gayest; among the grave, the gravest; and I always appeared to have good-breeding, or to be friends, whichever pleased and attached people to me: and accordingly I was soon connected with all the men of any fashion or figure in town.[63]

Letter CLXXXVI, LONDON, January 15, 1753
  A seeming ignorance is very often a most necessary part of worldly knowledge. It is, for instance, commonly advisable to seem ignorant of what people offer to tell you; and when they say, Have you not heard of such a thing? to answer No, and to let them go on; though you know it already. Some have a pleasure in telling it, because they think that they tell it well; others have a pride in it, as being the **sagacious** discoverers; and many have a vanity in showing that they have been, though very undeservedly, trusted. All of these types of people would be disappointed, and consequently displeased, if you said Yes, that you already knew the information. Seem always ignorant (unless to one's most intimate friend) of all matters of private scandal and **defamation**, though you should hear them a thousand times. . . . But even though you may pretend to be ignorant, you should always learn the thorough and extensive details. Seeming to be ignorant is the best method of procuring the details; for most people have such a vanity in showing a superiority over others, that they will tell you what they should not. Besides, seeming ignorance will make you pass as innocent of other motives. However, fish for facts, and take pains to be well informed of everything that passes; but fish judiciously, and not always, in the shape of direct questions. Too many direct questions will always put people on their guard, and, if asked too many times, will grow tiresome. You can pretend you heard a particular thing, upon which somebody will, kindly and officiously, set you right and give you more information. Or at other seem to know more than you do, in order to know all that you want; but avoid direct questioning as much as you can. All these necessary arts of the world require constant attention, presence of mind, and coolness.[64]

Key Terms

- **Proteus**—in Greek mythology, a god of rivers that could assume many forms.
- **Sagacious**—showing intelligence and shrewd judgment.
- **Defamation**—damaging the good reputation of someone.

Source D
Excerpts from *The Autobiography of Benjamin Franklin* (written from 1771–1790, published after Franklin's death) by Ben Franklin (1706–1790)[65]

Chapter II—Beginning Life as a Printer

While I was intent on improving my language, I obtained an English grammar book and Xenophon's *Memorable Things of Socrates*, which provided examples of logic and rhetoric. I was charmed with those examples, adopted them, and stopped my abrupt contradictions and argumentation with others, and instead pretending to be the humble inquirer and doubter. I had become a real doubter in many points of our religious doctrine, but I found this humble method safest for myself and very embarrassing to those against whom I used it; therefore I took a delight in it, practiced it continually, and grew very artful and expert in drawing people, even of superior knowledge, into concessions, the consequences of which they did not foresee, entangling them in difficulties out of which they could not extricate themselves, and so obtaining victories that neither myself nor my cause always deserved.

I continued this method some few years, but gradually left it, retaining only the habit of expressing myself in terms of modest diffidence. I never used the words "certainly," "undoubtedly," or any others that gave the impression that I was certain that I was correct. Instead, I would say that I "thought a thing to be so and so," or "it appears to me," or "I think it so or so, for such and such reasons'" or "if I am not mistaken." This habit of appearing humble, I believe, has been of great advantage to me. . . . A manner in which a person assumes to be right disgusts people, tends to create opposition, and to defeat the purpose of giving or receiving information or pleasure. For, if you talk to people in a **dogmatic** manner . . . modest, sensible men, who do not love to argue, will probably leave you undisturbed but you can seldom hope to recommend yourself in pleasing your hearers, or to persuade others.

Chapter VIII—Business Success and First Public Service

In order to secure my credit and character as a tradesman, I took care not only to be in reality industrious and **frugal,** but to avoid all appearances to the contrary. I dressed plainly; I was seen at no places of idle diversion. I never went out a fishing or shooting; a book, indeed, sometimes distracted me from my work, but that was seldom, and caused no scandal. To show that I was not above my business and willing to work hard, I sometimes carried large packages of paper for my business through the streets on a wheelbarrow myself. Thus people respected me as an industrious, thriving young man, and paying duly for what I bought, the merchants in the printing business were willing to do business with me and I went on swimmingly.

Key Terms

- **Dogmatic**—expressing personal opinions as an absolute certainty that cannot be questioned.
- **Frugal**—not wasteful, careful about spending too much money.

Source E
Excerpts from *A Vindication of the Rights of Woman* (1792) by Mary Wollstonecraft (1759–1797)[66]

Wollstonecraft argues that women have the ability to reason and should receive better educations that develop their natural abilities. She was responding to the belief that women should only learn how to keep house and be a wife, a view common in many of the advice books of the nineteenth century just as in The Whole Duty of a Woman *quoted earlier.*

Manners and morals are so nearly allied, that they have often been confounded; manners should be the natural reflection of morals. Yet, situations exist in which a young person develops artificial and dishonest manners and morality becomes an empty name.[67]

74 ~ Chapter Three

It is time to effect a revolution in female manners—time to restore to them their lost dignity—and make women, as a part of the human species, labor by reforming themselves to reform the world. It is time to separate unchangeable morals from local, artificial manners.[68]

Rakes know how to work on [a woman's] **sensibility**, whilst the modest merit of reasonable men has, of course, less effect on their feelings, and they cannot reach [the woman's heart] . . . because they have few sentiments in common. . . . And how can they [critics of female behavior and ability to reason] then expect women, who are only taught to observe behavior all their lives, and acquire manners rather than morals, to despise men for doing the same thing? Where are women suddenly to find judgment enough to appreciate an awkward but virtuous man, when his manners are unpolished and rebuffing and his conversation cold and dull, because it does not consist of pretty repartees, or well-turned compliments? In order to admire or esteem anything women must, at least, be educated in morality in some degree, in what we should admire; for we are unable to estimate the value of qualities and virtues above our comprehension.[69]

Key Terms

- **Rake**—a man of low morals who takes advantage of women.
- **Sensibility**—a social manner of the late eighteenth century that emphasized communicating one's emotions and displaying empathy and appropriate emotion, rather than just emphasizing only the formal good manners. A person with sensibility did not just follow the more formal behavior prescribed by politeness, but instead behaved with expressive actions such as sighing, trembling, or weeping, all emotions that were evidence of refined inner feelings and empathy for others. One's behavior (manners) directly mirrored one's emotional *and* moral state.

Source F
Excerpt from "To the Officers of the First Brigade for the Third Division of the Militia of Massachusetts, October 11, 1798," in *The Works of John Adams, Second President of the United States*, by John Adams (1797–1801)[70]

While our country remains untainted with the principles and manners which are now producing desolation in so many parts of the world; while she (the USA) continues sincere, and incapable of **insidious** and **impious** policy, we shall have the strongest reason to rejoice our local destination. But should the people of America once become capable of that deep insincerity towards one another, and towards foreign nations, which assumes the language of justice and moderation, while it is practicing **iniquity** and extravagance, and displays in the most captivating manner the charming pictures of **candor, frankness,** and sincerity, while it is rioting, and carelessly causing destruction, this country will be the most miserable place to live in the world.

Key Terms

- **Insidious**—gradually causing harm.
- **Impious**—not showing the proper respect.
- **Iniquity**—wickedness.
- **Candor**—openness and honesty.
- **Frankness**—expression of one's true feelings.

Source G
Excerpts from the novel *Sense and Sensibility* (1811) by Jane Austen (1775–1817)[71]

Elinor, this eldest daughter, whose advice was so effectual, possessed a strength of understanding, and coolness of judgment, which qualified her, though only nineteen, to be the counsellor of her mother, and enabled her frequently to counteract, to the advantage of them all, that eagerness of mind in Mrs. Dashwood (the mother of Elinor and Marianne) which must generally have led to **imprudence**. Elinor had an excellent heart;—her **disposition** was affectionate, and her feelings were strong; but she knew how to govern them: it was a knowledge which her mother had yet to learn; and which one of her sisters (Marianne) had resolved never to be taught.

Marianne's abilities were, in many respects, quite equal to Elinor's. She was sensible and clever; but eager in everything: her sorrows, her joys, could have no moderation. She was generous, amiable, interesting: she was everything but **prudent**. The resemblance between her and her mother was strikingly great.

Elinor saw, with concern, the excess of her Marianne's sensibility; but by their mother, Mrs. Dashwood it was valued and cherished. They encouraged each other now in **the violence of their affliction** (after the death of the father). The agony of grief which overpowered them at first, was voluntarily renewed, was sought for, and was created again and again. They gave themselves up wholly to their sorrow, seeking increase of wretchedness in every reflection that could afford it, and resolved against ever admitting consolation in future. Elinor, too, was deeply afflicted; but still she could struggle (to act normally), she could exert herself (to take care of daily duties). She could consult with her brother, could receive her sister-in-law on her arrival, and treat her with proper attention; and could strive to rouse her mother to similar exertion, and encourage her to similar **forbearance**.

Key Terms

- **Imprudence**—failure to show proper respect.
- **Disposition**—one's outlook on life, or mood.
- **Prudent**—being wise, considering one's actions and the effect of those actions in the future.
- **The violence of their affliction**—Marianne and her mother were showing extremely emotional grief at the death of Mr. Dashwood.
- **Forbearance**—self-control, restraint, tolerance.

The Primary Sources: Courtship and Dating

In the Classroom
Ask and discuss the following questions:

- Write three to five rules for socializing with a boy/girl in a romantic way. What words or phrases are used to name this system of rules?
    - The teacher should be careful to word the question with very neutral language so that students use the current words and same-sex relationships can be discussed. For example, dating is a term that is going out of fashion and students will likely have more up-to-date terms.
- Are the rules different for males and females?
- How are romantic relationships different in an era of social media and the Internet, as compared to previous generations before computers?
- Do different generations or different groups of people have different sets of rules for romantic relationships?
    - Ask students to do an Internet search for modern "dating advice for teens." Help students to categorize, compare, and contrast the advice collected. For example, is the advice following traditions of the past or recommending new ways to behave? Is the advice given by a religious authority or is it secular? Who is the target audience for the advice and is the person giving the advice from the target audience or not?

Introduce the shift from courtship to dating that occurred in the late nineteenth and early twentieth century, as described previously in this chapter. Examples of nineteenth-century "calling cards" can be digitally projected, like the examples pictured here. The calling card, or visiting card, was a small printed card, similar to the modern business card, with a person's name and, sometimes, his or her address. These cards were required for upper and striving middle-class people who wanted to be included in respectable middle- and upper-class society. The calling card was left at homes or sent to individuals for various social purposes, and many complicated rules governed its use.[72]

Students will also need to understand concepts of social status and class, the concepts of gender polarization, androcentrism, biological and religious essentialism, and the differences between sex and gender described in chapter 1.

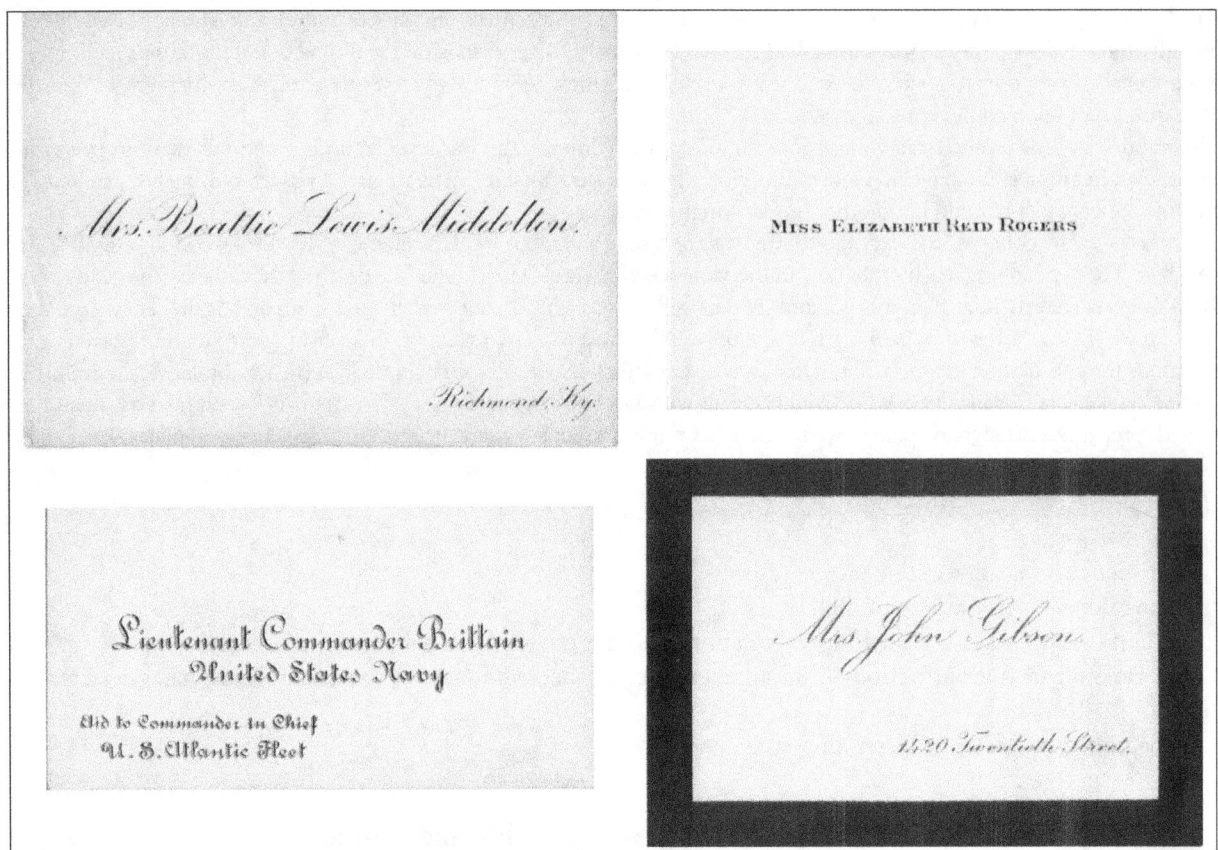

Figure 3.7. Visiting Cards, 1909. Complicated rules of etiquette governed the appearance and use of visiting cards. The black border on the card on the bottom right indicated that the person was in mourning due to the death of a family member.
(Courtesy of Eastern Kentucky University Special Collections and Archives, Richmond, KY.)

The excerpts below are from twelve different etiquette books spanning one hundred years. These primary sources can be used as a whole or introduced across several units that cover the decades of the twentieth century. You may wish to add a few modern sources from the twenty-first century. If the sources are introduced together, consider using a jigsaw strategy in which each student is assigned to read and analyze one or two sources, and then compare and contrast their assigned sources with different sources assigned to other students.

Provide students with copies of the primary sources and a reading guide for each assigned source (figure 3.8). After students have read and analyzed the sources individually, provide them with the summary reading guide (figure 3.9) in order to analyze change over time.

Source 1
Excerpts from *Manners and Social Usages* (1884) by Mary Elizabeth Wilson Sherwood (1830–1903)

This book was published in several editions in the late nineteenth and early twentieth century. Mary Sherwood also wrote The Art of Entertaining *(1892, 1893, and 1894) and* Etiquette, the American Code of Manners *(1884), several advice books for the home, numerous novels, and articles for* Harper's Bazaar *magazine. As a young woman, she was hostess for the social events of her father, a member of Congress, in their Washington DC home.*

> Bachelors should leave cards on the master and mistress of the house, and, in America, upon the young ladies. . . . It is a rule with sticklers for good-breeding that after any entertainment a gentleman should leave his card in person. . . . No gentleman should call on a lady unless she asks him to do so, or unless he brings a letter of introduction, or unless he is taken by a lady who is sufficiently intimate to invite him to call. A lady should say to a gentleman, if she wishes him to call, "I hope that we shall see you," or, "I am at home on Monday," or something of that sort.[73]

1. Source and Author	
2. Year of Publication	
3. Social status of author	
4. Age and role of intended audience *Parents, teenagers, single adults? Other groups?*	
5. Is intended audience male or female or both?	
6. Words/phrases that describe socially acceptable feminine qualities *Cite or circle the sentences or phrases that support your answer*	
7. Words/phrases that describe socially acceptable masculine qualities. *Cite or circle the sentences or phrases that support your answer.*	
8. Did the intended audience actually follow this advice? Why or why not?	
9. What were the consequences of not following this advice?	
10. To what groups of people might this advice NOT apply or be appropriate?	
11. Is the author upholding conservative traditions of the past OR advocating new patterns of behavior *Cite or circle the sentences or phrases that support your answer.*	
12. Is this advice still given today? If not, what is the modern expectation for behavior?	
13. Are the assumptions about sex roles and gender in this advice still present today? If not, what are the modern assumptions about sex and gender?	

Figure 3.8. Reading Guide—Courtship and Dating.

The following excerpts are from the 1912 edition of Manners and Social Usages, *published after the death of the author.*

The duties of a chaperon are very hard and unremitting, and sometimes very disagreeable. She must accompany her young lady everywhere; she must sit in the parlor when she receives gentlemen ; she must go with her to the skating-rink, the ball, the party, the races, the dinners, and especially to theatre parties ; she must preside at the table, and act the part of a mother [if there is no mother in the house] far as she can; she must watch the characters of the men who approach her charge, and endeavor to save the inexperienced girl from the dangers of a bad marriage, if possible. To perform this feat, and not to degenerate into . . . a dragon, or a Mrs. General . . . is a very difficult task.[74]

Gentlemen and ladies walk together in the daytime unattended, but if they ride on horseback a groom is always in attendance on the lady. In rural neighborhoods where there are not grooms, and where a young lady and gentleman go off for

	Late 1800s/ Early 1900s	1920s	1930s	1940s	1950s	1960s	1970s	1980s	Modern dating advice
Summary of female roles									
Summary of male roles									
Overall, do the sources from the decade assume gender polarization is natural?									
Overall, do the sources assume the differences in the roles of men and women are natural and to be accepted?									
Overall, do the sources acknowledge differences in social class or status?									
If differences in social class or status are acknowledged, how are the differences to be treated in dating situations?									

After considering the advice for courtship and dating provided to males and females over a period of one hundred years, answer the following:

- Why are men and women expected to follow different codes of etiquette?
- How do different expectations of behavior for men and women impact the lives of individuals?
- How are individuals treated that do not conform to societal gender expectations?
- Why do different groups of people (different cultures, social classes) have different codes of etiquette?

Figure 3.9. Reading Guide—Summary of Courtship and Dating.

a drive unattended, they have thrown Old-World etiquette out of the window, and must make a new etiquette of their own. Propriety, mutual respect, and American chivalry have done for women what all the surveillance of . . . Spanish and French chaperones has done for the young girl of Europe. . . .

A young lady should not write letters to young men, or send them presents, or take the initiative in any way. A friendly correspondence is very proper if the mother approves, but even this has its dangers. Let a young lady always remember that she is to the young man an angel to reverence until she lessens the distance between them and extinguishes respect. . . .

A young lady who is very prominent in society should not make herself too common; she should not appear in too many charades, private theatricals, tableaux, etc. She should remember the "**violet by the mossy stone**." She must also, at a watering-place remember that every act of hers is being criticized by a set of lookers-on who are not all friendly, and she must, ere she allow herself to be too much of a belle, remember to silence envious tongues.[75]

Key Term

- **Violet by the mossy stone**—reference to a poem by William Wordsworth; this phrase means the violet that is half hidden is the more beautiful—in other words, a girl should not show off or be too conspicuous.

Source 2
Excerpts from *Etiquette* (1922) by Emily Post (1873–1960)[76]

Emily Post published numerous books, articles, and newspaper columns on etiquette, as well as stories for magazines, novels, and travel books.

Chapter X—Cards and Visits

WHO was it that said—in the Victorian era probably, and a man of course—"The only mechanical tool ever needed by a woman is a hair-pin"? He might have added that with a hair-pin and a visiting card, she is ready to meet most emergencies.

Although the principal use of a visiting card, at least the one for which it was originally invented—to be left as an evidence of one person's presence at the house of another—is going gradually out of ardent favor in fashionable circles, its usefulness seems to keep a nicely adjusted balance. In New York, for instance, the visiting card has entirely taken the place of the written note of invitation to informal parties of every description. Messages of condolence or congratulation are written on it; it is used as an endorsement in the giving of an order; it is even tacked on the outside of express boxes. The only employment of it which is not as flourishing as formerly is its being left in quantities and with frequency at the doors of acquaintances.[77]

Not so many years ago, a lady or gentleman, young girl or youth, who failed to pay her or his "party call" after having been invited to Mrs. Social-Leader's ball was left out of her list when she gave her next one. For the old-fashioned hostess kept her visiting list with the precision of a bookkeeper in a bank; everyone's credit was entered or cancelled according to the presence of her or his cards in the card receiver. Young people who liked to be asked to her house were apt to leave an extra one at the door, on occasion, so that theirs should not be among the missing when the new list for the season was made up—especially as the more important old ladies were very quick to strike a name off, but seldom if ever known to put one back.

But about twenty years ago the era of informality set in and has been gaining ground ever since. . . . Visits to strangers, visits of condolence, and of other courtesies are still paid, quite as punctiliously as ever. But within the walls of society itself, the visit of formality is decreasing.[78]

Chapter XX—Engagements

In cities twenty-five years ago, a young girl had **beaux** who came to see her one at a time; they in formal clothes and manners, she in her "company best" to "receive" them, sat stiffly in the "front parlor" and made politely formal conversation. Invariably they addressed each other as Miss Smith and Mr. Jones, and they "talked off the top" with about the same lack of reservation as the ambassador of one country may be supposed to talk to him of another. A young man was said to be "devoted" to this young girl or that, but as a matter of fact each was acting a role, he of an admirer and she of a siren, and each was actually an utter stranger to the other.

Today no trace of stilted artificiality remains. The tête-a-tête of a quarter of a century ago has given place to the continual presence of a group. A flock of young girls and a flock of young men form a little group of their own—everywhere they are together. In the country they visit the same houses or they live in the same neighborhood, they play golf in foursomes, and tennis in mixed doubles. In winter at balls they sit at the same table for supper, they have little dances at their own homes, where scarcely any but themselves are invited; they play bridge, they have tea together, but whatever they do, they stay in the pack. In more than one way this group habit is excellent; young women and men are friends in a degree of natural and entirely platonic intimacy undreamed of in their parents' youth. Having the habit therefore of knowing her men friends well, a young girl is not going to imagine a stranger, no matter how perfect he may appear to be, anything but an ordinary human man after all. And in finding out his bad points as well as his good, she is aided and abetted, encouraged or held in check, by the members of the group to which she belongs.[79]

Key Term

- **Beaux**—plural of beau; boyfriends.

Figure 3.10. "Kiss Me Quick"—Currier and Ives Print. The printmaking firm Currier and Ives sold inexpensive lithograph prints depicting historical events, popular images, and portraits from 1834 to 1907. The images in figures 3.10 and 3.11 sent conflicting messages about the behavior of a courting couple.
Currier & Ives, published between and 1850 and 1900. (Courtesy of the Library of Congress.)

Figure 3.11. "No You Don't"—Currier and Ives Print. According to advice books from the eighteenth to the twentieth century, couples were expected to avoid sexual relations until after marriage, and the woman was expected to be a moral "gatekeeper" who said no. But published advice was not always followed. How did this pair of prints reflect and ignore the proper etiquette of courtship and why were expectations for men and women different?
Currier & Ives, published between and 1856 and 1907. (Courtesy of the Library of Congress.)

Source 3
Excerpt from *Hints on Etiquette* (1924) by Esther Floyd in *Little Blue Book No. 556*[80]

The Little Blue Books were extremely popular educational booklets printed from 1919 to 1978 on hundreds of different topics.

In New York and some other cities, young women in the "best society" do not dine in public or go to the theatre, with a man alone. In the Main Street towns, young men regularly escort young women to church, the theater, a dance, or anywhere that is proper for them to go at all, and nothing is thought of it. Except for something like a camping party, chaperons are unknown. Since even in New York, a young girl may go motoring for as many hours as she likes with a man and no chaperone, it would seem excessive strictness about chaperonage on other occasions is a little overdone.

 The warning to girls about going for long motor rides with men alone, sometimes returning after night-fall, has been sounded so often and reinforced by so many "horrible examples," that it should be superfluous to repeat it here. The mere danger of a girl's gaining the reputation of not being particular and careful of herself, should be enough, without any direr consequences. It is now quite the common thing in some places for the young man to stop his car in front of the girl's home and "honk" long and insistently if necessary (it seldom is) till she comes out. He condescends to open the door for her, she enters the car and they drive away. Her parents perhaps hardly know him by sight. He seldom if ever goes into her home—no need, so long as she will come when he "honks." Girls should not hold themselves so cheaply, and parents should not allow it while the girl is under their control.

Figure 3.12. Dating and the automobile, c. 1907. This photograph is one of a series created to accompany the 1905 song "In My Merry Oldsmobile." "She tries to learn the auto" is a line from the song. Complete lyrics and original recordings are available online and feature the slang of dating at the turn of the century.
Tom M. Phillips. She Tries to Learn the Auto. (Courtesy of the Library of Congress.)

Source 4
Excerpts from *Etiquette: The Blue Book of Social Usage* (1940) by Emily Post (1872–1960)[81]

Emily Post published numerous books, articles, and newspaper columns on etiquette, as well as stories for magazines, novels, and travel books.

Chapter 23—Modern Man and Girl

Letters from Readers—He is from over the car tracks
Question: My fiancé's parents live just a few blocks from our house, but as yet have not come to see me, or my family. It sounds snobbish to explain, but facts are facts. You see my family is "of society" and his family lives "on the other side of the car tracks." In this town the dividing car tracks are as definite as the boundaries between hostile countries. I know the members of his family hesitate to cross the tracks. I want them to like me and not to think my family or I feel above them in any way, but how can I be conciliatory without seeming patronizing? Should mother ask them to come to dinner—which might embarrass them—or should I go to see my fiancé's mother?

Answer: You may not want them to think that you feel above them, but you DO! Did you not feel above them, you would not fear to seem patronizing. And yet your belief that they would be embarrassed in being invited to your mother's house shows not their lack, my dear, but yours. If you were a truly great lady it would not even occur to you that anyone could be embarrassed under your roof—ever! To imagine that one or another side of the car tracks can grant a patent of superiority, or furnish proof of inferiority, is to acknowledge that the foundations for your own social position are very wobbly.

I know I am being brutal, but for the sake of your own character, as well as your whole future happiness, go out on those car tracks and take a good look at them. Ask yourself if you are really such a snob that you can't see the true values except as some of your friends happen to appraise them for you. And if the car track boundaries still seem to you those of a foreign country, break your engagement. If, on the other hand, you can overcome the car tracks, then forget them now and forever and go to see the family of the man you love and try to make *them* receive *you*!

Source 5
Excerpts from *When We Meet Socially, A Guidebook to Good Form in Social Conventions* (1940) by M'Ledge Moffett, PhD (1892–1969)—Dean of Women, State Teachers College, Radford, Virginia[82]

This book was written to be a textbook in a high school or university classroom.

Many changes are taking place in the forms for acceptable social conduct of men and women. The release of woman into the world of business, which brings her into frequent contact with men in many business, professional, and other non-social situations, has eliminated many former artificial courtesies. In place of the more stilted forms of a generation ago, behavior based on an attitude of equality and freedom marks the contacts of men and women today. Women expect to receive recognition and win courtesies from men because of *themselves* and not because they have a sex right to definite forms of courtesies.

1. *A woman always receives physical protection from a man.*
   (a) A man always walks on the curb side of the street.
   (b) A man assists a lady into all vehicles. He enters doors, buses, trains, and cars after her. . . .
   (d) The lady takes the arm of the man when physical support is needed and in cases of formal ushering.
   (e) A man draws out a chair from a table for a woman and waits until she is seated.
   (f) A man always offers a lady his seat in a crowded room. When the room is not crowded, he should rise and stand until she is seated. . . .
3. *A man must give a woman moral protection.*
   (a) A gentleman will in no way embarrass a woman by any physical contact which she indicates is not desired by her. Promiscuous petting in all of its manifestations is a violation of this principle.
   (b) No gentleman will escort a lady to a place where she may be embarrassed by other men or by the nature or reputation of the place.
   (c) A gentleman will respect the social code of the community in which he is calling upon the lady. This applies to hours and ways of calling, use of automobiles (as night driving, parking, so on), chaperonage, courtesies such as flowers, type of gifts, escorting her to public and private entertainments, and so forth.

At the beginning of an acquaintanceship, a gentleman should call at a lady's home and meet her family before extending social courtesies outside the home. If the home contact is impossible, he should ask the lady to invite a sister or intimate friend to accompany them. Many young people who do not have the protection of their own home or a suitable hostess available . . . arrange to "double date" with a couple who do have this protection.

Source 6
Excerpts from *Amy Vanderbilt's Compete Book of Etiquette, A Guide to Gracious Living* (1954) by Amy Vanderbilt (1908–1974)[83]

Amy Vanderbilt was considered an expert on etiquette after the publication of the first edition of her best-selling Amy Vanderbilt's Complete Book of Etiquette *in 1952. This book was updated and republished several times, the most recent edition in 1995.*

When does dating begin? Earlier and earlier, it seems. . . . Boy-and-girl dating may begin at about fourteen on a limited basis—early movies, dates at home of course, various sports, days at the beach, bicycle trips that bring the two home before dark, etc. Steady dating should be firmly discouraged throughout the early teens, because tastes are formed through a variety of contacts.

Dating, for boys, does bring with it increased financial responsibilities. While a certain amount of Dutch treating goes on, especially in group entertainment, a boy usually does pay for the entertainment of his special date. If his allowance is not adequate for his participation in the social activities of his high school group and if his parents cannot comfortably increase it, the after-school jobs must provide the difference. And boys should learn early to be unembarrassedly frank with girls about what entertainment they can afford to offer. Pretending to have more money than one actually has is an acutely uncomfortable business, and usually no one is deceived by the pretention.[84]

Chapter 15—Courtship and Engagements

Eventually, in the course of things, a girl begins to narrow her interest in young men to one young man. A fairly long courtship and a brief engagement seem to be a safe formula. The courtship period is casual and informal, without pledges on either side. It gives each a chance to know the other better—and yet make a graceful exit if that seems expedient.

Whenever possible, a girl should receive an attentive man in her own home and not see him exclusively in the artificial atmosphere of the theater, restaurants, and other places of amusement. He needs, if possible, to evaluate her with her family or at least in her own home, and to see her with her friends, to help him decide wither or not life with her would be comfortable and companionable as well as romantically satisfying.

If her relationships with her family are good and happy, no girl need to be ashamed to bring a suitor into the most modest home, even if he be from a more prosperous background. And, conversely, a man should be highly suspicious of a girl who does not wish him to meet her family and her intimate friends. It is important, too, for a girl to know and become familiar with his background and interests.

It is impossible for a man and woman to know whether they are really suited to one another if they spend all of their courtship time in the exclusive company of each other. Each should give the other an opportunity to expose to searching consideration his best and worst sides. They should see each other in the give and take of family life, or at least among close friends with kindred interests. Otherwise a resulting marriage is in the rude shocks and accusations of, "If I'd known such and such I'd never have married you!"[85]

Source 7
Excerpts from *The Art of Dating* (1958) by Evelyn Millis Duvall (1906–1998)[86]

Evelyn Millis Duvall wrote or was coauthor of a wide range of teen advice books and textbooks in the 1940s to 1970s and was active in organizations dedicated to marriage, child development, and sex education. She taught in the sociology department at the University of Chicago.

The Good-Night Kiss
Teen-agers tend to agree that a first date is too soon for a good-night kiss. Some sophisticated fellows say, "Sure I try, but I don't really expect to get a good-night kiss the first date." If such a fellow does get the kiss, he may wonder about how many other boys have also been favored. This is exactly the impression a girl wants to avoid. No girl wants to appear "too easy." She feels it's a better policy to give a boy something to come back for the next time.

Source 8
Excerpts from *McCall's Book of Everyday Etiquette, A Guide to Modern Manners* (1960)[87]

McCall's Magazine was a popular monthly women's magazine of the twentieth century, published from 1897–2002. The peak of its circulation was in the 1960s with over 8 million subscribers.

Men's treatment of women is based on a time when women were considered muscularly (hence mentally) the inferior sex. In return for knuckling under to this attitude of male superiority, women demanded and got many special considerations based on their "weakness" and "helplessness." Manners of men toward women are still to a great extent based on this ancient blackmail, although the reason for it has long since been disproven.[88]

Especially for Teen-agers
The conduct of teen-agers and what they are permitted to do varies so widely among communities and social groups that it is almost impossible to set down rules about ages, places, and times. The best rule to follow is that your children should be allowed to do pretty much what an average of their friends do. That is, on the question of what time to come home after a

date, you don't allow your daughter to stay out most of the night because one under supervised girl in her class does. Neither do you make her come home two hours earlier than most of the others just because your neighbor's daughter does. If you feel a need for moral support when you make the rules, consult other parents about their opinions.

Behavior Among Their Friends

You will have very little to say about this except for occasional advice. . . . You might point out that it is very bad manners for a boy to talk to other boys about his dates, or for girls to gossip about theirs. By the time your children are old enough to go out by themselves on dates, they should know how you feel about drinking and smoking. They may not adhere to your ideas exactly, but they may at least consider them if you haven't been an ogre about them in the past.

Parties and dates can hardly by classified by age. It depends on where you live, whom you know—and above all what the other kids do. But in general, the social life of the twelve- and thirteen-year-old is with a group rather than single couples and his dating activities are confined to the daylight hours unless he is with an adult, or chaperoned by one at a home party.

Girls of fourteen to sixteen (and slightly older boys, usually) go to the theatre and late movies, and occasionally even respectable night clubs. In the case of night clubs, they're often accompanied by an older couple or their parents. But you should teach your son that he neither goes himself nor takes a girl to a place with an unsavory reputation such as a pool hall or a questionable night club. Bowling alleys were formerly off-limits too, but this problem is now being solved by special teen-age bowling alleys or nights for young people in the regular ones. Soft drinks are served and no liquor is available. There are now a few night clubs which serve only soft drinks and close early, yet have the entertainment which teen-age boys and girls crave.[89]

Source 9
Excerpts from *Sex and the Single Girl* (1962) by Helen Gurley Brown (1922–2012)[90]

Helen Gurley Brown is best known as the editor of Cosmopolitan *magazine from 1965–1997. But her book* Sex and the Single Girl, *published one year before Betty Friedan's* The Feminine Mystique, *is what made her famous. Her book was very different from most advice books of the era that promoted the family and marriage. The book quickly made several best-seller lists in the United States and internationally, and she appeared on over thirty radio and television shows after the book was published.*

There is a more important truth that magazines never deal with, that single women are too brainwashed to figure out, that married women know but won't admit, that married men *and* single men endorse, and that is that the single woman, far from being a creature to be pitied and patronized, is emerging as the newest glamour girl of our times.

She is engaging because she lives by her wits. She supports herself. She has had to sharpen her personality and mental resources to a glitter in order to survive in a competitive world. . . . Economically she is a dream. She is not a parasite, a dependent, a scrounger, a sponger or a bum. She is a giver, not a taker; a winner, not a loser.

Why else is she attractive? Because she isn't married, that's why! . . . she has more time and often more money to spend on herself. She has the extra twenty minutes to exercise every day, an hour to make up her face for a date. . . .

Serving time as a single woman can give you the foundation for a better marriage if you finally go that route. . . . If you would like a good single life—since the married life is not just now forthcoming—you can't afford to leave any facet of you unpolished.

You don't have to do anything brassy or show-offy or against your nature. Your most prodigious work will be on *you*—at home. . . . You don't chase the glittering life, you lay a trap for it. You tunnel up from the bottom. . . . You must develop style. Every girl has one—it's just a case of getting it out in the open, caring for it and feeding it like an orchid until it leafs out. . . .

Brains are an asset but it doesn't take brainy brains like a nuclear physicist's. Whatever it is that keeps you from saying anything unkind and keeps you asking bright questions even when you don't quite understand the answers will do nicely. A lively interest in people and things (even if you aren't that interested) is why bosses trust you with new assignments, why men talk to you at parties . . . and sometimes ask you on to dinner.

Fashion is your powerful ally. Let the "secure" married girls eschew shortening their skirts and wear their classic cashmeres and tweeds until everybody could throw up. You be the girl other girls look at to see what America has copied from Paris.

Your figure can't harbor an ounce of baby fat. It never looked good on anybody but babies.

You must cook well. It will serve you faithfully.[91]

Source 10
Excerpt from *Modern Etiquette* (1963)[92]

Teen Dating—General Rules

- There are only three situations in which a girl may properly ask a boy for a date: 1) when she's giving a party or a small get-together; 2) when she's been asked to bring an escort to a party; 3) when an affair is **"girls' bid."** *Otherwise, a boy does the asking!*
- Blind dates are permissible, but only if they've been arranged by someone the girl knows well (and, even then, it's wise to go out with another couple).

Figure 3.13. **The Etiquette of Dancing, 1942.** Numerous rules of etiquette governed dancing by men and women throughout history. What rules of etiquette were the men and women in this photograph expected to follow related to invitations, clothing, and behavior before, during, and after the dance? Compare those expectations for behavior to modern dancing etiquette. In the past and today, how are people who do not conform treated?

Fenno Jacobs, photographer. Southington, CT. Amusement park. May 30, 1942. (Courtesy of the Library of Congress.)

- Pick-ups are *not* permissible. However if, for example, at the library, a boy and girl should recognize each other from school, church, etc., the boy may properly introduce himself, and ask the girl for a date. If she chooses, she may proper accept. In this situation, too, it is wise to "double" on the first date.
- Girls who act like ladies are treated like ladies. Which means a girl can't expect a boy to behave like a gentleman if she opens doors for herself, gives her order to the waiter instead of to her date, etc. However, conversely, a girl doesn't embarrass a boy who forgets (or perhaps doesn't know) good manners. For example, she pauses to allow him to open a door, but if he doesn't she opens it herself.
- At a dance, a girl always dances the first and the last dance with her date; makes certain they both say hello and goodbye to the chaperones.
- After dancing with another boy, a girl *doesn't* say "Thank you." She waits until the boy says it, then answers, "you're welcome—I enjoyed it too" (or other words to that effect).

It is the girl's responsibility to suggest going home—and up to her, too, to see that the suggestions sticks.

Dos and Don'ts

Girls

A wise girl accepts a date enthusiastically, doesn't break it if a boy she likes better asks later; is dressed prettily, properly, on time; introduces the boy to her parents if they haven't met; doesn't behave conspicuously; doesn't flirt with other boys; listens when her date is speaking; patches make-up in private, but doesn't spend hours doing it; doesn't giggle or talk endlessly with other girls; tells her date she had a good time (whether she did or didn't).

Boys

A wise boy plans a date ahead—and lets the girl in on the plan so she knows how to dress; picks her up promptly; goes to the door (*never* honks a car horn) when he arrives; opens doors for the girl; helps her on and off with her coat; stands when she leaves or returns to the table; asks what color gown she's wearing if the occasion necessitates flowers; doesn't flirt with other girls; makes certain he has enough money for the night's entertainment; tries, but doesn't fight, for a goodnight kiss.

Key Term

- **Girl's bid**—An event or dance in which the girls invite the boys—similar to a Sadie Hawkins Dance, named after a *Li'l Abner* comic strip published in 1937. Sadie Hawkins and the other unmarried women of Dogpatch got to chase the bachelors and "marry up" with the ones that they caught.

Source 11
Excerpts from *Amy Vanderbilt's Etiquette* (1972) by Amy Vanderbilt (1908–1974)[93]

Amy Vanderbilt was considered an expert on etiquette after the publication of the first edition of her best-selling Amy Vanderbilt's Complete Book of Etiquette *in 1952. This book has been updated and republished several times; the most recent edition in 1995.*

Behavior During Engagements

Good manners always dictate that men and women be restrained about public demonstrations of their physical feeling toward one another. While it is my conviction that decisions about premarital sexual relations are a private matter, a couple does have obligations toward themselves, society, and their parents. First, they should exercise considerable discretion in their conduct. And second, any girl thinking of taking this important step, be she engaged or not, should consult a gynecologist, or at least her family doctor, to received instruction about contraception. It may surprise you to learn that in one state alone one out of every four girls is pregnant when she marries. It is not possible to estimate how many of these marriages are forced. But it is wise to note that necessity is not a good basis for marriage, and that not all engagements lead inevitably to marriage.[94]

A Girl and her Car

When a girl is driving, the young man still shows her the same courtesy as if he were in the driver's seat. The traditional courtesies in the matter are passing but the girl should at least hesitate to see whether a boy expects to help her out of a car before jumping out on her own. Sometimes a boy who has prepared himself for a courteous gesture feels snubbed if the girl barges ahead like a militant woman. Few girls like to be overprotected, but behavior on their part that denigrates the masculine role can also be destructive to the relationship. Men like to think of themselves as strong and protective. Would it hurt a girl hockey player to go along with this notion if it makes her date feel ten feet tall?[95]

Source 12
Excerpts from *Emily Post's Etiquette*, 14th edition (1985) by Elizabeth L. Post (1920–2010)[96]

Elizabeth L. Post was the granddaughter-in-law of etiquette writer Emily Post. She succeeded Emily Post at The Emily Post Institute and revised the works of Emily Post from 1865 to 1992, as well as writing on etiquette for several magazines.

Breaking the Ice

The changing relationship between men and women in general is challenging the established order of "boy asks girl" for a date. The girls say, "Why should we sit at home and wait to be invited out? Why, if we are equal to men, shouldn't we be free to ask them out?"

There is a certain amount of justice in this attitude, but I believe it can be self-defeating. Men or boys may be flattered by a woman who pursues them, but they may also feel that their masculinity is being threatened. If a young woman wants a young man to like her—and presumably she does if she wants to ask him out—she will be much wiser to let him *think* that it is his idea than to be too obvious. Of course she *can* do all the asking she wants, and she probably won't even be criticized with the current approval of woman's independence, but she may find that she is alienating the very person she wants to impress. A young woman who knows how to use her femininity and her charm to attract the man she wants, instead of displaying her independence and "strength" to bowl him over, has a far better chance of success. The same general rule applies to telephone calls and to writing letters.

The girl who wants to make a boy aware of her, without seeming to be pushy, can:

- Persuade a mutual friend to invite them both to a small party.
- Go to all school events in which he takes part.
- Join clubs and organizations to which he belongs.
- Ask a girl who knows him to arrange a double date.

Going Steady

When a boy and girl date each other consistently, and they have an agreement that neither is to date anyone else, they are "going steady"; this may be formalized by an exchange of friendship rings or identification bracelets.

For several reasons, this in an unfortunate practice. A wise young person should widen rather than narrow his or her circle of friends. Unfortunately, many girls fear not having a date for Saturday night, and some boys are afraid to be told "No" when they call a girl for a date, so they decide to protect themselves by having ready-made dates. But these young people are restricting the development of their own experience when they limit their dating friendships. Only by meeting other young people of varied backgrounds and interests can a boy or girl gain enough insight to be capable of making a good judgment regarding more permanent relationships.

The constant "togetherness" of going steady also poses a sexual problem. Boys and girls are put in a position where it is difficult, if not impossible, to resist their urges, even though they may want to.

Extending the Theme

Analyze Modern Etiquette Advice

Ask students to collect examples of twenty-first-century etiquette advice related to a specific topic from the Internet, magazines, newspapers, or books. For example, students might collect advice on behavior related to dating, table manners, or special occasions. Ask students to look for patterns in the rules that are prescribed. Do the same rules appear over and over, or are there variations? What rules are missing? Who is writing the advice? Who is the audience?

Is the advice similar to other advice or are new manners proposed? After students identify patterns, ask them to analyze those patterns using the lenses of sex, gender, culture, social status, or generational values. Also, direct students to consider how local and regional culture can influence manners and social behavior. For example, how might romantic socializing among students be different in a city with public transportation and in a rural or suburban setting in which people must travel by car?

Oral History Interviews

Encourage students to do oral history interviews with family members or other adults from previous generations. Assist students in writing interview questions in preparation for the interview that focus on the themes of generational change, differences in manners between social status groups and cultures, or the differing expectations of behavior for men and women.

Create Etiquette Manuals

Students can write etiquette manuals describing the socially acceptable manners in their home or school (descriptive) or create new rules for a utopian world they wish existed (prescriptive). Ask students to analyze the patterns in their own etiquette guides, comparing and contrasting their own enculturation from family, friends, and media, and reflecting upon the process that resulted in their own expectations for behavior.

Evaluate Self-improvement Books

The self-improvement book is the modern best-selling equivalent of the etiquette book of previous centuries. Economic insecurity, the uncertain job markets of the late twentieth and early twenty-first centuries, and a new emphasis on emotional well-being or "happiness" as a requirement for personal success are the economic and cultural shifts that drive the sales of these books.[97]

Ask students to research and categorize the types of self-help books available for sale. Students can visit stores or websites of popular booksellers and search for the "self-help" or "self-improvement" sections. Ask students to read the titles and book descriptions and categorize the books by status or background of the author, intended audience, or promised outcomes if the advice is followed. Students should consider in what circumstances the promised outcomes will probably not occur, even if the advice is followed.

Follow up with discussion of the impact of self-help books on the lives of readers and the agency of individuals to make changes in their own lives or in a wider society. For example, can individuals always make a radical change in their lives when confronted with difficult challenges inherent in the wider society, such as poverty, lack of employment in one's community, or economic barriers to a higher education or relocation? Does success or failure depend solely upon an individual?

In a recent analysis of the self-help genre, a sociologist argued that many of these books sell an unattainable fantasy. The self-help message that wealth, social success, and personal happiness are available to everyone, as long as the individual works hard enough at it and follows the advice in the self-help book, suggests that all failures are personal shortcomings.[98] In other words, self-help books assume that individuals have *all* of the agency to make their lives a success without acknowledging that inequities exist, such as lack of wealth, racial or sex discrimination, or differing social status.

Notes

1. J. D. Salinger, *The Catcher in the Rye* (Boston: Little, Brown, and Company, 1951), 87.
2. Micki McGee, *Self-Help, Inc.: Makeover Culture in American Life* (Oxford: Oxford University Press, 2005), 11.
3. C. Dallett Hemphill, *Bowing to Necessities: A History of Manners in America, 1620–1860* (New York: Oxford University Press, 2002), 3–4.
4. H. R. French, "The Search for the 'Middle Sort' of People in England, 1600–1800," *The Historical Journal* 43, no. 1 (2000): 282.
5. Christina Kotchemidova, "From Good Cheer to 'Drive-by Smiling': A Social History of Cheerfulness," *Journal of Social History* 39, no. 1 (Autumn 2005): 6, http://www.jstor.org/stable/3790528.
6. John F. Kasson, *Rudeness and Civility: Manners in Nineteenth-Century Urban America* (New York: Hill & Wang, 1990), 258.
7. Jorge Arditi, *A Genealogy of Manners: Transformations of Social Relations in France and England from the Fourteenth to the Eighteenth Century* (Chicago: University of Chicago Press, 1998), 4.
8. *Oxford English Dictionary Online*, s.v. "courtesy, n.," March 2016, http://www.oed.com/view/Entry/43220?rskey=rXkcKQ&result=1&isAdvanced=false.
9. *Oxford English Dictionary Online*, s.v. "civility, n.," December 2015, http://www.oed.com/view/Entry/33581?redirectedFrom=civility.
10. *Oxford English Dictionary Online*, s.v. "etiquette, n.," March 2016, http://www.oed.com/view/Entry/64853?redirectedFrom=etiquette.
11. Norbert Elias, *The History of Manners: The Civilizing Process*, vol. 1, trans. Edmund Jephcott (New York: Pantheon Books, 1978).

12. Full text available online: Baldassare Castiglione, *The Book of the Courtier* at https://archive.org/details/bookofcourtier00castuoft.

13. Esther Aresty, *The Best Behavior: The Course of Good Manners: From Antiquity to the Present, as Seen through Courtesy and Etiquette Books* (New York: Simon & Schuster, 1970), 62–75.

14. Beth Bailey, "Manners and Etiquette," in *Encyclopedia of American Social History*, vol. 2, Mary Kupiec Cayton, Elliott J. Gorn, and Peter W. Williams, eds. (New York: Charles Scribner's Sons, 1993), 1349–53.

15. Philip Carter, "Polite 'Persons': Character, Biography and the Gentleman," *Transactions of the Royal Historical Society*, 12 (2002): 333–54, http://www.jstor.org/stable/3679351.

16. Carter, "Polite 'Persons': Character, Biography and the Gentleman," 337.

17. Ibid., 344.

18. Full text available online: Richard Allestree, *Ladies Calling* at https://archive.org/details/ladiescallingin00allegoog.

19. Full text available online: *The Whole Duty of a Woman* at https://archive.org/details/wholedutyawoman00unkngoog.

20. Ingrid H. Tague, *Women of Quality: Accepting and Contesting Ideals of Femininity in England, 1690–1760* (Woodbridge, Suffolk, UK: Boydell & Brewer, 2002), 23–24, http://www.jstor.org/stable/10.7722/j.ctt81gd7.7.

21. Carter, "Polite 'Persons': Character, Biography and the Gentleman," 345.

22. Ibid., 346.

23. Ibid., 352; Arthur M. Schlesinger, *Learning How to Behave: A Historical Study of American Etiquette* (New York: The Macmillan Company, 1946), 9, 11–12.

24. *Oxford English Dictionary Online*, s.v. "etiquette, n.," March 2016, http://www.oed.com/view/Entry/64853?redirectedFrom=etiquette.

25. Alexander Hamilton, *Gentleman's Progress: The Itinerarium of Dr. Alexander Hamilton, 1744*, ed. Carl Bridenbaugh (Chapel Hill, University of North Carolina Press, 1948), 184; full text online: Early Americans Digital Archive at http://mith.umd.edu/eada/html/display.php?docs=hamilton_itinerarium.xml, section 614.

26. Full text available online: Alexis De Tocqueville, "Chapter XIV, Some Reflections on American Manners," in *Democracy in America* at http://xroads.virginia.edu/~hyper/detoc/ch3_14.htm.

27. Full text available online: Frances Trollope, *Domestic Manners of Americans* at https://archive.org/details/domesticmannerso00troliala.

28. Bailey, "Manners and Etiquette," 1348–49.

29. Schlesinger, *Learning How to Behave*, 18.

30. Kasson, *Rudeness and Civility*, 44.

31. Ibid., 44–54.

32. Hemphill, *Bowing to Necessities*, appendix.

33. Karen Halttunen, *Confidence Men and Painted Women, A Study of Middle-Class Culture in America 1830–1870* (New Haven, CT: Yale University Press, 1982), 191–97.

34. Mark C. Carnes, "The Rise and Consolidation of Bourgeois Culture," in *Encyclopedia of American Social History*, vol. 1, eds. Mary Kupiec Cayton, Elliott J. Gorn, and Peter W. Williams (New York: Charles Scribner's Sons, 1993), 616.

35. Hemphill, *Bowing to Necessities*, 222.

36. Linda Kerber, "The Republican Mother: Women and the Enlightenment: An American Perspective," *American Quarterly* 28, no. 2 (1976): 187–205.

37. Barbara Welter, "The Cult of True Womanhood: 1820–1860," *American Quarterly* 18, No. 2, Part 1 (Summer 1966), 151–52.

38. Nancy F. Cott, *The Bonds of Womanhood: 'Woman's Sphere' in New England, 1780–1835* (New Haven, CT: Yale University Press, 1997), 63–64, eBook Collection, EBSCOhost, accessed August 10, 2016.

39. Full text available online: Lydia Maria Child, *The Mother's Book* (1831) at https://archive.org/details/mothersbook1831chil.

40. Full text available online: Lydia Sigourney, *Letters to Mothers* (1838) at https://archive.org/details/letterstomother00sigogoog.

41. Hemphill, *Bowing to Necessities*, 218–19.

42. Schlesinger, *Learning How to Behave*, chapter V, "Relax!" 49–61.

43. Ibid., 49–50.

44. Lynn Dumenil, *The Modern Temper, American Culture and Society in the 1920s* (New York: Hill and Wang, 1995), 85–86.

45. Warren Susman, *Culture as History, The Transformation of American Society in the Twentieth Century* (New York: Pantheon Books, 1973, 1984), 273–77, 280.

46. Cas Wouters, "Etiquette Books and Emotion Management in the Twentieth Century: Part One: The Integration of Social Classes," *Journal of Social History* 29, no. 1 (Autumn 1995), 107–124, http://www.jstor.org/stable/3788711.

47. Leonore Davidoff, *The Best Circles, Society Etiquette and the Season* (London, UK: Croom Helm, 1973), 60.

48. *Oxford English Dictionary Online*, s.v. "snob, n.1," March 2016, http://www.oed.com/view/Entry/183348?rskey=IQofDo&result=1&isAdvanced=false.

49. Emily Post, *Etiquette: The Blue Book of Social Usage* (New York, NY: Funk & Wagnalls Company, 1940), x.
50. Full text available: E. Azalia Hackley, *The Colored Girl Beautiful* (1916) at https://archive.org/details/coloredgirlbeaut00hack.
51. Full text available: Silas X. Floyd, *Floyd's Flowers, or Duty and Beauty for Colored Children* (1905) at https://catalog.hathitrust.org/Record/100207574.
52. Full text available: Edward S. Green, *National Capital Code of Etiquette* (1920) at https://archive.org/details/nationalcapitalc00greerich.
53. Katharine Capshaw Smith, "Childhood, the Body, and Race Performance: Early 20th-Century Etiquette Books for Black Children," *African American Review* 40, no. 4 (Winter 2006): 795–811, http://www.jstor.org/stable/40033754.
54. Bailey, "Manners and Etiquette," 1353.
55. Bailey, *From Front Porch to Back Seat*, 13–18.
56. Bailey, "Manners and Etiquette," 1353–55.
57. Bailey, *From Front Porch to Back Seat*, 8.
58. Margaret Visser, *The Rituals of Dinner: The Origins, Evolution, Eccentricities, and Meaning of Table Manners* (New York: Grove Weidenfeld, 1991), 353–57.
59. Shel Silverstein, *Where the Sidewalk Ends* (New York: Harper Collins Publishers, 1974), 37.
60. John Locke, *Some Thoughts Concerning Education*. Vol. XXXVII, Part 1. The Harvard Classics. (New York: P. F. Collier & Son, 1909–14) sections 41–50, http://www.bartleby.com/37/1/5.html.
61. *The Whole Duty of a Woman*. (London: T. Read, 1737), 21, https://archive.org/stream/wholedutyawoman00unkngoog#page/n29/mode/2up.
62. Philip Dormer Stanhope, 4th Earl of Chesterfield, *Letters to His Son. On the Art of Becoming a Man of the World and a Gentleman* (The Project Gutenberg EBook: 2004, updated 2012), http://www.gutenberg.org/files/3361/3361-h/3361-h.htm.
63. Ibid., "LETTER CLXXXII," http://www.gutenberg.org/files/3361/3361-h/3361-h.htm#link2H_4_0184.
64. Ibid., "LETTER CLXXXVI," http://www.gutenberg.org/files/3361/3361-h/3361-h.htm#link2H_4_0188.
65. Benjamin Franklin, *Autobiography of Benjamin Franklin* (New York: Henry Holt and Company, 1916), http://www.gutenberg.org/files/20203/20203-h/20203-h.htm.
66. Mary Wollstonecraft, *A Vindication of the Rights of Woman* (The Project Gutenberg EBook: 2002), http://www.gutenberg.org/cache/epub/3420/pg3420-images.html.
67. Ibid., dedication.
68. Ibid., chapter 3.
69. Ibid., chapter 6.
70. John Adams, "To the Officers of the First Brigade for the Third Division of the Militia of Massachusetts, October 11, 1798," in *The Works of John Adams, Second President of the United States: With a Life of the Author, Notes and Illustrations*, Vol. 9 (Boston: Little, Brown, 1854), 228–29; Google Play Books, https://play.google.com/store/books/details?id=-Wh3AAAAMAAJ&rdid=book--Wh3AAAAMAAJ&rdot=1.
71. Jane Austen, *Sense and Sensibility*, in *The Works of Jane Austen* (London, UK: Allan Wingate, 1962), chapter 1, 2–3. Full text available online: http://austen.com/sense/.
72. Additional texts available online about visiting cards: L. N. Howard, *Etiquette of Visiting Cards* (Brooklyn, NY: Collins and Co., 1880), https://archive.org/details/etiquetteofvisit00howa; Abby B. Longstreet, *Cards: Their Significance and Proper Uses* (New York: Frederick A. Stokes & Brother, 1889) http://babel.hathitrust.org/cgi/pt?id=hvd.hn39xi;view=1up;seq=7.
73. Mary E. Sherwood, *Manners and Social Usages* (New York: Harper and Brothers, 1884), 16–17, https://archive.org/stream/mannerssocialus00sher#page/16/mode/2up.
74. Ibid., 147.
75. Mary E. Sherwood, *Manners and Social Usages* (New York: Harper and Brothers, 1912), 276–77, 279.
76. Emily Post, *Etiquette in Society, in Business, in Politics and at Home* (New York: Funk & Wagnalls Company, 1922), http://www.bartleby.com/br/95.html.
77. Ibid., 73.
78. Ibid., 80–81.
79. Ibid., 299–300.
80. Esther Floyd, *Hints on Etiquette: Little Blue Book No. 556* (Girard, KS: Haldeman-Julius Company, 1924), 24–25.
81. Emily Post, *Etiquette: The Blue Book*, 375.
82. M'Ledge Moffett, *When We Meet Socially, A Guidebook to Good Form in Social Conventions* (New York: Prentice-Hall Inc., 1940), 37–40.
83. Amy Vanderbilt, *Amy Vanderbilt's Compete Book of Etiquette, A Guide to Gracious Living* (Garden City, NY: Doubleday & Company, Inc., 1954).

84. Ibid., 538–39.
85. Ibid., 115.
86. Evelyn Millis Duvall, *The Art of Dating* (New York: Association Press, 1958), 183, http://hdl.handle.net/2027/mdp.39015023172102.
87. Margaret Gevans and editors of *McCall's Magazine*, *McCall's Book of Everyday Etiquette, A Guide to Modern Manners* (New York: Golden Press, 1960).
88. Ibid., 11.
89. Ibid., 26–28.
90. Helen Gurley Brown, *Sex and the Single Girl* (New York, NY: Bernard Geis Associates, 1962), 5–10.
91. Ibid., 5–10.
92. *Modern Etiquette*, Dell Purse Books (New York: Dell Publishing Co., Inc., 1963), 61, 63.
93. Amy Vanderbilt, *Amy Vanderbilt's Etiquette* (Garden City, NY: Doubleday & Company, Inc., 1972).
94. Ibid., 17–18.
95. Ibid., 713.
96. Elizabeth L. Post, *Emily Post's Etiquette*, 14th edition (New York: Harper & Row, 1985), 313, 316.
97. McGee, *Self Help*, introduction.
98. Ibid., 13.

Additional Resources

Aresty, Esther. *The Best Behavior: The Course of Good Manners: From Antiquity to the Present, as Seen through Courtesy and Etiquette Books*. New York: Simon & Schuster, 1970.

    A description of advice literature from ancient Egypt to twentieth-century America, with a very useful bibliography of courtesy books from all time periods.

Bailey, Beth L. *From Front Porch to Back Seat: Courtship in Twentieth-Century America*. Baltimore: Johns Hopkins University Press, 1989.

    A scholarly but readable book that is excellent for the preparation of more lessons or units on the shift from courtship to dating in the late nineteenth and twentieth centuries.

Carson, Gerald. *The Polite Americans, A Wide-Angle View of Our More or Less Good Manners over 300 Years*. New York: William Morrow & Company. 1966.

    Very readable overview with a few images and an excellent bibliography for finding more primary or secondary sources on the topic of manners.

Coontz, Stephanie. *Marriage, a History: How Love Conquered Marriage*. New York: Penguin Books, 2005.

    A history of marriage from ancient to modern times that relates marriage to wider cultural, political, and economic themes. I highly recommend this book to all teachers interested in social history.

Coronet Instructional Films. Short videos on marriage, dating, and other topics from the 1940s, 1950s, and 1960s. Students will love them! Titles include *What to Do on a Date* (1951); *Dating Do's and Don'ts* (1949); and *Are You Popular?* (1947). Many are available at Internet Archive, https://archive.org/.

"Glory of Woman: An Introduction to Prescriptive Literature." Duke University Libraries, http://guides.library.duke.edu/c.php?g=289854&p=1931558.

    This excellent website provides additional information about prescriptive literature and an extensive bibliography of works from 1630 to the present.

Peril, Lynn. *Pink Think, Becoming a Woman in Many Uneasy Lessons*. New York: W. W. Norton and Company, 2002.

    Highly recommended for the teacher, but some content may be too mature for middle and high school students. The author combines her own experiences growing up in the mid-twentieth century with an examination of various items from that period—advice books, teen magazines, textbooks, toys, clothing, beauty products, and fiction—that conveyed the "pink think" message. "Pink think" is defined as "a set of ideas and attitudes about what constitutes proper female behavior."

    This book is easy to read, provides ideas for primary source objects and texts that can be studied by students, and is very funny. The author includes a chapter on the expectations for boys, a helpful resource that can be used to remind students that gender expectations limit both men and women, forcing them to act in strange ways and creating artificial lines between them.

Schlesinger, Arthur M. *Learning How to Behave: A Historical Study of American Etiquette Books.* New York: The Macmillan Company, 1946.
    Older, but short and very readable history of American manners from a well-known historian who was doing social history before it became popular.

CHAPTER FOUR

Exploring More Themes

The previous chapters outline the social history of manners and vacations and provide primary source excerpts selected to encourage students to analyze two different themes relevant to the lives of students through the lenses of popular culture, sex, gender, and social class. Hopefully, these chapters have inspired you to introduce thematic teaching in your classroom and research additional themes that are of interest to you. This final chapter provides some guidance on how to research themes, locate relevant primary sources, and organize the information and sources around essential questions that are relevant to the courses you teach and the lives of students.

Choosing a Theme

Choose a theme that interests you, is applicable to the classes that you teach, and is of interest to students, in that order. If you choose a theme of little interest to you, thematic instruction will become a burden, not an adventure. The themes in this book are of interest to me personally, and they are relevant to the issues of sex, gender, and social class, concepts that I believe should be addressed in the classroom. Furthermore, since I prefer social history over political or economic history, the research and teaching focuses on themes relevant to the lives of everyday people. Your interests may be different. If I had been required to research and locate primary sources related to the history of government regulation of tourism and travel, the results would have disappointing.

Relevance to your teaching assignments is also important. Thematic teaching can be integrated with any set of teaching standards. If you teach several different classes, consider themes that can be relevant across each course. At first glance, you may think that your personal interests may not align directly with the content you are assigned to teach. For example, you may teach about ancient civilizations but prefer modern themes. Consider how to expand your theme. For example, if you are interested in travel by air or rail, expand your theme to transportation in the preindustrial world. Brainstorm with other teachers to choose themes that may also be relevant across the curriculum.

A partnership between the social studies and literature teachers can result in cross-disciplinary connections. For example, students might read travel literature in one class and study why vacations became more popular as the middle class expanded in the nineteenth century. If you are unable to find a teacher who is willing to become a thematic partner, then examine the curriculum of other courses and make connections in your own teaching to the content your students are learning in other disciplines. Your colleagues will be impressed and more interested in thematic partnerships when mutual students say, "We learned about this in Mr./Ms. _____'s class!"

Any theme you choose should have relevance to the lives of your students so that they can make past-present connections and critically analyze the theme as it pertains to their own lives. Consider surveying students about their interests; you are sure to find at least one area in which your interests, the interests of your students, and the required curriculum overlap.

For example, students may express interest in various forms of current popular music. This interest can be used to develop several different units and lessons related to types of popular music across time and cultures; how cultures interact and impact one another, using music as an example; the interaction of folk, popular, and elite cultures; or music as an important vehicle of social and political commentary through history. Music from the past can be examined through the lenses of social class, ethnicity, race, or sex and gender, and students may consider their own favorite artists and songs in a new light.

Social history is the underlying thread that connects the themes that interest me, but themes are adaptable. A social history theme can be expanded to highlight enduring political, economic, or geographic issues. For example, travel for leisure can be used as a framework to examine many topics from many academic disciplines. Government policies impact travel for leisure both positively and negatively. Worldwide political unrest, natural disasters, and epidemics impact vacation patterns, to the detriment of some destinations and to the advantage of others.

Themes can be selected that highlight persistent problems or challenges faced by society, such as war or poverty; ongoing debates about who should hold political power; economic issues such as taxes, wages, or debt; or issues usually considered within the realm of the natural sciences or professional studies—agriculture, business, architecture, engineering, technology, or medicine.

How to Research a Theme

Researching a theme over time is rewarding, but it can also be time-consuming. Begin with a focus on a time period that is most relevant to one particular class or unit that you teach and then move outward. My interest in the theme of vacations began when I learned that mineral spring resorts in my state of Kentucky were popular tourist destinations before the Civil War. I was able to make my research on nineteenth-century Kentucky immediately relevant to a place-based education and local history course I was teaching. Then, my research grew outward in time and scope from there. Over time, you can locate more resources and increase the depth and breadth of your knowledge to make connections to more units that you teach.

Keep the End in Mind: The Essential Question

A theme is a vehicle to help students connect historical information to the critical analysis of wider issues, current events, local history, or daily life and culture. The essential question provides the focus for the themed lesson or teaching unit; it is the equivalent of a thesis in an essay or book. A thesis and an essential question are both theories or propositions to be discussed, proven, or disproven. Without good essential questions, your theme may disintegrate into just a bunch of facts.

Good teaching in social studies is not just about relaying facts, dates, and information. Good teaching is using facts and concepts about a topic to help students scrutinize the bigger picture of life. For example, students will think it is hilarious when they learn that adults in the fifteenth century must have been farting, belching, and picking their nose at the table on a regular basis, since so many advice books addressed those topics. But these facts have little relevance to the modern world. The bigger essential questions are why have expectations for behavior changed, what caused the change, and why do we reject or accept the expectations of our culture?

If you have not used essential or compelling questions as unit and lesson organizers, read the work of Jay McTighe and Grant Wiggins on essential questions[1] and review the purpose of compelling questions in the *College, Career, and Civic Life (C3) Framework*. Throughout the process of researching the theme and choosing primary sources, continually brainstorm, record, and revise possible questions. Pay special attention to the theses of the scholarly books and articles that you read during your research, as these can often be adapted for the classroom.

The best essential questions will often go through several revisions as you research and develop lessons. In the end, you will have overarching essential or compelling questions that relate to your discipline, the lives of your students, and the critical thinking and writing skills you want to teach, and that make your theme relevant to the big and important issues of modern life.

Doing the Research—Secondary Sources

Books

Try beginning your research on a theme with a search for books. Books that provide a history of a particular topic through time have become very popular; books have been published about the history of sugar, salt, cod, and medicine, just to name a few. If social history is your main interest, try general searches of libraries and bookstores that include "social history of" to discover the wide range of titles available.

If you are uncertain about a topic, consult the *Encyclopedia of American Social History*,[2] a three-volume set that provides a comprehensive overview of numerous social history topics. The two-volume *The Oxford Encyclopedia of American Social History*[3] summarizes the most up-to-date scholarship on a topic. Both include short bibliographies of influential works on each topic by historians and social scientists.

In your research, be conscious of the hierarchy of books on history, which ranges from popular titles written by professional writers or journalists to very specialized books written by professional scholars. Popular titles can offer interesting and easy-to-read overviews of a theme. But keep in mind that these are often written by people who are not trained historians. The authors may summarize, speculate, or assume things that are not accurate for the time period that is covered. Many are written from other secondary works, without reference to the primary sources used by historians.

For example, popular biographies about historical queens often overemphasize the romantic lives of monarchs and attribute modern assumptions about love, marriage, or other issues that are anachronistic and not supported by surviving primary sources. Popular histories are usually written in narrative style. They tell the story chronologically with interesting facts and details, but may not have a wider, overarching thesis that connects the person or event to political, economic, or social themes. Plus, popular titles rarely include endnotes or footnotes, and these bibliographic notes are a great help when researching a theme and searching for primary sources.

Scholarly books or monographs (books on one particular historical topic) can be much more valuable for this type of research. Books in this category are written by specialists in their field of study, and many work as university professors. Scholarly books are built around a thesis, an argument that is proven using evidence from primary sources or other research data. Scholarly authors also build their theses on previous scholarly books and journal articles by referencing the previous scholarship, accepting or rejecting it, and pointing out flaws in reasoning. Footnotes or endnotes document the primary and secondary sources that are used.

Pay close attention to the sources listed in the endnotes or footnotes. The references can lead you to more relevant books and articles on your topic and a wealth of primary sources that can be used in your classroom. The previous chapters include endnotes. Consult these sources for more information about each theme.

Occasionally, scholarly works may have been written with a general reader in mind and do not include footnotes or endnotes. Most of these do include extensive bibliographies. For example, historian Jack Larkin's *The Reshaping of Everyday Life, 1790–1840*[4] is one of my favorite social histories. While the chapters are not footnoted, the bibliography is extensive and is divided into sections for primary sources and secondary sources. It is one of several excellent books in the Everyday Life in America series with volumes on every period of American history.

The Daily Life through History series by Greenwood Press are examples of books that summarize scholarly primary and secondary sources but are written in a style that is appropriate for students. These books are written by a wide range of authors, and each includes an extensive bibliography. One caution about this series—in the ones I've reviewed, the authors do not always clearly explain how the lives of people in different social classes differed, and students may assume that everyone in a particular period lived like the middle or upper classes.

But scholarly books can be more challenging to find and read than popular titles. Scholarly books are usually more expensive than popular titles, so preview a scholarly title before you buy. You may find some scholarly titles in your local community library, but the best source is university libraries. Access to a university library can vary depending upon your location, but always check at your school library or nearest community library about their interlibrary loan services. Many libraries will get titles for you on loan from other libraries for free or at low cost. More and more scholarly books are available in e-book formats for purchase, as well as through libraries.

Scholarly books can be very long, very dense, and may use specialist terminology—all barriers when time is valuable. When reading a scholarly book or article, always locate the thesis of the author first. It is the framework that holds the facts, concepts, and primary sources together. An understanding of the thesis will help determine if the work will be useful to develop your theme, make reviewing the content of middle chapters easier, and assist in formulating your own essential questions for the classroom. Some authors make the thesis easy to find, others spread it out over several pages. Read the introduction and first chapter and go straight to the final, summary chapter to find the thesis. Now, you are ready to review the middle chapters and assess the argument of the author.

Articles

Magazine and journal articles are also valuable resources for expanding knowledge of your theme and locating primary sources. Popular magazines like *American History*, *National Geographic*, or *Smithsonian* provide overviews of topics, but may not lead to additional secondary sources or primary sources. Scholarly journal articles, like scholarly books, are written by experts but are not easily located on the Internet or on the shelf at the local library or bookstore. Most are accessible through giant databases such as JSTOR (my favorite) or EBSCOhost, which includes Academic Search Complete.

Scholarly journals exist for every academic discipline and profession and publish new research in the field. Most are peer-reviewed, which means the articles are reviewed by specialists in the field for accuracy and relevancy before they are published. You may want to start your search with scholarly articles rather than books because it is easier to access the full text of articles online and they take less time to read.

If you locate a book that will be difficult to obtain, you may find articles by the same author with much of the same information. Reviews of scholarly books are published in academic journals and are more useful than the starred reviews by general readers on the websites of popular booksellers. Academic reviews are written by scholars and focus upon the thesis of the book and how it contributes to research in that particular field of study. Search for "review" and the name of the book in academic databases.

The Internet

The Internet and digital resources have dramatically changed the nature of doing research in recent years. Some of the tips provided here may appear old-fashioned in a world where Google seems to offer the answer to everything. But the quality of information from general websites ranges from terrific to terrible, and for many topics, terrible information seems to be much more prevalent and easy to find.

Furthermore, the Internet changes every day, so my best advice is to use information from websites and blogs very carefully. Wikipedia can be an excellent starting point to get a quick overview of a topic, but always scroll to the reference list at the bottom of a Wikipedia entry. The reference list can lead to useful secondary and primary sources, or it can reveal which information might not be reliable.

Only use information from the web that comes from reliable sources and cites those sources. Sadly, many sites for teachers contain undocumented historical information full of misconceptions and errors. The preferred websites or blogs are those of museums or other reputable academic organizations. You will discover excellent ideas, information, and references related to your favorite themes by subscribing to the social media feeds of museums, libraries, and archives.

Doing the Research—Locating Primary Sources

Digitization technology and the Internet have made more primary source materials available to more people than ever before. Availability and access to quality historical sources is no longer a problem. The challenge that teachers face is finding what is relevant and narrowing down the possibilities in a reasonable amount of time. Every teacher has entered the Internet labyrinth in search of quality teaching materials and looked up from the computer hours later disoriented, overwhelmed, and exhausted. The following are a few tips that can focus the search and save time.

First, search for quality lesson plans or units with primary sources that can be adapted to the theme being researched. Museums, libraries, and archives are creating and posting more and more teaching units and lessons that use the primary sources in their collections. Also, be sure to check the primary source resources already available in your school in published curriculum materials, textbook resources, and subscription databases. Usually, the English/language arts teachers are the first to learn about new primary source resources available because they have been adapting curriculum to the *Common Core Standards for Literacy* longer than social studies teachers.

As you research your chosen theme in the secondary sources, note the primary sources referenced by historians both in the text and in the footnotes. If a primary source that relates to your theme is quoted in the text, record that quote and all of the information provided about that primary source in the text, endnotes, and bibliography. The endnotes and/or bibliography will reference either a published version of a primary source or the original manuscript and its location.

Using this information, conduct an Internet search using the title of the source or a quote from the source. You may locate all or part of the primary source online. Many books with expired copyrights (published before the 1920s) are available in their entirety in online archives such as Internet Archive (https://archive.org/), HathiTrust's Digital

Library (https://www.hathitrust.org/), or Digital Public Library of America (https://dp.la/). Access to the materials in these archives is free, and users can create accounts to bookmark works to which they want to return. Often the original text can be viewed online and several different downloadable formats are offered.

Google Books is a useful tool that offers many out-of-copyright books in digital formats for free. You may also find primary sources online on the websites of organizations dedicated to providing these sources for teaching purposes. The Internet History Sourcebooks Project[5] by Fordham University is an example, with both full text and primary source excerpts arranged by historical eras and topics. Be sure to check with your school, community, and local university libraries. Many subscription databases are free to users through libraries and offer a wide variety of primary documents that can be used by students, teachers, and researchers (but not reproduced for profit without permission).

Primary sources that are not available online may be published in their entirety or excerpted in collections of primary sources. For example, many Greek, Roman, and medieval sources that were originally in manuscript format in languages other than English have been translated and edited by scholars. Edited editions of primary sources are especially helpful as they provide information about a source, its author, and the context in which the document was produced.

More and more collections of primary source excerpts, arranged by topics and themes, are published to be used as textbooks. These textbooks are generally intended for use in college classes, but the sources in these collections can be shortened and adapted for reading by younger students. Quick searches of online bookstores using the key words "primary source collection," "primary source reader," or "primary source textbook" can provide many available options related to your theme.

Some primary sources used by historians are only available in their original form and housed in museums and libraries. You may discover that a primary source has been digitized and made available online since the publication of the book or article in which the primary source was referenced. If not, and the primary source is just too good to pass up, contact the archive and inquire about the item. The staff may be willing to digitalize it for you.

Many smaller local institutions have archives of primary sources that may not be listed on websites. Call or visit the archives of local universities, historical societies, libraries, and museums and discuss the theme you are researching with the staff. Try visiting an archive at least once, as it can provide insight into the process of historical research used by historians.

Local historical societies and small museums are overlooked treasure troves of primary sources—letters, diaries, scrapbooks, photographs, local publications, and ephemera—that can be used to teach a social history theme in a local context. In most cases, these local institutions are thrilled to work with teachers to showcase their collections, and the staff will know about local history and have primary sources that you didn't even know existed! They may also be eager to work with your students on projects related to their collections.

Historical newspapers that served your city or state are especially valuable for making connections between national and international historical events and the local community. More and more historical newspapers are available online, in their original format, and in searchable databases. The Library of Congress offers Chronicling America, http://chroniclingamerica.loc.gov/, a free searchable database of American newspapers from across the nation from 1836 to 1922.

Some online newspaper archives, such as newspapers.com and the *New York Times* historical database, are open only to subscribers. Individuals must pay to access the collections, but your school, community, or university library may hold a subscription. State and local historical societies and state archives may provide access to a wider selection of local newspapers. If local newspapers are not available online, it is well worth the time to use the old-fashioned technology of microfilm to read issues from at least a few key years associated with your theme.

Many non-text primary sources are also available and are equally important in teaching. Images, film, art, and pictures of artifacts are available on museum and archive websites. As you do your research, note the images that are referenced or reproduced in the books or journal articles. Most will include the source of the image, and in many cases, you can locate that same image, with documentation that includes the date, artist, and context in which it was published or presented.

Beware of general searches for images using search engines like Google. Many of the images are undocumented and may not be what they appear. Some images have been altered or are being used to illustrate a time period or concept they do not represent. For example, paintings of historical subjects may have been produced decades or even centuries after the event and say more about the myth surrounding the event than what really occurred. *Examining the Evidence: Seven Strategies for Teaching with Primary Sources* by Hilary Mac Austin and Kathleen Thompson[6] provides excellent advice and strategies for locating and teaching with primary source images.

Figure 4.1. Example of a social history primary source donated by a friend. This postcard, mailed in 1930, is a primary source that documents the history of vacations, the popularity of mineral springs, tourism in Tennessee, and the history of a local community. Today, Whittle Springs Middle School is located on property that once belonged to the resort.
(Courtesy of David Wilson.) For more information about Whittle Springs, see Chrystal B. Talbott, "Hotel Plays Big Role in Whittle Springs' Past," Go Knoxville. accessed July 27, 2016, http://www.knoxnews.com/entertainment/life/chrystal-talbott-hotel-plays-big-role-in-whittle-springs-past-ep-510359495-355442281.html.

Social history primary sources from the last century can be found in unlikely places. My collection of ephemera comes from junk stories, yard sales, and items bound for the trash. I've been interested in etiquette books, old postcards, women's magazines, and road maps for years and have built an impressive collection from thrift and used bookstores. My budget is limited, and I certainly don't own any first edition texts from the seventeenth century or medieval manuscripts related to pilgrimage, but I have a collection of items that can be shared and analyzed with students.

It is likely that the theme you choose may be related to a hobby or collection that you already have. Tell your friends about your research, and they may have items to contribute. One of my friends contributed a stack of old magazines from the 1950s and 1960s that I can use to illustrate a number of different themes. Ask your relatives, and they may remember a box of family papers or other ephemera in the attic.

As you assemble primary sources related to your theme, keep in mind that the farther back in time you go, the more difficult it is to find information and relevant primary sources about the lives of regular people. But this shortage of evidence provides the opportunity for students to learn more about the work of historians, how they make conclusions about the past, and the changing nature of historical knowledge as new discoveries and interpretations are made.

Reading and Interpreting the Primary Sources

As you read the secondary sources related to your theme and note the primary sources used by historians, your list of related primary sources is likely to grow very quickly. Reading, interpreting, and selecting the ones appropriate for the classroom can seem overwhelming due to the number, the length of many of the documents, or archaic language used in many primary sources. The following suggestions may be helpful.

Archaic and unfamiliar words or references in primary sources are a challenge faced by historians, teachers, and students. Words fall out of use, meanings change, and references to other people, places, or things lose their meaning outside of the time in which they were created. After all, will a reader in two hundred or two thousand years recognize the humor in quotes from twentieth-century television shows? In some cases, dictionaries or Internet searches can help to discover the meaning of the word, phrase, or reference. Internet searches can turn up some surprising results, but always question the source as some of the interpretations may be very wrong.

Many primary sources originally created in manuscript form or that have been translated into English have been published in critical editions—modern articles or books by an expert in the language and history of the source. Critical editions include extensive notes explaining antiquated terms and references. The same primary sources might be available on the Internet but without these detailed explanations.

Primary Source from a Local Historical Society. Photograph of the Monticello—Burnside, Kentucky, stagecoach (c. 1903). This photograph documents the history of a local community that was not served by a railroad, as well as the history of travel for leisure and business prior to the era of trains, automobiles, and airplanes. The stagecoach stopped service in 1915, long after most stagecoach lines had ceased to exist.
(Courtesy of the Wayne County Historical Society, Monticello, KY.)

Primary source translations available on the web are often from older, out of copyright translations, and while some of these translations are excellent, others may be in dated language and not take into account newer historical findings. For example, for the excerpts in this book, the author used recent critical editions of the medieval epics *The Pilgrimage of Charlemagne* and *William in the Monastery* that had been translated and commented upon by experts in medieval history.

The number and length of primary sources can also be a challenge when studying social history themes. In order to understand a time period, social historians often read as many different publications from an era as possible. For example, a historian studying nineteenth-century etiquette might read every available etiquette manual from the eighteenth and nineteenth centuries in order to assess continuity and change over time.

Historians studying vacations might read as many published and unpublished accounts of leisure travel as possible. But middle and high school teachers, no matter how dedicated to their theme, must teach students for the majority of every working day and grade papers at night. Reading every available primary source book, magazine, or newspaper on a topic is just not possible. Here is a shortcut: Read in their entirety a few of the primary sources cited most by historians and look for recurring themes. Historians will identify many themes relevant to their theses, but you are likely to find additional information that will be relevant to your students. You will be able to enter into the mind of the people of that era, and as you read, you can choose short excerpts for your students to read and analyze.

This can work with any large set of similar sources. For example, if your theme is sports, read the entire sports section of historical newspapers from just a few issues, maybe one newspaper from each month from a key year, or one newspaper from each year for twelve years, to gauge change over time.

Reading a set of primary sources in order to find recurring themes that represent attitudes or issues of an era is a key skill practiced by historians and is the focus of several of the student activities in this book. Here is a modern example from popular culture that can help your students understand how to analyze a set of primary source patterns that reflect the wider social, political, and economic issues.

I like zombie movies, but after watching just a few zombie movies, I discerned several predictable elements. For example, zombies are usually created by an out-of-control virus, most zombies are very slow, and the people who get killed by zombies usually die because they are standing around talking about their feelings instead of being alert to zombie attacks. A scholar of popular culture would ask, "How do these recurring elements reflect the culture of the late twentieth and early twenty-first centuries?" An answer could be that the out-of-control virus represents modern fears of antibiotic resistant diseases and biological warfare.

Ask your students to discern the patterns in zombie movies and TV shows and how those patterns reflect wider issues in modern culture. They will most likely see patterns and make relevant connections between recurring zombie themes and wider culture very quickly. The products of popular culture from the past—magazines, newspapers, prints, and even surviving medieval pilgrim badges—have similar themes and connections to the wider culture in which they were produced.

Another shortcut—if a long primary source is digitalized, learn to use the "search text" or "find" functions of the Internet browser or online archive and the search function for PDF documents. Search for key terms related to your theme. Be sure to use terms relevant to the time period being researched. For example, "vacation" defined as travel for leisure may not be referenced in documents from the early 1800s, but similar terms such as "travel," "resort," or "summer stay" may yield relevant results.

Consider the unique characteristics of the medium in which the primary source originally appeared. Manuscripts, books, newspapers, and magazines all have a unique history that is relevant to the interpretation of the text they contain, and good histories of all of these media have been written.[7] For example, magazines are a relatively "new" form of communication that began to be published in the eighteenth century. As with the history of manners and vacation, the story of the history of magazines involves technological innovation, commercialization, government policy, social class, ethnicity, race, sex, and gender.

Furthermore, much of the information about manners and vacations was conveyed through magazines. Information about the magazine in which an article first appeared provides many clues about the intended audience of the source. In the early years, magazine publishers depended upon costly subscriptions fees, which limited the number of readers to the upper classes. In the late nineteenth century, when publishers discovered the real profits came from advertising revenues, magazine prices fell and circulation boomed to include many more groups of people.[8] As magazines featured more and more advertising, the ads as well as the articles influenced perceptions of vacation and proper etiquette.

Creating Themed Units and Lessons

After you have researched your theme and collected related primary sources, you will be faced with the difficult task of narrowing down the information and sources to those that focus upon essential questions. A warning: you will probably have far too much material and deciding what to leave out is difficult. You will have wonderful, entertaining, and interesting information and sources that must be set aside. I personally have reams of secondary and primary source material related to vacations and manners in my collection that I sadly laid aside when making the final decisions about what to include in this book.

Choose the best essential questions for the lessons or units you plan to create from your list of possible essential questions and consider how the information and primary sources you have gathered can be used to answer those questions. Reflect on whether your best essential questions really connect to wider issues relevant to students and the content and skills that must be taught. Decide if the question is intended to lead students to make connections between the theme and issues in their own lives, to national or international current events, or to local issues. Choose one purpose; don't try to connect to everything in just one lesson.

Often students will make the additional connections naturally. You may want to sort the material you have assembled into physical or electronic folders by essential question to help in the selection of the best one. Also, remember that the essential question can serve as the focus of a wide range of assessments at the end of the lesson or unit. Once you have selected the essential question, start the work of planning the lesson or unit.

The next steps are choosing the best teaching strategies and learning activities for your students, making final decisions about which primary sources to include, editing sources, and creating reading guides. In order to narrow down the themed information and sources and to keep your units or lessons focused, continually ask yourself the following questions:

1. Will this information or primary source help students explore and answer the essential question(s)?
2. Will this information or primary source help students learn the content and skills I need to teach?

If a source is related to the essential question, but appears to be too long or difficult for your students, do not be shy about cutting, chopping, and annotating if needed. In other words, don't make my early mistake and throw the entire novel *Uncle Tom's Cabin* at students who were unprepared or unwilling to read it. If a source is long or written in dated or laborious language that is beyond the reading level of most of the students in your class, select relevant excerpts and simplify the language if needed. But don't make it too easy; it is better for students to be challenged than to be bored. If two different sources are saying the same thing, but one is written in easier language or is shorter, then both can be used to differentiate the reading assignment based on student reading levels.

Vocabulary skills are stressed in the *Common Core Standards for Literacy*, and primary source analysis can be an excellent opportunity to help students improve those skills. Therefore, if you edit a source, do not remove too many of the words that will challenge students. So as not to overwhelm students, I often choose a few words the majority of the students will not know and provide simple definitions in advance. But during the lesson, I ask students to identify other unknown words and determine their meanings based on their context in the text, and follow up with discussions of those words.

Reading and notetaking guides for students are crucial for three reasons. First, they clue students in to the most important parts of the text, something that is essential for a struggling reader and appreciated by all students. Second, requiring students to take notes on key points, or "cite the evidence,"[9] assists students in crafting an answer to the essential question. Furthermore, the note-taking guide can be used as a formative assessment. Finally, reading and notetaking guides provide a framework for small group discussion among students.

Many generic primary source analysis guides, reading guides, and note-taking formats that can be used with any reading or source are available and most are satisfactory. But you may prefer to create guides that are tailored to specific primary sources and that lead students in answering the essential question or focus on the key content or skill that is to be learned in the lesson. A generic guide that asks what, where, when, and why can be too broad for some sources, provide little assistance for struggling readers, and fail to help students connect the source to broader themes.

Conclusion

I hope you incorporate some form of thematic teaching into your classroom and are inspired to research and incorporate your own favorite themes in teaching. I cannot promise that thematic instruction will solve all of your classroom challenges. But you will start seeing relationships to your favorite themes everywhere you go. Your friends will be amazed, at least some of your students will be interested, and your administrators will be impressed with your ability to relate events in everyday life to wider culture. You may start planning vacations around visits to sites related to your themes and filling bookshelves, cabinets, and computer hard drives with photos, articles, books, and ephemera related to your favorite themes. But most importantly, you will be reminded why you love teaching—because you can learn new things and share your excitement about learning with students.

Notes

1. Jay McTighe and Grant Wiggins, *Essential Questions: Opening Doors to Student Understanding* (Alexandria, VA: Association for Supervision & Curriculum Development, 2013). For an overview see "Essential Questions: Opening Doors to Student Understanding," http://www.ascd.org/Publications/Books/Overview/Essential-Questions.aspx.

2. Mary Kupiec Cayton, Elliott J. Gorn, and Peter W. Williams, eds. *Encyclopedia of American Social History*, 3 vols. (New York: Charles Scribner's Sons, 1993).

3. Lynn Dumenil, ed. *The Oxford Encyclopedia of American Social History*, 2 vols. (Oxford/New York: Oxford University Press, 2012).

4. Jack Larkin, *The Reshaping of Everyday Life, 1790–1840*, Everyday Life in America Series, ed. Richard Balkin (New York: HarperPerennial, 1988).

5. Paul Halsall, ed. Internet History Sourcebooks Project. http://legacy.fordham.edu/halsall/index.asp.

6. Hilary Mac Austin and Kathleen Thompson, *Examining the Evidence: Seven Strategies for Teaching with Primary Sources* (North Mankato, MN: Maupin House/Capstone Professional, 2015).

7. Asa Briggs and Peter Burke, *A Social History of the Media from Gutenberg to the Internet*, 3rd ed. (Malden, MA: Polity Press, 2009) is recommended.

8. John Tebbel and Mary Ellen Zuckerman, *The Magazine in America, 1741–1990* (New York/Oxford: Oxford University Press, 1991).

9. "Cite specific textual evidence to support analysis of primary and secondary sources" is the first standard listed for grades 6–12 in the *Common Core English Language Arts Standards for History/Social Studies*. Common Core State Standards Initiative (2016) http://www.corestandards.org/ELA-Literacy/RH/introduction/. Accessed July 21, 2016.

Works Cited

Adams, John. "To the Officers of the First Brigade for the Third Division of the Militia of Massachusetts, October 11, 1798." In *The Works of John Adams, Second President of the United States: With a Life of the Author, Notes and Illustrations*, Vol. 9. Boston: Little, Brown, 1854. Google Play Books, https://play.google.com/store/books/details?id=-Wh3AAAAMAAJ&rdid=book--Wh3AAAAMAAJ&rdot=1.
"Amusement Parks and Theme Parks." In *Oxford Encyclopedia of American Social History*, Vol. 1, edited by Lynn Dumenil. Oxford. UK/New York: Oxford University Press, 2012: 37–39.
Arditi, Jorge. *A Genealogy of Manners: Transformations of Social Relations in France and England from the Fourteenth to the Eighteenth Century*. Chicago: University of Chicago Press, 1998.
Aresty, Esther. *The Best Behavior: The Course of Good Manners: From Antiquity to the Present, as Seen through Courtesy and Etiquette Books*. New York: Simon & Schuster, 1970.
Aron, Cindy S. *Working at Play: A History of Vacations in the United States*. Oxford/New York: Oxford University Press, 1999.
Austen, Jane. *Northanger Abbey*. In *The Works of Jane Austen*. London: Allan Wingate, 1962.
———. *Sense and Sensibility*. In *The Works of Jane Austen*. London: Allan Wingate, 1962.
Austin, Hilary Mac and Kathleen Thompson. *Examining the Evidence: Seven Strategies for Teaching with Primary Sources*. North Mankato, MN: Maupin House/Capstone Professional, 2015.
Bailey, Beth L. *From Front Porch to Back Seat: Courtship in Twentieth-Century America*. Baltimore: Johns Hopkins University Press, 1989.
———. "Manners and Etiquette." In *Encyclopedia of American Social History*, Vol. 2, edited by Mary Kupiec Cayton, Elliott J. Gorn, and Peter W. Williams, 1345–56. New York: Charles Scribner's Sons, 1993.
Barber, Sarah and Corinna Peniston-Bird. "Introduction." In *History Beyond the Text: A Student's Guide to Approaching Alternative Sources*. Abingdon, UK: Routledge, 2009.
Barron, Brigid and Linda Darling-Hammond. "How Can We Teach for Meaningful Learning?" In *Powerful Learning: What We Know about Teaching for Understanding*, edited by Linda Darling-Hammond, 11–70. San Francisco: Jossey-Bass, 2008.
Belasco, Warren James. *Americans on the Road, From Autocamp to Motel, 1910–1945*. Baltimore: The Johns Hopkins University Press, 1979.
Bem, Sandra Lipsitz. *The Lenses of Gender, Transforming the Debate on Sexual Inequality*. New Haven, CT: Yale University Press, 1993.
Berkowitz, Michael. "A 'New Deal' for Leisure: Making Mass Tourism During the Great Depression." In *Being Elsewhere: Tourism, Consumer Culture, and Identity in Modern Europe and North America*, edited by Shelley Osmun Baranowski and Ellen Furlough, 185–212. Ann Arbor: University of Michigan Press, 2001.
Boorstin, Daniel. *The Image: A Guide to Pseudo-Events in America*. New York: Harper & Row, 1964, 1961.
Briggs, Asa and Peter Burke. *A Social History of the Media from Gutenberg to the Internet*. 3rd ed. Malden, MA: Polity Press, 2009.
Brown, Helen Gurley. *Sex and the Single Girl*. New York: Bernard Geis Associates, 1962.
Brown, Peter. *The Cult of the Saints: Its Rise and Function in Latin Christianity*. Chicago: University of Chicago Press, 1982.
Buck Institute for Education. "Why Project Based Learning (PBL)?" Accessed April 28, 2016. http://www.bie.org.
Burgess, Glyn S., ed. and trans. *The Pilgrimage of Charlemagne (Le Pèlerinage de Charlemagne)*. Vol. 47, series A of the Garland Library of Medieval Literature. New York: Garland Publishing, Inc., 1988.

Works Cited

Burke, Peter. *Popular Culture in Early Modern Europe*. New York: New York University Press, 1978.

Butcher, Jim. *The Moralisation of Tourism: Sun, Sand . . . and Saving the World?* London/New York: Routledge, 2003.

Carnes, Mark C. "The Rise and Consolidation of Bourgeois Culture." In *Encyclopedia of American Social History*, Vol. 1, edited by Mary Kupiec Cayton, Elliott J. Gorn, and Peter W. Williams, 605–20. New York: Charles Scribner's Sons, 1993.

Carter, Philip. "Polite 'Persons': Character, Biography and the Gentleman." *Transactions of the Royal Historical Society*, 12 (2002): 333–54. http://www.jstor.org/stable/3679351.

Center for Place-Based Learning and Community Engagement. "What Is Place-Based Education?" Accessed April 28, 2016. http://promiseofplace.org/what_is_pbe.

Coffey, Thomas F., Linda Kay Davidson, and Maryjane Dunn, eds. and trans. *The Miracles of Saint James*. New York: Italica Press, 1996.

Coleman, J. Winston. "Old Kentucky Watering Places." *The Filson Club History Quarterly* 16 (January 1942): 1–26.

Common Core Standards Initiative. "English Language Arts Standards." Accessed April 28, 2016. http://www.corestandards.org/ELA-Literacy/.

Coontz, Stephanie. *The Way We Never Were: American Families and the Nostalgia Trap*. New York: Basic Books, 1992, 2002.

Cott, Nancy F. *The Bonds of Womanhood: 'Woman's Sphere' in New England, 1780–1835*. New Haven, CT: Yale University Press, 1997. eBook Collection, EBSCOhost. Accessed August 10, 2016.

Cross, Gary S. and John K. Walton. *The Playful Crowd: Pleasure Places in the Twentieth Century*. New York: Columbia University Press, 2005.

Davidoff, Leonore. *The Best Circles, Society Etiquette and the Season*. London, UK: Croom Helm, 1973.

Davidson, Linda Kay and Maryjane Dunn-Wood. *Pilgrimage in the Middle Ages: A Research Guide*. New York: Garland Publishing, 1993.

De Vitry, Jacques. *The History of Jerusalem A.D. 1190*. Translated by Aubrey Stewart. London, UK: Palestine Pilgrims' Text Society, 1885. https://archive.org/details/cu31924028534422.

Dumenil, Lynn. *The Modern Temper, American Culture and Society in the 1920s*. New York: Hill and Wang, 1995.

Duvall, Evelyn Millis. *The Art of Dating*. New York: Association Press, 1958. http://hdl.handle.net/2027/mdp.39015023172102.

Edwards, Richard Henry. *Christianity and Amusements*. New York: Association Press, 1915. https://play.google.com/store/books/details?id=Zy83AAAAMAAJ&rdid=book-Zy83AAAAMAAJ&rdot=1.

Einhard. *The Life of Charlemagne*. Translated by Lewis Thorpe. London/New York: Penguin Books, 1969.

Elias, Norbert. *The History of Manners: The Civilizing Process*. Vol. 1. Translated by Edmund Jephcott. New York, NY: Pantheon Books, 1978.

Ellis, Arthur K. and Carol J. Stuen. *The Interdisciplinary Curriculum*, Larchmont, NY: Eye on Education, 1998.

Ferrante, Joan M., trans. *Guillaume d'Orange: Four Twelfth-Century Epics*. New York/London: Columbia University Press, 1974.

Floyd, Esther. *Hints on Etiquette: Little Blue Book No. 556*. Girard, KS: Haldeman-Julius Company, 1924.

Fogarty, Robin. *The Mindful School: How to Integrate the Curricula*. Palatine, IL: Skylight Publishing, Inc., 1991.

Fogarty, Robin and Brian Pete. *How to Integrate the Curricula*. 3rd ed. Thousand Oaks, CA: Corwin Press, 2009.

Franklin, Benjamin. *Autobiography of Benjamin Franklin*. New York: Henry Holt and Company, 1916. http://www.gutenberg.org/files/20203/20203-h/20203-h.htm.

French, H. R. "The Search for the 'Middle Sort' of People in England, 1600–1800." *The Historical Journal* 43, no. 1 (2000): 277–93.

Fried, Stephen. *Appetite for America: Fred Harvey and the Business of Civilizing the Wild West—One Meal at a Time*. New York: Bantam, 2011. Kindle.

Fry, Richard and Rakesh Kochhar. "Are You in the American Middle Class? Find Out with Our Income Calculator." Pew Research Center, September 10, 2012. Accessed May 4, 2016. http://www.pewresearch.org/fact-tank/2016/05/11/are-you-in-the-american-middle-class/.

Gabriele, Matthew. *An Empire of Memory: The Legend of Charlemagne, The Franks, and Jerusalem before the First Crusade*. Oxford, UK: Oxford University Press, 2011.

Gassan, Richard. *The Birth of American Tourism: New York, the Hudson Valley, and American Culture, 1790–1835*. Amherst: University of Massachusetts Press, 2008.

Genovese, Eugene D. *Roll, Jordan, Roll: The World the Slaves Made*. New York: Vintage Books, 1976.

Gevans, Margaret and editors of McCall's Magazine. *McCall's Book of Everyday Etiquette, A Guide to Modern Manners*. New York: Golden Press, 1960.

Gibson, Jamesha. "Preservation Glossary. Today's Word: Heritage Tourism." (Blog) Last modified June 17, 2015. Accessed July 22, 2016. https://savingplaces.org/stories/preservation-glossary-todays-word-heritage-tourism#.V5ImQ6K1Zlc.

Gilbert, Dennis. *The American Class Structure in an Age of Growing Inequality*. 9th ed. Thousand Oaks, CA: Sage, 2015.

Gorky, Maxim. "Boredom." *The Independent* 63, no. 3062 (August 8, 1907): 309–17. https://babel.hathitrust.org/cgi/pt?id=pst.000020207205;view=1up;seq=331.

Grigsby, John L. *The Gab as a Latent Genre in Medieval French Literature, Drinking and Boasting in the Middle Ages*. Cambridge: Medieval Academy of America, 2000.

Halbwachs, Maurice. "Conclusions of the Legendary Topography of the Gospels in the Holy Land." In *On Collective Memory*, edited and translated by Lewis A. Coser. Chicago: University of Chicago Press, 1992.

Halttunen, Karen. *Confidence Men and Painted Women, A Study of Middle-Class Culture in America 1830–1870*. New Haven, CT: Yale University Press, 1982.

Hamilton, Alexander. *Gentleman's Progress: The Itinerarium of Dr. Alexander Hamilton, 1744*. Edited by Carl Bridenbaugh. Chapel Hill: University of North Carolina Press, 1948.

Hemphill, C. Dallett. *Bowing to Necessities: A History of Manners in America, 1620–1860*. New York: Oxford University Press, 2002.

Herlihy, David. *Medieval Households*. Cambridge, MA/London: Harvard University Press, 1985.

Hill, Rosalind, trans. *Gesta Francorum et Aliorum Hierosolimitanorum—The Deeds of the Franks and the Other Pilgrims to Jerusalem*. London: Thomas Nelson and Sons Ltd., 1962.

Hoade, Eugene, trans. "The Itineraries of Fr. Simon Fitzsimons (1322–23)." In *Western Pilgrims*. Jerusalem: Franciscan Printing Press, 1970.

Holt, Felicia. "Promiscuous Bathing." *Ladies' Home Journal* (August 1890), 6. https://babel.hathitrust.org/cgi/pt?id=mdp.39015012341569;view=1up;seq=280.

Hubert, Philip G. Jr. "Open Letters: Camping Out for the Poor." *The Century* 44, no. 4 (August 1892): 632–34. http://ebooks.library.cornell.edu/cgi/t/text/pageviewer-idx?c=cent;cc=cent;rgn=full%20text;idno=cent0044-4;didno=cent0044-4;view=image;seq=643;node=cent0044-4%3A30;page=root;size=100.

Hunt, E. D. "Travel, Tourism and Piety in the Roman Empire: A Context for the Beginnings of Christian Pilgrimage." *Echos De Monde Classique* 28 no. 3 (1984): 391–417.

Kasson, John F. *Rudeness and Civility: Manners in Nineteenth-Century Urban America*. New York: Hill & Wang, 1990.

Kerber, Linda. "The Republican Mother: Women and the Enlightenment: An American Perspective." *American Quarterly* 28, no. 2 (1976): 187–205.

Kornblith, Gary J. and Carol Lasser. "More Than Great White Men: A Century of Scholarship on American Social History." *OAH Magazine of History* 21, no. 2 (April 2007): 8–13.

Kotchemidova, Christina. "From Good Cheer to 'Drive-by Smiling': A Social History of Cheerfulness." *Journal of Social History* 39, no. 1 (Autumn 2005): 5–37. http://www.jstor.org/stable/3790528.

Kovalik, Susan and Karen Olsen. *ITI: The Model, Integrated Thematic Instruction*. Federal Way, WA: Susan Kovalik & Associates, 1993.

Kyvig, David E. and Myron A. Marty. *Nearby History, Exploring the Past Around You*. 3rd ed. Lanham, MD: Altamira Press/Rowman & Littlefield, 2010.

Lake, Kathy. "Integrated Curriculum." School Improvement Research Series VIII. Portland, OR: Northwest Regional Educational Laboratory, 1994. Accessed April 28, 2016. http://educationnorthwest.org/webfm_send/528.

Larkin, Jack, *The Reshaping of Everyday Life, 1790–1840*. New York: HarperPerennial, 1988.

Locke, John. *Some Thoughts Concerning Education*. Vol. XXXVII, Part 1. The Harvard Classics. New York: P. F. Collier & Son, 1909–14. http://www.bartleby.com/37/1/5.html.

Margry, Peter Jan. *Shrines and Pilgrimage in the Modern World: New Itineraries into the Sacred*. Amsterdam, Netherlands: Amsterdam University Press, 2008.

McGee, Micki. *Self-Help, Inc.: Makeover Culture in American Life*. Oxford: Oxford University Press, 2005.

McTighe, Jay and Grant Wiggins. *Essential Questions: Opening Doors to Student Understanding*. Alexandria, VA: Association for Supervision & Curriculum Development, 2013.

Modern Etiquette. Dell Purse Books. New York: Dell Publishing Co., Inc., 1963.

Moffett, M'Ledge. *When We Meet Socially, A Guidebook to Good Form in Social Conventions*. New York: Prentice-Hall Inc., 1940.

Morin, Rich and Seth Motel. "A Third of Americans Now Say They Are in the Lower Classes." Pew Research Center, September 10, 2012. Accessed May 4, 2016. http://www.pewsocialtrends.org/2012/09/10/a-third-of-americans-now-say-they-are-in-the-lower-classes/.

Murphy, Denis, trans. *Pilgrim's Guide*, 2011. https://sites.google.com/site/caminodesantiagoproject/home.

National Council of Social Studies. *College, Career, and Civic Life (C3) Framework for Social Studies State Standards: Guidance for Enhancing the Rigor of K–12 Civics, Economics, Geography, and History*. Silver Spring, MD: National Council of Social Studies, 2013. Accessed April 28, 2016. http://www.socialstudies.org/c3.

Paulding, James Kirke. *A Book of Vagaries Comprising the New Mirror for Travellers and Other Whim-Whams*. Edited by William I. Paulding. New York: C. Scribner, 1868. https://archive.org/details/bookvagaries00paulrich.

Pansanias, *Description of Greece*. Full text available at http://persens.tufts.edu/hopper/text?doc=Persens%3Atext%3A1999.01.0160.

Peiss, Kathy. *Cheap Amusements: Working Women and Leisure in Turn-of-the-Century New York.* Philadelphia: Temple University Press, 1986.

Pool, Kevin R., ed. and trans. *The Chronicle of Pseudo-Turpin, Part IV of the Liber Sancti Jacobi (Codex Calixtinus).* New York: Italica Press, 2014.

Popp, Richard K. *The Holiday Makers, Magazines, Advertising, and Mass Tourism in Postwar America.* Baton Rouge: Louisiana State University Press, 2012.

Post, Elizabeth L. *Emily Post's Etiquette.* 14th ed. New York: Harper & Row, 1985.

Post, Emily. *Etiquette: The Blue Book of Social Usage.* New York: Funk & Wagnalls Company, 1940.

———. *Etiquette in Society, in Business, in Politics and at Home.* New York: Funk & Wagnalls Company, 1922.

Resor, Cynthia W. "Richard I Takes the Cross: The Twelfth-Century Culture of Crusade." PhD diss., University of Kentucky, 2002. ProQuest (ProQuest document ID 251650215).

The Right Question Institute. "Right Question Strategy." Accessed July 15, 2016. http://rightquestion.org/about/strategy/.

Roberts, Patricia L. and Richard D. Kellough. *A Guide for Developing Interdisciplinary Thematic Units.* Upper Saddle River, NJ: Pearson, 1996, 2000, 2004, 2006.

Rugh, Susan Sessions. *The Golden Age of American Family Vacations: Are We There Yet?* Lawrence: University of Kansas Press, 2008.

Salinger, J. D. *The Catcher in the Rye.* Boston: Little, Brown, and Company, 1951.

Schlereth, Thomas J. *Victorian America: Transformations in Everyday Life, 1879–1915.* New York: Harper Collins, 1991.

Schlesinger, Arthur M. *Learning How to Behave: A Historical Study of American Etiquette.* New York: The Macmillan Company, 1946.

Schroeder, Fred. E. H. "The Discovery of Popular Culture Before Printing." Introduction in *5000 Years of Popular Culture, Popular Culture Before Printing,* edited by Fred. E. H. Schroeder. Bowling Green, OH: Bowling Green University Popular Press, 1980.

Schudson, Michael. "The New Validation of Popular Culture: Sense and Sentimentality in Academia." *Critical Studies in Mass Communication* 4 (1987): 51–68.

Sears, John F. *Sacred Places, American Tourist Attractions in the Nineteenth Century.* New York/Oxford: Oxford University Press, 1989.

Sedgwick, Catharine Maria. *The Travellers: A Tale Designed for Young People.* New York: E. Bliss and E. White, 1825. https://archive.org/details/travellersatale00sedggoog.

Shaffer, Marguerite S. *See America First, Tourism and National Identity, 1880–1940.* Washington, DC: Smithsonian Books, 2001.

Sherwood, Mary E. *Manners and Social Usages.* New York: Harper and Brothers, 1884. https://archive.org/stream/mannerssocialus00sher#page/16/mode/2up.

Silverstein, Shel. *Where the Sidewalk Ends.* New York: Harper Collins Publishers, 1974.

Smith, Katharine Capshaw. "Childhood, the Body, and Race Performance: Early 20th-Century Etiquette Books for Black Children." *African American Review* 40, no. 4 (Winter 2006): 795–811. http://www.jstor.org/stable/40033754.

Stanhope, Philip Dormer, 4th Earl of Chesterfield, *Letters to His Son. On the Art of Becoming a Man of the World and a Gentleman.* The Project Gutenberg EBook: 2004, updated 2012. http://www.gutenberg.org/files/3361/3361-h/3361-h.htm.

Starkie, Walter. *The Road to Santiago, Pilgrims of St. James.* New York: E. P. Dutton & Co., 1957.

Stearns, Peter N. "Social History Present and Future." *Journal of Social History* 37, no. 1 (Autumn 2003): 9–19. http://www.jstor.org/stable/3790307.

Sumption, Jonathan. *Pilgrimage, An Image of Mediaeval Religion.* Totowa, NJ: Rowman and Littlefield, 1975.

Susman, Warren. *Culture as History, The Transformation of American Society in the Twentieth Century.* New York: Pantheon Books, 1973, 1984.

Sutherland, Daniel E. *The Expansion of Everyday Life, 1860–1879.* New York: Harper Collins, 1989.

Tague, Ingrid H. *Women of Quality: Accepting and Contesting Ideals of Femininity in England, 1690–1760.* Woodbridge, Suffolk, UK: Boydell & Brewer, 2002. http://www.jstor.org/stable/10.7722/j.ctt81gd7.7.

Tebbel, John and Mary Ellen Zuckerman. *The Magazine in America, 1741–1990.* New York/Oxford: Oxford University Press, 1991.

The Whole Duty of a Woman. London: T. Read, 1737. https://archive.org/stream/wholedutyawoman00unkngoog#page/n29/mode/2up.

Theilmann, John. "Medieval Pilgrims and the Origins of Tourism." *Journal of Popular Culture* 20, no. 4 (Spring 1987): 93–102.

Thompson, Hugh. "The Vacation Savings Movement." *Munsey's Magazine* 49 (May 1913): 257–59. https://babel.hathitrust.org/cgi/pt?id=uc1.b2870653;view=1up;seq=259.

Tosh, John. *The Pursuit of History: Aims, Methods and New Directions in the Study of History.* 6th ed. London and New York: Routledge, Taylor & Francis Group, 2015.

Uminowicz, Glenn. "Sport in a Middle-Class Utopia: Asbury Park, New Jersey, 1871–1895." *Journal of Sport History* 11, no. 1 (Spring 1984): 51–73.

Utne Reader, March/April 1992.

Vanderbilt, Amy. *Amy Vanderbilt's Complete Book of Etiquette, A Guide to Gracious Living.* Garden City, NY: Doubleday & Company, Inc., 1954.

———. *Amy Vanderbilt's Etiquette.* Garden City, NY: Doubleday & Company, Inc., 1972.

Visser, Margaret. *The Rituals of Dinner: The Origins, Evolution, Eccentricities, and Meaning of Table Manners.* New York: Grove Weidenfeld, 1991.

Walpole, Ronald N. "The Pèlerinage de Charlemagne, Poem, Legend, and Problem." *Romance Philology* 8 (1954–55): 173–86.

Welter, Barbara. "The Cult of True Womanhood: 1820–1860." *American Quarterly* 18, No. 2, Part 1 (Summer 1966): 151–74.

Wineburg, Samuel S. and Pamela L. Grossman. *Interdisciplinary Curriculum: Challenges to Implementation.* New York: Teachers College Press, 2000.

Wollstonecraft, Mary. *A Vindication of the Rights of Woman.* The Project Gutenberg EBook: 2002. http://www.gutenberg.org/cache/epub/3420/pg3420-images.html.

Wouters, Cas. "Etiquette Books and Emotion Management in the Twentieth Century: Part One: The Integration of Social Classes." *Journal of Social History* 29, no. 1 (Autumn 1995): 107–24. http://www.jstor.org/stable/3788711.

Yezierska, Anzia. "The Free Vacation House." *The Forum* (December 1915): 706–41. http://www.unz.org/Pub/Forum-1915dec-00706.

Index

Page references for figures are italicized.

Adams, John, 62, 74
Addison, Joseph, 61
advice literature, 6, 56, 58–60, 67, 69, 70; as a business, 63; courtship and dating, 75–87; defined, 56; differences by ethnicity or race, 60, 63, 67, 69; differences by sex, 58, 60, 61, 63, 66, 68–69, 75–87; Enlightenment, impact on, 60–63, 70–75; influenced by technological change, 57; middle class, 56, 63–66; nineteenth-century authors of, 64; social stratification of, 59–60, 65; twentieth-century themes, 6–7
African American: advice manuals/etiquette, 60, 63, 67, 69; vacation, 24, 25–26, 28, 29, 54
agency, 2, 7, 14, 24, 29, 31, 88; defined, 6–7
Alcott, Louisa May, 65
Allestree, Richard, 61, 72
American Guide Series, 24, 48
amusement parks, 22–23, 24, 25, 29, 45–46, 47–48, 68
anachronism, 6, 9, 31, 95
androcentrism, 8, 75; defined, 7
Animal Farm, xiii
archaic language, xiv, 5, 70, 99–101
aristocracy, 58, 66
Asbury Park, New Jersey, 44–45
assumptions, 2, 4, 7, 8, 11, 18, 56, 69, 95. *See also* expectations
Astor, Caroline, 66
Atlantic City, New Jersey, 24, *45*
Austen, Jane, 1, 19, 62, 74–75
Austin, Hilary Mac, 97
The Autobiography of Benjamin Franklin, 73
autocamping. *See* camping
automobile: courtship and dating, 69, *81*, *82*; vacation, 22, 24, *27*, 49. *See also* motel

Bailey, Beth, 69, 91
Barnum, P. T., 21
Barron, Brigid, 10
beach, vacation destination, 24, 29, 43–44, *44*

Becker, Elizabeth, 50
Becket, Thomas, shrine of, 16
Bennet, Elizabeth. *See Pride and Prejudice*
Bierstadt, Albert, 19
Book of St. James, 34–35, *36*, 37–38
The Book of the Courtier, 57, 58
Boorstin, Daniel, 39–40
borscht belt. *See* Jews, vacation
bourgeoisie, 6
The Bronze Bow, xiv
Brown, Helen Gurley, 84
Buddhism, 15

calling card, 74, *76*, *79*. *See also* visiting card
Callixtus II (pope), 34–35, 36
camp meeting, 19, 21, 44
camping, 22, 29, 43–44
Cane Ridge Revival, Kentucky. *See* camp meeting
Canterbury Tales, 16
Carnegie, Dale, 67
Casa, Giovanni della, 58
Castiglione, Baldassare, 58, 60
The Catcher in the Rye, 55
cemetery, rural or garden as tourist destination, 19
Central Park, New York, 22
chaperone, role in courtship and dating, 69, 78, 80, 84, 86, 23, 27, 69
Charlemagne, 31, 32–39
Chateaubriand, François-René de, 18
Chaucer, Geoffrey, 16
Chautauqua, 21
Chesterfield, 4th Earl of, 58, 62, 72
Child, Lydia Maria, 66
chivalry, 31, 63, 78
Christianity, 4, 7, 15
Chronicle of Pseudo-Turpin, 34, 36
Chronicling America (newspaper database), 97

Church, Frederic, 19
Civil Rights Act of 1964, 26, 39
Civilian Conservation Corps, 24
civility, 60, 61; defined, 58
cleanliness, association with manners, 69
Cluniac monasticism, 34
Codex Calixtinus, 34, 36
cohort. *See* social generation
Cole, Thomas, 19
collective memory, 14, 18, 30–32, 50; defined, 18
The Colored Girl Beautiful, 67
Common Core State Standards, xiv, xv, 1, 96, 101
compelling question. *See* essential question
conduct manual. *See* advice literature
Coney Island, New York, 22, 25, 45–46, 68
Cook, Thomas, 21, 40
courtesy, defined, 57–58, 61
courtship, 5, 60, 68–69, 69, 75, 77, 78, 80, 91
critical analysis, xv, 1, 2, 7, 10, 11, 12, 30, 31, 57, 93, 94
critical thinking. *See* critical analysis
crusade, medieval, 16, 18, 30–35, 54
cult of domesticity. *See* republican motherhood
cult of true womanhood. *See* republican motherhood
cultural circuit, 14, 15, 29, 50n1; defined, 50n1
cultural continuum, 3–4, 3
cultural meta-message, 56; defined, 9
Currier and Ives, 80

Daily Life through History series, 95
Darling-Hammond, Linda, 10
dating, 5, 60, 68–69, 75, 77, 78, 80, 87, 91
Description of Greece, 14
Dickens, Charles, 19
differentiation, 8, 10
Digital Public Library of America, 97
dime museum, 22, 23
Dirty Dancing (movie), 24
Disney, Walt, 25
Disneyworld, California, 25
Downton Abbey, 66
Dreamland, Coney Island, New York, 23

Egypt, Egyptian, 4, 8, 18, 58, 91
Einhard, 32, 34, 35
elite culture/upper class, 3–5, 6, 10, 14, 16, 23, 27, 29, 59–60, 63, 66, 67, 93
enculturation, 2, 88; enculturation, defined, 9
Encyclopedia of American Social History, 95
Enlightenment, 55, 60–63, 66; primary sources, 70–75
ephemera, as a primary source, 97–99
epic, medieval, 4, 32–35, 52n57, 100; compared to action movies, 32
Erie Canal, 19, 41
essential question, xv, xvi, 10, 31, 40, 70, 93, 94, 101; defined, xv

essentialism, biological or religious, 7–8, 61, 75
etiquette, defined, 58, 62. *See also* manners; advice literature
Examining the Evidence: Seven Strategies for Teaching with Primary Sources, 97
expectations, 7, 9, 14, 15, 29, 40, 55, 56, 58, 59, 69, 80, 85, 88, 91, 94. *See also* assumptions

fair use copyright, xv
familial generation, defined, 8
fiction. *See* novels as primary sources
Federal Aid Highway Act of 1956, 24, 39, 48, 49
Federal Writers' Project, 24
Flagler, Henry Morrison, 21
Flesichmann's Resort. *See* Jews, vacation destinations
Floyd, Silas X., 67
Floyd's Flowers, or Duty and Beauty for Colored Children, 67
folk culture, 4–5, 93
Franklin, Benjamin, 62, 73
"freak" shows, 22–23, 25
Freud, Sigmund, 4, 66

Garden of Eden, 7, 66
Gassan, Richard, 15. *See also* vacation, "societally defined boundaries"
gender polarization, 8, 69, 75; defined, 7
gender (i.e., feminine/masculine), 1, 2, 5, 7–9, 14, 39, 55, 60, 69, 75, 87, 91, 93, 94, 100; gender, defined, 7, 12n14; difference from sex, 7, 12n14
generation gap, defined, 8
generational change, 2, 57, 60, 88; defined, 8
geography, five themes of, 50
Gorky, Maxim, 45–46
Grand Canyon, 22, 23
Greece, Ancient, xiv, 7, 14, 30, 37, 58, 73, 97
The Green Book, 26, 28
Green, Edward S., 67
Greenbriar, West Virginia. *See* White Sulphur Springs, Virginia
Greenword Park, Nashville, Tennessee, 24. *See also* African American, vacation

Hackley, E. Azalia, 67
hagiography, 17, 30
Halbwachs, Maurice, 18
Hamilton, Alexander (physician), 62
Harvey, Fred, 21, 22, 23
HathiTrust Digital Library, 96
Hawthorn, Nathaniel, 19
Hemphill, C. Dallett, 64
heritage tourism, 13, 26, 49
Highland Beach, Maryland, cover photograph, 24. *See also* African American, vacation
Hinduism, 15
Hiroshima, xiii
history and fiction, relationship of, 1, 18, 32–35; historical research, comparison of popular and scholarly books, 96;

comparison of popular and scholarly journals, 96; locating non-text primary sources, 97–98; internet, 96–97; museums and archives, 97. See also novels as primary sources
The History of Manners, 58
"history with a literary turn." See cultural history
The Hobbit, xiv
hotel, 15, 19, 21, 22, 23, 24, 25, 40, 42, 43, 44. See also motel
Holt, Victoria, xiii
Holy Land, as pilgrimage destination, 15–16, 18, 32, 34
hot springs. See mineral springs
How to Win Friends and Influence People, 67
Howells, William Dean, 65
Hume, David, 61
hydropathy, 2, 19

Idlewild, Michigan, 24. See also African American, vacation
Il Galateo: The Rules of Polite Behavior, 58
The Image: A Guide to Pseudo-Events in America, 39
immigrants: manners, 40, 60, 63; vacation, 24, 29, 45, 48
Industrial Revolution, 3, 9, 14, 63
industrialization, 6, 9, 59
inquiry arc, xv
intellectual history, 3
interdisciplinary/integrated instruction, xiv, 10; defined, 10; interdisciplinary/integrated instruction, vacation, 49–50; interdisciplinary/integrated instruction, manners, 58, 87
Internet Archive, 96
Internet History Sourcebooks Project, 97
Interstate Highway Act of 1956. See Federal Aid Highway Act of 1956
Irving, Washington, 19
Islam, modern 7, 15; as perceived by medieval crusaders, 18, 32–36

James, Saint, 16, 17, 32, 34–38. See also Santiago de Compostela
Jaques, Brian, xiv
Jefferson, Thomas, 61
Jerusalem Delivered, 18
Jerusalem, as pilgrimage destination, 16–18, 32, 34, 36, 37
Jews, vacation destinations, 24, 26, 43, 54; Jews, vacation, 24, 25, 26, 29, 42–43, 48, 54
Johnson, Samuel, 61
Judaism, 7
The Jungle, xiv

Kellerman's Resort, 24. See also *Dirty Dancing* (movie); Jews, vacation destinations
Kerber, Linda, 66
Kerouac, Jack, 50
Knott's Berry Farm, California, 25

Ladies Calling, 61, 72
Ladies' Home Journal, 43, 68

Lake, Kathy, 10
Land of Cockaigne, xvi, xviin6
language shift over time, 2, 5, 56–58, 60–62. See also semantics
Larkin, Jack, 95
leisure travel, defined, 14–15
Letters to His Son on the Art of Becoming a Man of the World and a Gentleman, 62, 72
Letters to Mothers, 66
lexicon, 5
Life of Charlemagne, 32, 35
literacy instruction, xiv–xv, 1, 96, 101
literacy rates, 9
Little Women, 65
Locke, John, 3, 60–61, 70
lower class, 3–6, 16, 25, 64, 65, 68
Luna Park, Coney Island, New York, 22

magazines, as primary sources, 4, 5, 15, 22, 25, 55–56, 63, 70, 87, 96, 98–100
male-centeredness. See androcentrism
Mammoth Cave, Kentucky, 19, 49
Mandeville, Sir John, 18
Mandeville's Travels, 18
manners: contrast between colonial American and English, 62–63; elite/nobility, 50–60, 66; Enlightenment, impact of, 60–63, 66, 70–75; essential questions, 55, 70; interdisciplinary connections, 58, 87; key terms, 57–58; nineteenth-century American, 63–66; Renaissance, 58; self-control, 58; twentieth-century American, 66–69
Mansfield Park, 62
Manual of Social and Business Forms, 59, 64
marriage, 24, 25, 61, 68, 69, 80, 77, 83, 84, 86, 91
Marx, Karl, 3, 6
Marzano, Robert, 10
mass media, 2, 4, 9, 14, 18, 25–26, 29, 66, 69
McAllister, Ward, 66
McTighe, Jay, xv, 94
mental map, 50
middle class: defined, 4, 6, 56; etiquette, 59–60, 63–64, 66–69, 75; vacationing, 21–27, 29, 29, 54
middling sort/middle sort of people, 6, 56, 59, 62. See also middle class
A Midwife's Tale, 3
mineral springs, 2, 19, 21, 42, 98
Moran, Thomas, 19
Morland, Catherine, 1
motel, 22, 24, 25, 26, 40, 48–49, 49, 54. See also hotel
The Mother's Book, 66

National Association for the Advancement of Colored People (NAACP), 26
National Capital Code of Etiquette, 67
National Council of Social Studies College, Career, and Civic Life (C3) Framework, xv, 1, 94

National Parks, United States, 21, 50, 49, 26
National Trust for Historic Preservation, 49
"native" culture, 5, 9
"new social history." *See* social history
New York Times historical database, 97
newspapers, as primary sources, 5, 15, 21, 22, 27, 30, 42, 55–56, 60, 61, 63, 70, 87, 91, 97
Niagara Falls, 19, 41, 50
nobility/nobles, 4, 6, 16, 32, 38, 39, 57, 58. *See also* elite culture
Norbert, Elias, 57, 58
Northanger Abbey, 1
nostalgia, associated with manners, 57
novel, sentimental or novel of sensibility, 62
novels as primary sources, xiii, xiv, 1, 5, 19, 34, 41, 61, 62, 65, 66, 74, 101, 109

Ocean Grove, New Jersey, 21, 44
Oil Embargo (1973), 24, 54, 69
On the Road, 50
oral history, 50n1, 88
Orwell, George, xiii
Overbooked, The Exploding Business of Travel and Tourism, 50
Oxford Encyclopedia of American Social History, 95
Oxford English Dictionary, 5, 57, 67

Pausanias, 14
peasant, 4, 6, 58
periodization of history, 9
personality, and manners, 67
Pickering, Debra, 10
Picturesque America, 20
pilgrim badge, 17–18, *17*, 100
Pilgrim's Guide to Santiago de Compostela, 35, 37–38
Pilgrimage of Charlemagne, 32–35, 37, 100
pilgrimage: defined, 15; destinations, 15–18. *See also* Holy Land; Jerusalem; Rome; Santiago de Compostela; medieval, 15–18, 30–32, 54; medieval and collective memory, 30–48; medieval pilgrimage as vacation, 15–18; medieval, primary sources, 32–39, 100; motivation, 16; promotion of, 17, 29, 31, 34; symbols in art, *17*
place-based education, xiv, xvi, 1, 94; related to manners, 87–88; primary sources from the local community, 97–99; vacation, 48–50; "taking action," xvi
Plutarch, 14
politeness, as a form of behavior, 60, 61–63
popular culture, 2, 3–5, 4, 6, 9, 14, 29, 31, 33, 53, 93, 100
Post, Emily, 79, 81
Potter, Harry, 33
prescriptive literature, defined, 56
Price, Fanny. *See Mansfield Park*
Pride and Prejudice, 19
primary source excerpts: courtship and dating, 75–87; Enlightenment, 70–75; medieval, Europe, 35–39; vacation, United States, 41–48

primary sources: critical analysis of medieval primary sources, 30; identifying themes in, 100; interpretation, 99–100; locating, 96–98; medieval primary sources, special problems, 30–31; relationship to teaching standards, xiv–xvi, 96, 101
printing: impact of the invention, 2, 9–10, 14; impact on social history, 4, 9–10, 14, 59
Prohibition, 57, 66
project-based learning, 10
proletariat, 6
public memory. *See* collective memory

Question Formulation Technique, 31

railroad. *See* transportation; vacation, promotion by railroad companies
reading guides, xi, xvi, 101; examples, *31, 41, 71, 77, 78*; developing, 101
relic, 15–17, 31, 34–36, 38. *See also* pilgrimage; saint
religion, teaching in public schools, 31
Renaissance, 5, 9, 30, 57, 58, 60
republican motherhood, 41, 66
The Reshaping of Everyday Life, 1790–1840, 95
Riesman, David, 67
The Rise of Silas Lapham, 65
road maps, 25, 30, 50, 54
Roman Catholic Church, medieval, 4, 16–18, 29, 34, 36–38
Roman, Rome (ancient), xiii, 7, 14, 16, 30, 32, 58, 97; pilgrimage site, 16, 54

saint, 15–18, 30–39. *See also* hagiography; relic; pilgrimage
Salinger, J. D., 55
Santa Fee Railroad, 22, 23
Santiago de Compostela, 16–17, 34–35, 37–38. *See also* James, St.
Saratoga Springs, New York, 19, 42
Schlesinger, Arthur, 66, 91
Sedgwick, Catharine Maria, 41, 66
"See America First" campaign, 21
segregation, vacation, 24, 25, 26, 29, 43, 54
self-improvement/self-help, 55, 56, 67, 88
semantics, 5. *See also* language shift over time
Sense and Sensibility, 62, 74–75
sensibility, as a form of behavior, 60, 61–62, 63, 74
servant, domestic or household, 56
Sex and the Single Girl, 84
sex education, 83
sex (i.e., female/male), 1, 2, 5, 7–9, 14, 21, 24, 44, 56, 60, 63, 64, 66, 69, 75, 82, 83, 84, 87, 93, 100; defined, 7; difference from gender, 7, 12n14
sexual behavior, 58
Shakespeare, William, 4
Sherwood, Mary Elizabeth Wilson, 76
Short Stories for Colored People Both Old and Young, 67
Sigourney, Lydia, 66

Silverstein, Shel, 70
slavery, 7, 32
snob, changing definition, 67
social class, 1, 5, 6, 7, 8, 93, 94, 95, 100; defined, 6; etiquette, 55, 56, 66, 67, 68; vacation, 14, 15, 24, 39, 42
Social Darwinism, 7, 65
social generation, 8
social historian, 2, 11, 19, 64, 66, 100; work of, 3–7, 64, 67, 100
social history: challenges related to teaching, 2, 3, 60; classroom, in the, xiii–xiv, 1–2; cultural history, related to, 3–5; defined, 3; developing themes for classroom, 93–95; glasses (lenses), 2, 8, 9, 11, 19, 69, 87, 93, 94; key concepts related to, 5–11; "new social history," xiii–xiv, 3; popular culture, related to, 3–5; primary sources, 95–100; relevance, xiii, 1, 93
social media, 2, 4, 9, 15, 70, 75, 96
social memory. *See* collective memory
social myth, defined, 18. *See also* urban legend
social status, 5; defined, 6; etiquette, 59, 60, 67, 75, 87, 88
social stratification, 2, 6, 9, 40, 59
Some Thoughts Concerning Education, 60, 70
Song of Roland, 32, 34, 35
Spartacus (movie), 32
Speare, Elizabeth G., xiv
The Spectator, 61
Spencer, Herbert, 7, 65
standards (teaching): aligning instruction to, xiv–xvi, 1, 2, 11, 93; national, xv, 1, 94, 96, 101
Steele, Richard, 61
Steeplechase Park, Coney Island, New York, 22
subtext. *See* cultural meta-message
Sumption, Jonathan, 18, 54
Susman, Warren, 67

Taft, William Howard, 46–47
Tasso, Torquato, 18
Taylor, Preston, 24
technological change, impact of, 1, 2, 3, 4, 6, 8, 9–10, 14, 57, 59–60, 66, 69, 100
television shows: primary sources, 1, 3–5, 10, 14, 15, 25, 30, 32, 57, 62, 66, 69, 84, 100; role in dating behavior, 69
temperance, 24, 48, 66
textbooks: as instructional materials, xiii, 1, 2, 10; to teach manners, 63, 82, 83, 91; primary source collections, 54, 97
thematic instruction, xiv, 10–11; advantages, 11; approaches in the classroom, xiv; defined, 10; developing, 93–102; interdisciplinary/integrated instruction, relationship to, xvi, 2, 10–11, 50, 94; purpose, xiv, 1; relationship to teaching standards, xiii; selecting themes, 93–94
thematic unit, xiv, 10, 93–94, 96; creating units, 101
Thompson, Kathleen, 97
Tocqueville, Alexis de, 63
Tolkien, J. R. R., xiii, xiv

Tomlinson, Carol Ann, 10
tourism, defined, 15; mass tourism; 29, 39–40; moral tourism, 29
tourist or traveler?, 26–29, 39–40
transportation: manners, impact on, 87; "societally defined boundary" of vacation, 15; theme for the classroom, 93, 99; vacation, impact on, 2, 15, 18, 19, 22, 24, 29, 39–40, 48, 50. *See also* automobile
Travelguide, 26
Turpin, Archbishop, 37. *See also Chronicle of Pseudo-Turpin*
Twelve Peers, 34–35, 37. *See also* Charlemagne

Ulrich, Laurel Thatcher, 3
Uncle Tom's Cabin, xiv, 101
United States Travel Bureau, 24
urban legend, 18, 51n22. *See also* social myth
Utne Reader, xiv

vacation: American vacations, history of, 19–29, 39–47; boardinghouse, 21, 23, 24, 47; classism/tourist or traveler, 26–29, 39–40; commercialization, 14, 21, 22, 29, 40; environmental conservation, 50; essential questions, 14, 29, 31, 40; family, 25–26, *27*; guidebook, 14, 15, 19, 26, 30, 40, 50; history of the word vacation, 15; interdisciplinary teaching of, 50; pilgrimage, compared to, 15–19; paid, 21, 24, 25, 40, 49; place-based instruction, 48; promotion of, *13*, 14–15, 17, 22, 24, 25, 29, 31, 49, 50; promotion by railroad companies, 22, 23; resorts, 2, 19, 21–22, 24, 27, 48, 94; savings plans, 26; segregation, 24, 25–26, 28, 29, 42–45; "societally defined boundaries," 15; societies/clubs, 24, 47–48
Van Gogh, Vincent, 4
Vanderbilt, Amy, 82, 87
vernacular, 5
visiting card, 74, 76, 79. *See also* calling card
Visser, Margaret, 69
Vitry, Jacques de, 16

water cures. *See* hydropathy
watering places. *See* mineral springs
Weber, Max, 6
Wharton, Edith, 66
White Sulphur Springs, Virginia, 19
The Whole Duty of a Woman, 72
Wiggins, Grant, xv, 94
William in the Monastery, 100, 32, 34, 38
William of Orange, 34, 37–39
Wollstonecraft, Mary, 61, 73–74
working class, 5, 6;
etiquette, 56, 57, 63, 64, 66, 68; vacation, 19, 21, 22, 23, 24, 25, 29, 40, 43, 44, 45
World's Fair, 21

zombies, 100

About the Author

Cynthia Williams Resor taught high school social studies and sixth grade before deciding to pursue her dream of obtaining a PhD in history. She is currently a professor at Eastern Kentucky University and has taught undergraduate and graduate teacher education courses, social studies for teachers, medieval history, US history survey courses, humanities, and has led study abroad classes. She has also conducted a wide variety of professional development sessions, published several articles in various journals related to history and social studies education, and served as a history consultant for a Teaching American History grant.

   Cynthia loves history, especially the history of daily life and ordinary people, and she is always trying to spread her enthusiasm about history inside and outside of the classroom. She worked as a costumed interpreter, a "fake" Shaker, at the Shaker Village at Pleasant Hill in central Kentucky and loves to surprise her students by appearing in class in historical costumes. She is obsessed with genealogy and local history and makes her students visit local historical sites. She forces her family and friends to visit old cemeteries and take vacations with her that revolve around historical themes and locations. She lives in an old house, collects old stuff, names her dogs and chickens after historical people, and is probably a dangerous driver because she listens to historical novels in the car. Her dream job is to be a tour guide with a time machine.

www.ingramcontent.com/pod-product-compliance
Lightning Source LLC
Chambersburg PA
CBHW080940300426
44115CB00017B/2891